Critical Human Ge

'Critical Human Geography' is an international series which provides a critical examination and extension of the concepts and consequences of work in human geography and the allied social sciences and humanities. The volumes are written by scholars currently engaged in substantive research, so that, wherever possible, the discussions are empirically grounded as well as theoretically informed. Existing studies and the traditions from which they derive are carefully described and located in their historically specific context, but the series at the same time introduces and explores new ideas and insights from the human sciences as a whole. The series is thus not intended as a collection of synthetic reviews, but rather as a cluster of considered arguments which are accessible enough to engage geographers at all levels in the development of geography. The series therefore reflects the continuing methodological and philosophical diversity of the subject, and its books are united only by their common commitment to the prosecution of a genuinely human geography.

Department of Geography MARK BILLINGE
University of Cambridge DEREK GREGORY
England RON MARTIN

i

Critical Human Geography

PUBLISHED

Recollections of a Revolution: Geography as Spatial Science
Mark Billinge, Derek Gregory and Ron Martin (*editors*)

*Capitalist World Development: A Critique of Radical
Development Geography*
Stuart Corbridge

The Arena of Capital
Michael Dunford and Diane Perrons

*Regional Transformation and Industrial Revolution: A
Geography of the Yorkshire Woollen Industry*
Derek Gregory

Social Relations and Spatial Structures
Derek Gregory and John Urry (*editors*)

Geography and the State: An Essay in Political Geography
R. J. Johnston

*Spatial Divisions of Labour: Social Structures and the Geography
of Production*
Doreen Massey

*Conceptions of Space in Social Thought: A Geographic
Perspective*
Robert David Sack

*The Urban Arena: Capital, State and Community in
Contemporary Britain*
John R. Short

FORTHCOMING

A Cultural Geography of Industrialisation in Britain
Mark Billinge

Between Feudalism and Capitalism
Robert Dodgshon

Regions and the Philosophy of the Human Sciences
Nicholas Entrikin

Strategies for Geographical Enquiry
Derek Gregory and Ron Martin

The Geography of De-Industrialisation
Ron Martin and Bob Rowthorn (*editors*)

Capitalist World Development

A Critique of Radical Development Geography

Stuart Corbridge

MACMILLAN

First published 1986

Published by
MACMILLAN EDUCATION LTD
Houndmills, Basingstoke, Hampshire RG21 2XS
and London
Companies and representatives
throughout the world

Printed in Hong Kong

British Library Cataloguing in Publication Data
Corbridge, Stuart
Capitalist world development: a critique of
radical development geography. — (Critical
human geography)
1. Economic development — Social aspects
2. Economic development — Political aspects
I. Title   II. Series
330.9   HD82
ISBN 0–333–32405–6
ISBN 0–333–32406–4 Pbk

Contents

v

List of Figures

List of Tables

List of Abbreviations Used

ATP	Aid–Trade Provision (UK)
CMP	Capitalist Mode of Production
ECLA	(UN) Economic Commission for Latin America
GATT	General Agreement on Trade and Tariffs
GDP	Gross Domestic Product
GNP	Gross National Product
IBRD	International Bank for Reconstruction and Development
IGBA	International Group on British Aid
IMF	International Monetary Fund
LDCs	Less Developed Countries
LIBOR	London Inter-bank Offered Rate
MIC	Middle Income Countries
MIT	Massachusetts Institute of Technology
NASA	National Aeronautics and Space Administration
NICs	Newly Industrialising Countries
NIDL	New International Division of Labour
NIEO	New International Economic Order
PCMPS	Pre-capitalist Modes of Production
RIO	Reshaped International Order
SCP	Simple Commodity Production
SDR	Special Drawing Rights
TNCs	Transnational Companies
UN	United Nations
UNCTAD	UN Conference on Trade and Development

Acknowledgements

This book was originally to have been written with Steve Jones. Though Steve had to drop out of the project my first debt is to him, and to his burgeoning family, for continued support and friendship. I am also indebted to Ben Farmer, Derek Gregory and Ron Martin for reading through the entire text in draft form, and to Alan Gilbert, John Harriss, Gerry Kearns and Derek Reeve for reviewing particular draft chapters. All of them offered valuable comments and whilst I alone am responsible for the book's thesis I hope they will recognise the imprint of at least some of their remarks. I must also thank Stephen Pratt of the Geography Department of Huddersfield Polytechnic for his help in drawing the diagrams.

Finally, my greatest thanks go to my family: to my parents, to Jane and Dave, to my wife Joan Simms, and to our cat Hattie. One of them, at least, promises to be a silent critic.

STUART CORBRIDGE

The author and publishers wish to thank the following who have kindly given permission for the use of copyright material.

Croom Helm Ltd for extracts from *The Geography of Multinationals* by Taylor and Thrift.

Norman Girvan for extracts from *Corporate Imperialism: Conflict and Expropriation* (1976). Reprinted by permission of Monthly Review Press.

Hutchinson Publishing Group Limited for extract from *Modern World Development: A Geographical Perspective* by M. Chisholm (1982).

The Institute of Development Studies for extracts from T. Dyson and N. Crook 'Causes of Seasonality in Vital Events' in R. Chambers, R. Longhurst and A. Pacey (eds), *Seasonal Dimensions to Rural Poverty* (1981) London, Frances Pinter.

The Institute for Food and Development Policy for extract from their book *Aid as Obstacle*.

Longman Group Limited for extract from *Theoretical Population Geography* by R. Woods (1982).

Methuen & Co. for extract from *Regions in Question: Space, Development Theory and Regional Policy* by C. Gore (1984)

National Westminster Bank for extracts from 'Transnationals and the Third World: Changing Perceptions' by S. Lall in *National Westminster Bank Quarterly Review* (1984).

Oxford University Press for extract from *Agriculture and Structural Transformation* by B. F. Johnston and P. Kilby (1975).

James Petras for extract from *Critical Perspectives on Imperialism and Social Class in the Third World* (1978). Reprinted by permission of Monthly Review Press.

A. P. Thirlwall for extracts from *Growth and Development*, 2nd edition 1978 (3rd edition 1983) Macmillan Publishers Ltd.

Universe Books for extract from *The Limits to Growth: A Report for the Club of Rome's Project on the Predicament of Mankind*, by Donella H. Meadows, Dennis L. Meadows, Jørgen Randers, William W. Behrens, III. A Potomac Associates book published by Universe Books, N.Y. 1972. Graphics by Potomac Associates.

Verso/New Left Books for extracts from *Imperialism: Pioneer of Capitalism* by B. Warren (1980); and extracts from *The Dollar and Its Rivals* by R. Parboni (1981).

Butterworths and Edward Arnold for permission to reproduce material published in *Applied Geography*, *Political Geography Quarterly* and *Progress in Human Geography*.

Every effort has been made to trace all the copyright holders, but if any have been inadvertently overlooked the publishers will be pleased to make the necessary arrangement at the first opportunity.

Part I
Capitalism and Development: Grand Theories

1
Introduction

What are the consequences for development geography of adopting a radical perspective on differential development? More exactly, what are the consequences of adopting a view of events which emphasises a necessary conflict of interest between metropolitan capitalism and the development of the periphery of the modern world system? This book hopes to throw some light on these questions. It presents a critical review of radical development studies, and more especially of radical development geography. We might define this as a paradigm which archetypally, or perhaps in caricature, holds to four basic propositions. These are: that capitalism cannot or will not promote the development of the Third World; that capitalism alone is ultimately responsible for the world's demographic and environmental 'ills'; that capitalism is incapable of promoting the independent industrialisation of the South; and that the fundamental cleavage shaping the capitalist world system lies between North and South.[1]

Of course these are not the only defining features of radical development geography, and there are nuances and secondary questions which are not explicit in this simple preface. Nevertheless, the thrust of these remarks should make it clear that this book takes an ambivalent view of the new paradigm. The book argues that radical development studies have failed to live up to their early promise, and that they have too often traded dogma and determinism for the real insights that a radical perspective is capable of offering. The purpose of this introduction is to summarise the arguments that can be made in support of this judgement. Before these arguments are broached, however, it is necessary to signpost two assumptions on which the book is based.

3

Assumptions

The book's first assumption is that radical development geography is a recognisable and important branch of our discipline. This can be 'demonstrated' with the aid of two simple content analyses. Figure 1.1 reveals the general growth of interest in aspects of economic development in selected geographical journals over the period 1955–64 to 1974–83. Writing of the first period, David Keeble complained, in 1967, 'of an apparent and remarkable lack of interest in the study of the phenomena of economic development' (Keeble, 1967, p. 243). This lack of interest was borne out by the fact that 'of 251 major articles published between 1955 and 1964 inclusive in what is probably the most relevant professional journal, *Economic Geography*, only ten were explicitly concerned in whole or part with problems of economic development' (ibid). Moreover, within the pages of 'the more general journal of the *Annals of the Association of American Geographers*, the percentage falls still further, to 2.5 per cent (i.e. 6 articles out of 242)' (ibid).

Today these statistics are far behind us. Over the ten-year period 1974–83, the percentage of *Economic Geography* articles dealing with economic development issues rose to 16 per cent, whilst the *Annals* boosted its coverage to a respectable 13 per cent (at a time of multiplying sub-disciplines).[2] More significantly, this new-found interest in development, which infected other social sciences too, was extended to other journals. Had Keeble reviewed the contents pages of the *Tijdschrift voor Economische en Sociale Geographie* over the years 1955–64, he would have found that a mere 7 per cent of its articles were concerned with economic development. Over the period 1974–83 this percentage stands at 26 per cent, and its coverage continues to rise. Similar tales can also be told of *Antipode* (a newcomer), *Geography* and *Professional Geographer*.

Development geography, then, has come of age. But what is of more interest is the sort of development geography now being produced, and which lies behind this renaissance.[3] Back in the mid-1960s Keeble looked to the likes of Rostow and Hirschman, Hoselitz and North,[4] to provide a series of models around which the new development geography could be written. Not without reason, he saw in such modernisation theory an intellectual vigour

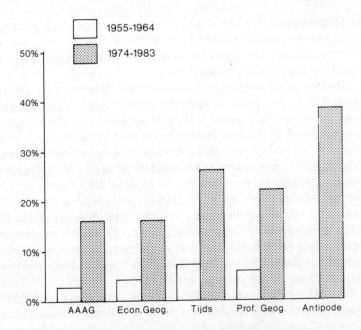

NOTE AAAG — *Annals of the Association of American Geographers*

Econ. Geog — *Economic Geography*

Tijds — *Tijdschrift voor Economische en Sociale Geographie*

Prof. Geog — *Professional Geographer*

FIGURE 1.1 *Articles devoted to aspects of economic development in selected geographical journals, 1955–64 and 1974–83 (%)*

which would tear development geography away from its suffocating dependence on a 'predominantly idiographic approach' (Keeble, 1967, p. 245) and for a while this prophecy did seem to be coming true. For a few short years development geography was infused with the sort of spatial algebra then driving the 'new geography', and some development geographers did begin to map out the optimistic logic embodied in the linear stages theories of the modernisation school. Many readers will remember such landmark studies as Gould's (1970) article on 'Tanzania 1920–63: The Spatial Impress of the Modernisation Process', or Soja's text on

The Geography of Modernization in Kenya (1968). Both of these looked to the development of East Africa in terms of a process of polarised urbanisation in which innovations would diffuse down an emerging central-place hierarchy.

However, this marriage of statistics and space – what David Slater (1973) described as 'spatial dualism theory' – did not last long. As the 1970s wore on it became apparent that this perspective was blind to the historical reproduction of systems and processes of inequality, and that the basis of a future development geography was more likely to be found in the antithesis of Keeble's favoured vision. Figure 1.2 seems to confirm this judgement.[5] Of the 168 articles published in the *Annals*, in *Economic Geography* and in the *Tijdschrift* between 1974 and 1983, fully 65 of the 97 offering a clear set of theoretical statements (as opposed to simply describing a given space-economy) subscribed to one or more of radical development geography's four defining features – the percentage rising as the years passed by.

Now this is obviously a crude way of measuring any paradigm's 'success' since I have divided these articles into just two competing schools of thought and thereby accentuated the divisions between them. But my concern here is to establish an *archetypal* 'radical development geography' rather than to provide a sustained commentary on the writings of particular individuals, which may well depart from the general model set out in these pages. What matters is that such an archetype is recognisable, at least in its essentials, and that an increasing number of individuals are being influenced by some of its central propositions.[6]

The book's second assumption should be less controversial. It is, simply, that the 'strong points' of radical development geography are well understood and are in need of little further elaboration. This being the case, I see little point in rehashing the debates of the early 1970s, pointing out how the new radicalism met and defeated the swelling ranks of modernisation theory on this point, that point and the other; on the fallacies of the 'take-off' model, on the dubious assumptions of diffusionism and trickle-down and on the dangers of overpopulation. These debates were more than adequately dealt with ten years ago by Harold Brookfield (1975) and there can be little basis, in the 1980s, for acting on John Browett's extraordinary claim that 'The impact of the diffusionist paradigm has been so pervasive that today as in 1974. . . . there are few textbooks which are not firmly wedded to its ideology'

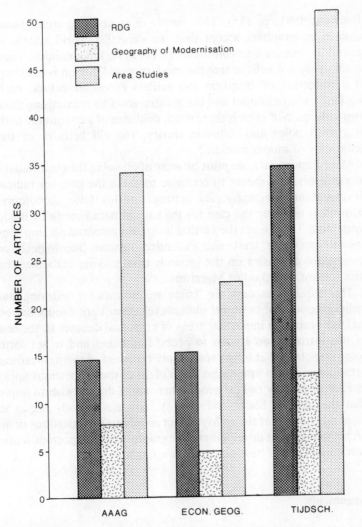

NB   This figure includes double-counted radical/areal and modernisation/areal articles

NOTE   AAAG — *Annals of the Association of American Geographers*

Econ. Geog — *Economic Geography*

Tijds — *Tidjschrift voor Economische en Sociale Geographie*

FIGURE 1.2   *Theoretical perspective of articles on economic development published in selected geographical journals, 1974–83*

(Browett, 1981, p. 155). This simply does not ring true.[7] Most modern geographers accept that the capitalist world system is racked by massive and continuing (if changing) inequalities. They certainly do not believe that the modern world system is made up of a collection of atomistic and selfless economic actors, each working for equilibrium and the greater good by maximising their own utilities. Nor even is there much evidence of a continuing faith in growth poles and diffusion theory, the old bedrock of the geography of modernisation.[8]

More importantly, we must be wary of allowing the clear failings of modernisation theory to continue to make the case for radical development geography. By setting up this false dichotomy, Browett is allowing the case for the radical paradigm to be made by default. The danger then is that its main claims and assumptions are accepted on trust and defended against 'ideological' or 'bourgeois' criticisms on the grounds that it alone embodies the true scientific method of Marxism.

This is quite unacceptable. There are grounds for believing that radical theories of capitalist underdevelopment are deeply flawed and are occluding important areas of empirical debate. In the rest of this introduction I want to probe this belief and to set forth some questions that might reasonably be asked of the new radical orthodoxy. I must emphasise that not all of these questions apply to each and every radical geographer, and I do not wish to imply that the likes of Slater and Harvey have not already begun to respond to some of them. My object is only to ask questions of an archetypal radical development geography in the expectation that certain issues will be cleared up as a result.

Arguments

This book argues that radical development geography is now closing as many doors as it once opened. It suggests that if radical development geography is to maintain its credibility it must give up four particular failings which now scar it. These failings are a tendency to oppositionism, a tendency to determinism, a tendency to spatial over-aggregation, and a tendency to epistemological confrontation.

Oppositionism

The curse of oppositionism is at the root of each of the three following failings, and I would define it as the tendency to confront a given argument simply by standing it on its head. Rather than accepting some parts or clauses of an argument the entire corpus is rejected and turned upside down (though its axle, or logic, is often retained).

This tendency is all too apparent in radical development studies and we shall have cause to examine its consequences in each of the four main chapters. In Chapter 2 it is capitalism itself which is at issue. I will argue that many radical geographers have arrived at their definitions of capitalism by subverting the vision of the capitalist world economy so publicly promoted by the likes of Rostow. Following Frank and certain other neo-Marxists, they have defined capitalism so that it must actively promote the underdevelopment of the Third World. In this way modernisation theory is rejected *tout court*, but its basic logic is unknowingly accepted. Capitalism either promotes development by definition or it promotes underdevelopment by definition. In neither model is there anything approaching a middle ground, nor is there any real space for mediating factors.

In Chapter 3 the oppositionism is evident in radical development geography's critique of demographic and environmental determinism. I suggest that radical geography has moved too easily from the (correct) recognition that population growth does not cause underdevelopment, to the (incorrect) claim that population growth rates are irrelevant to patterns of differential development. A similar lack of logic is evident in the critique of environmental determinism. In Chapter 4 the concerns of neo-Marxism are back on the agenda. This time I challenge the view that capitalism is incapable of promoting the industrialisation of the Third World. This deterministic view is shown to have emerged in opposition to the equally bland, but this time optimistic, view that capitalism can, will and must promote the industrialisation of the periphery. Finally, Chapter 5 explores the logic and the implications of the core-periphery and North-South models which radicals hold in common with their 'opponents'. Contrasting the diffusionist sentiments of the original centre-periphery models with the core versus periphery claims of the Left, I argue that both schools of thought are committed to models of the world economy which are so spatially generalised as to be of little practical use in guiding contemporary geopolitics.

Determinism

A second flaw in the make-up of radical development geography is its determinism. Though scornful of environmental or demographic determinism, it is evident that many radical theorists of development – and not just geographers – have adopted their own unhelpful and unnecessarily deterministic models of capitalism and its effects. Once again the roots of these models can be traced back to a desire to confront an opponent's vision – but their consequences are still with us.

Within contemporary radical development geography there are two main accounts of the relationship between capitalism, development and underdevelopment. On the one hand there is the neo-Marxist account which was favoured by radical geography from the first and which has been given a new lease of life by the recent adulation of Wallerstein. In this model capitalism is shown as a system of global production and exchange – especially exchange – in which the centre necessarily exploits the periphery to secure its own future growth. The possibility that capitalism might promote the development of the Third World is rejected as absurd because of the function that the South *must* play in this overall system. A precondition for peripheral development is thus a disengagement from the capitalist world system, but even this is thought to be forbidden by the all-powerful metropolitan authorities.

Set against this there is the more classically Marxist model developed by the so-called structural Marxists or Althusserians.[9] In this more sophisticated model it is allowed that underdevelopment is not directly promoted by the fact of it being capitalist. The idea that development and underdevelopment are two sides of the same capitalist coin is rejected on the grounds that this contradicts the rather progressive vision of capitalism first advanced by Marx, Lenin and Luxemburg. Instead, the Third World is said to be underdeveloped because it is not capitalist enough. The metropolitan powers are believed to preserve pre-capitalist relations of production in the periphery, (and the political systems appropriate to them, such as tribalism or apartheid), because this is the most rational way for them to secure and reproduce a cheap labour force.

Undoubtedly there is much to be said for this model, particularly as it is developed by some members of the French school – notably Meillassoux. Nevertheless, the model is still couched in a deterministic framework. Modes of production in the periphery are said to be articulated with the metropolitan capitalist mode of production in such a way that developments in the former (where a degree of relative autonomy is enjoyed) must always be subordinate 'in the last instance' to the determining needs and requirements of the centre. In practical and political terms the implications of such theorising are again deeply pessimistic, for it suggests that economic and political action in the periphery will only be brooked to the extent that it has the assent of the centre. Once more this is by definition. Capitalism is presented in such a way that its reproduction is eternal, and it must be based on the continuing domination of the periphery by the centre. The possibility that this system might at points be challenged is not considered in this theoretical system. Similarly, there is no conception that the relationship between 'capitalism' and the 'Third World' could be theorised in less teleological and less deterministic terms. (One alternative I will suggest runs as follows: capitalist relations of production are understood to depend upon, or to presuppose, the prior establishment of certain conditions of existence – but these conditions of existence cannot be supposed to be provided as of right or in any predetermined form. In this fashion the prevailing rationalist conception of capitalism is undone and we can begin to contest the pessimistic logic that is spread by the Althusserian view of capitalism as a self-reproducing totality.)[10]

Spatial over-aggregation

A third weakness of the radical paradigm is its willingness to conceive of the capitalist world system in terms of North versus South, or core versus periphery. I have already suggested that an emphasis upon these enormous spatial aggregates has its roots in a confrontation with earlier centre-periphery models. It can also be traced back to the influence of Wallerstein, whose popularity in geography is itself a function of his use of very clear spatial metaphors. What is at issue, though, are the consequences of this vision. In my view, an exclusive emphasis upon just two spatial blocs obscures many other important fractures that have developed in the post-war international economic and political system. In Chapter 4 we will have cause to trace out these developments in terms of the selective industrialisation of the Third World. In fact I will join others in questioning the current validity of the term *the* Third World.[11] Nevertheless, we are also concerned with the North, or the core. In Chapter 5 I argue that whilst the North does oppose the South in many contexts and arenas, this is not the whole story. For various reasons there are now cracks appearing in the North – to such an extent that rivalries between the trilateral powers may yet provide certain Southern countries with a degree of leverage in their quest for international trading and monetary reforms.

Epistemological confrontation

Finally, there is the question of epistemological confrontation. Given what has already been said about radical development geography it is to be expected that it will face an increasing barrage of criticism in the years to come. As less convinced scholars finally cut through the walls of jargon, so they will come to a more informed challenge of some of radical geography's sacred cows: on the facts of Third World industrialisation, for example, or on the relevance of population and other resource factors.

The question is, how will radical geography deal with these points? Michael Chisholm has already indicated what he expects to be the answer. In the introduction to his book on *Modern World Development*, Chisholm suggests that radical geographers must take much of the blame for the 'apparent dialogue of the deaf which [now] seems to characterise much writing [in our field]' (Chisholm, 1982, p. 11). Sadly I must concur. Though I am less convinced than Chisholm that this stand-off has its roots in questions of scale or in interdisciplinary disputes, I do detect in many radical writings a predisposition to arrogance and contempt rather than to engagement and debate. The roots of this seem to me to lie in epistemological invective. Given that the emerging radical orthodoxy is steeped in a rationalist philosophy of science, the tendency is for its proponents to ward off all criticism by decrying the methodological basis of their assailant's case. Much like the empiricist who would reject as ideological (and therefore unscientific) all knowledges not steeped in basic 'facts' or data, the rationalist rejects as ideological all knowledges not produced by prescribed procedures. In this case the favoured methodology is Marxism, or what Harvey and many others like to call 'scientific Marxism'. Unless critics have grasped the basic truth of Marxism, the argument goes, there can be no point in taking their criticisms seriously.

It is possible that this is an overstatement. Nevertheless this tendency to confrontation is quite apparent in Chapter 3, where David Harvey is seen to dismiss Malthusianism on the grounds that it is not Marxist, rather than on the grounds that it is racked by contradictions. My grounds for rejecting such procedures are quite straightforward. Following Hindess and Hirst I will argue that all forms of epistemological discourse, or 'argument', can be dismissed because of their 'ultimate circularity and dogmatism' (Hindess and Hirst, 1977, p. 13). The epistemological project consists of setting up a uniquely privileged, or 'scientific' level of discourse, in which the privilege itself (be it the pure facts of the empiricist, or the proper procedures of the rationalist) can only be demonstrated 'by means of discourses that are themselves held to be privileged' (ibid, p. 14). It follows that if radical development geography is ever to meet a rising tide of criticism it must first give up this easy, but pernicious, option and begin again to confront and engage the arguments of less committed colleagues.[12] A dialogue of the deaf is of no value to anyone: not to radical development geography, and certainly not to those poor people in the Third World whose future depends in part upon the political guidance offered by informed theory.

Structure, style and content

Thus far I may have given the impression that this book is not only polemical but excessively theoretical. I hope that this is not the case. What I have just sketched out are the underlying themes of the book; the four points of attack which guide the text from chapter to chapter. The organisation of the book, however, is not in terms of oppositionism, determinism, over-aggregation and epistemology. Since these are recurrent points of reference such a structure would hardly make sense. Instead, I would ask readers to keep these general themes in mind as their implications are explored in four more specific, and for the most part quite empirical, review papers: on Capitalism, Development and Underdevelopment (Part I, Chapter 2); on Capitalism, Determinism and Development (Part II, Chapter 3); on Capitalism, Industrialisation and Development (Part II, Chapter 4) and on Capitalism, Interdependency and Development (Part II, Chapter 5).

Chapter 2 is the cornerstone of the book. At this point the concept of capitalism itself is under review and we examine how radical development theorists (within and outside geography) have sought to deploy this key concept to 'explain' global patterns of differential development. The chapter traces through the genesis and elaboration of two contrasting accounts of capitalism and its effects in the Third World. Both these accounts – the neo-Marxist and the structural Marxist – are criticised on several grounds, and I conclude with some thoughts on how the relationship between capitalism, development and underdevelopment might be theorised in less grandiose and less deterministic terms.

Chapters 3, 4, and 5 explore the empirical and political consequences of adopting the intellectual frameworks outlined in Part I. The focus of Chapter 3 is on the way in which radical development geography has confronted, and in turn theorised, the 'physical' factor in economic development: be this demographic or environmental. I will argue that radical scholars have done sterling work in trashing the sterile determinisms of the Malthusians and the environmentalists, but that in challenging the idea that physical factors cause underdevelopment they have leapt too quickly to the view that capitalism alone determines underdevelopment. By a careful review of the recent environmental and demographic literature I hope to show that this is not the case. More generally, I hope to show that not all demographic and environmental effects can be referred back to, or read off from, some 'essentialising'[13] conception of capitalism. They must instead be understood as important conditions of existence of capitalist development in the Third World. To deny this by resorting to epistemological claims can only be counter-productive.

Chapter 4 takes up a further aspect of the radical's deterministic vision of capitalism and its effects: that of industrialisation. Again, the general point which I wish to make is a simple one. I suggest that capitalism is capable of promoting a selective and 'developmental' industrialisation of the Third World, and I argue that this process cannot be understood solely in terms of restructuring and relocation theories (whereby Northern transnational companies – TNCs – are said to integrate the newly industrialising countries – NICs – into a metropolitan-dominated new international division of labour). Some room must also be found for positive government actions in particular Southern countries, and for the prompting role of particular class structures in the periphery. In support of these central claims the chapter ranges quite widely. Specifically, it reviews the debates which continue to surround the work of Bill Warren, and it takes up the subsequent controversies that have emerged concerning the role of the TNCs and the significance of the NICs.

Finally, Chapter 5 takes issue with the North–South, core versus periphery visions of radical development theory. The differentiation of the South, of course, is one of the themes of Chapter 4. In Chapter 5 the focus is on the possible future disintegration of the core. Having once more indicated a set of common assumptions shared by the radical, Keynesian and neo-classical accounts of interdependency, I trace out those recent intra-Northern bloc rivalries over trade and finance that point up the need for a more disaggregated model of the world's geopolitical economy. For purposes of presentation this discussion is centred on an analysis of the reactions to the two Brandt reports, in which I draw on the writings of Riccardo Parboni, an Italian socialist who deals persuasively with the geopolitics of international relations.

Let me conclude with a few words about style and omissions. Given the aims of this book it will be apparent that its structure is dictated by two clear points of departure. On the one hand there are the basic underlying themes of oppositionism, determinism and so on. On the other hand there are the contexts in which these themes are explored and their consequences mapped out – on population and the environment, on industrialisation and on global geopolitics. Together these vectors impose a very definite style on the book. At the most basic level it means that it cannot hope to be a textbook in the conventional sense of that word. Less obviously it demands that a few topics are given extensive treatment, rather than a large number of topics being given the rudest of once-overs. The reason for this is that the primary purpose of the book is to provide a critical human geography. The job of each chapter, therefore, is to present a debate, or more often a series of debates, illustrative of one or two central themes. It is the dialogue that matters here; the engagement more than the exposition.

Two consequences follow from this and they need to be signposted well in advance. First, it is inevitable that much has had to be left out. To readers expecting an informed discussion of capitalist agriculture in the Third World, or of the urban problem in the periphery, or of migration and urban bias, let me offer my apologies right away. Unfortunately Salman Rushdie is right when he maintains that 'every story one chooses to tell is a kind of censorship, it prevents the telling of other tales' (Rushdie, 1983, p. 71). In this book I have allowed the censor's axe to fall on those topics which I have discussed elsewhere (urban bias)[14] and on those topics – the 'urban arena' – where radical geography's contribution has been most successful.[15] More positively, I can say that I have chosen to concentrate on those debates which seem to me to highlight the general themes under examination here. Thus the chapter on environmental and demographic factors is a particularly useful field within which to probe the (possibly contradictory) conditions of existence of capitalist development. To put it another way, this chapter helps to highlight the failures of an over-determining model of capitalism and its effects. By contrast, Chapters 4 and 5 both take issue with the suggestion that capitalism must have such and such a spatial effect at a global scale: that it must prevent the industrialisation of the South, and that it must lead to the perpetual opposition of North and South in political arenas.

That being said, let me say, finally, that whilst Chapters 3–5 are written in support of a wider argument, they are also written with an eye to some degree of internal coherence and comprehensiveness. As a result it should be possible to read each chapter as a review in its own right, which may be a bonus factor.[16] At the same time readers will have to work a little harder at moving between the chapters, reminding themselves of the general themes which link Part I to Part II. They will also have to make some allowance for the lack of professional geography in some sections of the latter chapters. Sadly, it remains the case that geographers have had little to say about a number of the key issues which are now informing development studies. Partly as a result of the limited successes which I will be documenting here, radical geography has remained content with a rather limited reading of today's development agenda.

2
Capitalism, Development and Underdevelopment

Introduction

This chapter examines the concepts of capitalism upon which radical development geography has based itself, and from which its major strengths and weaknesses derive.

Section 2.1 presents a brief genealogy of the neo-Marxist account of capitalism and the development of underdevelopment. This tradition has long been influential within radical geography where it made its mark mainly through the ideas of Gunder Frank and others in the Latin American school of underdevelopment theory.[1] However, whilst the views of Frank (and Wallerstein) deserve our consideration, the neo-Marxist agenda was first established by Paul Baran. As a result we must begin with an act of recovery. Our first task is to retrace the intellectual roots of Paul Baran's work and to uncover the background against which he wrote *The Political Economy of Growth*. Only then will we see how far neo-Marxism has moved from its classical roots and how it comes to be dominated by a theory of under-consumptionism and by an emphatic mistrust of monopoly capital. In Baran's work we will also discover the basically quantitative model of development and underdevelopment for which Gunder Frank is so rightly famed. From Baran onwards neo-Marxism has been concerned with the production and transfer of a physical surplus. It is less concerned with class relations of production and with capitalism's insistent quest for the more efficient production of relative surplus-value.[2]

In section 2.2 these neo-Marxist ideas are subjected to a critique. Following Robert Brenner (and others) I argue that the neo-Marxist account is unable to grasp what is truly significant about capitalism and capitalist development. Instead, it has built upon Baran to provide a stagnationist and zero-sum theory of development and underdevelopment which is little more than a mirror image of the modernisation account it claims to surpass. Whilst the spatial dimensions of this thesis are attractive to geography it must be clear that neo-Marxism is riddled with tautology and teleology. It has no conception of the qualitative dynamic at the heart of Marx's theory of capitalist development, and it is surprisingly insensitive to basic world geography.

In section 2.3 an outline sketch of the major classical theories of capitalist development is presented: those of Marx, Lenin and Luxemburg. This may seem a topsy-turvy way of proceeding but in the development studies literature an appreciation of classical Marxism was sought only as the failings of neo-Marxism became apparent. In radical development geography this quest for a more 'scientific' Marxism was led by David Slater, and this section of the chapter is much dependent upon his guide to early post-Frankian development studies.

Section 2.4 shows Slater's influence beginning to recede. At this point our attention shifts to the second major contemporary account of capitalist development and underdevelopment. This is the structural Marxist account toward which Slater's (1977) article begins to look, and which has been most fully developed without the borders of geography. The chief concern of this paradigm is with the articulation of modes of production. Moving on from Lenin and Luxemburg, the structuralists have sought to interpret the continuing underdevelopment of the Third World in terms not of the presence of metropolitan capitalism (as per neo-Marxism) but in terms of its absence. In other words the structural Marxists accept the classical Marxist thesis that capitalism is a force for development and not underdevelopment. It is a revolutionary and progressive social force. At the same time they are faced by the fact of continuing underdevelopment in wide swathes of the Third World, and they seek to explain this in terms of the preservation of pre-capitalist modes of production (PCMPs) in the periphery. In those parts of the Third World where capitalism is deemed to be present, these theorists talk of a dependent form of development within a New International Division of Labour (NIDL) (see Chapter 4). As ever there are many variants within this broad tradition and this chapter cannot hope to sketch out more than a few of them. For various reasons the contributions under review here are those of P. P. Rey, Claude Meillassoux and Harold Wolpe.

In section 2.5 these structuralist views are themselves subjected to a critique. On the one hand I accept that the rigour and internal logic of these accounts is a vast improvement upon neo-Marxism. On the other hand I am not convinced that such theorising is the last word in radical development thinking. In my judgement there are problems with an account which depends so heavily upon Althusserian structuralism. In formal terms these problems are those of rationalism and structural causality. Less opaquely, we are faced with the old problem of determinism. The new account of articulation (or *dependencia*)[3] might admit the interaction of different modes of production, but it continues to suggest that what happens in the Third World is done at the First World's bidding. The implication is that the underdevelopment of the periphery, or even its selective 'development', occurs because it happens to 'suit' the core. For various reasons metropolitan capitalism is thought to have an interest in the continuing misdevelopment of the periphery.

To my mind this is not far removed from the functionalism that radicals feign to despise. Once more capitalism is conceived as a totality, and its metropolitan component is endowed with semi-mythical powers and with something like a quest *vis-à-vis* the periphery. At no point is it suggested that the underdevelopment of the periphery might not be in the interests of 'the core', and at no point is it allowed that both development and underdevelopment in the Third World may be partly the responsibility of the Third World's own structures and agencies.

It is to combat this determinism that the final section of the chapter advances a third 'radical' account of capitalism and its effects. This account is based upon the work of Cardoso and that of Hindess and Hirst (and colleagues). What it proposes is a far more diffuse reading of capitalist development and underdevelopment. In place of a self-reproducing mode of production this third theory focuses upon specific relations of production and their conditions of existence. More especially, it recognises two points. First, it recognises that there are no general laws of capitalist development which can be read off in explanation of differential development. In this account, for example, there are no necessary barriers to the industrialisation of the Third World that are given in the concept of capitalism itself. Second, it recognises that any effects that capitalism may have in the Third World will be mediated by conditions of existence whose production and reproduction are not necessarily at its beck and call. In this way some space is cleared for a consideration of (say) demographic and environmental problems in the Third World – problems that have been all but ignored by those accounts holding capitalism alone and *per se* responsible for underdevelopment. It further acknowledges that these conditions of existence cannot always be assumed to be reproduced in the best interests of capital. Very often they might be produced in forms which pose severe problems for capital accumulation and development.

2.1 Neo-Marxist accounts of capitalist development and underdevelopment

Radical geography made its appearance at a time when the ideas of Gunder Frank ruled the roost in left-wing development circles. It is hardly surprising, therefore, that the first radical geographers rendered the underdevelopment question in terms that were explicitly Frankian. Terry Cannon, for example, confidently proclaimed that underdevelopment obtained as a result of 'the antagonistic relations between two groups of countries' (Cannon, 1975, p. 213). More expansively, Richard Peet drew on Frank to maintain that:

> the development of the central regions is predicated on the underdevelopment of peripheries both within capitalist countries and in the Third World. The early functions of the Third World periphery included supplying raw materials to the metropolitan countries, providing markets for their industrial products, and serving as an outlet for surplus capital which if invested in the First World would yield a lower rate of profit. The economies of the colonial and dependent countries were transformed to fit this international division of labour. Subsequently, center and periphery became locked together with the

center appropriating surplus value [*sic*] from the periphery (Peet, 1978, p. 22).

For all Frank's undoubted importance, however, and for all that he and Wallerstein later added to neo-Marxism, the basic concepts of this paradigm were formulated by Paul Baran.

Baran

It is important to establish the status of Paul Baran as 'the true father of neo-Marxism' (Palma, 1978, p. 899), but not just for reasons of historical record. What is truly important about Baran's work, and what lends it a touching irony, is that Baran coined the vocabulary of Neo-Marxism in the context of a discourse which was not primarily addressed to the underdevelopment question. What really concerned Baran was the apparent irrelevance of classical Marxism in the United States of the mid- to late -1950s. Classical Marxism, he said, made its appeal to the working class and to the intelligentsia in terms of its theory of workplace exploitation and by way of its predictions of imminent systemic collapse. In the years of post-war Keynesian boom these ideas seemed rather hollow. Baran reasoned that if the case for democratic socialism was to be re-established in the metropolis it would have to be done on the back of a revamped and 'updated' Marxism.

It was against this background that Baran wrote *The Political Economy of Growth* (first published in 1957). This was an account of capitalist development which emphasised the stagnation (not the dynamism) of metropolitan monopoly capitalism, and its necessary tendencies to waste and a militaristic imperialism as ways of ridding its endemic over-production. In Baran's hands the case against capitalism becomes an essentially quantitative one. His case for democratic socialism depends upon an analysis of the contrasting ways in which the physical surplus was and would be distributed under capitalism and socialism.

Let us now rehearse Baran's thesis in more detail before rejoining the disciplinary fold. *The Political Economy of Growth* begins with an influential distinction between competitive and monopoly capitalism. It also contrasts the production and use of an actual and a potential economic surplus. Baran argues that under competitive capitalism (and under democratic socialism) there is only a small divergence between the actual economic surplus that a society produces and the potential economic surplus that could be produced if resources were more productively deployed and if non-essential consumption were at a minimum.[4] Compared with the pre-existing feudal system, competitive capitalism is said to be marked by an admirable freedom from guilds and other unnecessary restrictions. More positively, the free play of market forces ensures that the striving of individual entrepreneurs to 'get ahead, to accumulate and to enlarge their enterprises, necessarily serve[s] as a powerful engine of expansion' (Baran, 1973, p. 159). Simply to stay alive the capitalists have to 'improve their methods of production, to promote technological progress and to make full use of its results, as well as to increase and diversify their output' (ibid). Market forces also see to it that 'aggregate output [will] normally encounter adequate demand' (ibid). When these features are combined with thrift on the part of the capitalist, and restraint on the part of government, then it is clear, says Baran, that this is a rational economic system. It is a system which brings actual and potential economic surpluses into harmony, and which is reasonably described by the main tenets of perfect competition theory.

The problem is that all good things come to an end.[5] Baran argues that it is a contradiction of competitive capitalism that it contains within it the seeds of its own destruction. Its very thrust to rationalisation and to capital-intensiveness lays the foundations of a system where perhaps one or two, or three or four, firms can begin to use their economies of scale to stifle growth and competition.

Baran suggests that this dawning of the age of monopoly capitalism occurred towards the end of the last century and that the entire world is now living with its ill-effects. Characteristically Baran's argument is made at two levels. At a micro level it turns on a belief that monopolistic and oligopolistic enterprises have no need to be price competitive and that they have a positive bias against innovation. The reason for this is that the conditions and assumptions of perfect competition theory no longer apply. Baran notes that the modern enterprise is not a price-taking family firm whose initial ease of entry into a given industry is offset only by a compulsion to accept average rates of profit. It is, rather, a giant corporation well able to generate an enormous economic surplus but unable to distribute it beyond a small group of controlling capitalists. More pertinently, it is a price-setting institution. Sheltering behind all manner of legal obstacles and government concessions, and simple economies of scale, the modern monopoly inhabits a protected world far removed from that aired by the sharp winds of competition. As a result, says Baran:

> *In any given situation* an expansion of output is likely to be contrary to the monopolist's profit-maximisation policy. Depending on the prevailing elasticity of demand for his product (and the shape of the marginal revenue curve derived therefrom), an increase in output may fail to increase his total profits or may even reduce them below their pre-output expansion level (Baran, 1973, p. 198. Emphasis in the original).

Of course there is rather more to it than this. Baran acknowledges that a monopolist, like any other capitalist, is always interested in reducing his costs of production. But this is offset by certain other monopolistic considerations (such as the desire to preserve the value of existing investment). In any case the detail of this debate need not concern us. What matters is that Baran is driven to uphold Alvin Hansen's contention that 'The problem of our generation is, above all, the problem of inadequate investment outlets' (Baran, 1973, p. 182, quoting Hansen, 1944, p. 379). In Baran's judgement there is a contradiction between the monopolistic firm's capacity to generate an economic surplus and its willingness to reinvest that surplus to secure future development and full employment. Under the regime of the giant firm the actual and potential economic surpluses begin to diverge.

This same contradiction is then traced out at a macro level. Baran suggests that where the organisation of economic life is dictated by large firms taking socially sub-optimal decisions, it must follow that monopoly capitalism itself is prone to stagnation and massive long-run unemployment. Once more:

> *In any given situation* the volume of investment tends to be smaller than the volume of the economic surplus that would be forthcoming under full employment. There is consequently a tendency towards unemployment and stagnation, a tendency towards over-production that was precisely identified by Marx a

hundred years ago (Baran, 1973, p. 207. Emphasis in the original).

Do note this qualification 'in any given situation'. Baran makes it clear that the foregoing is a static description of the macro-economics of monopoly capitalism. In a dynamic analysis an underemployment equilibrium is neither satisfactory nor stable. Indeed he suggests that the social and political repercussions of spiralling unemployment will so threaten the West's existing order that 'the mere continuation of the "given situation" does not represent a practical option that is available for any length of time to the capitalist class' (Baran 1973, p. 209).

The question then is, what does constitute a practical option (putting to one side the 'rational' solution of socialism)? Baran is in no doubt that it is statism and imperialism. To be exact, because 'individual firms cannot be expected to function as Santa Claus to their workers and buyers in order to increase mass consumption' (Baran, 1973, p. 211) and because not even the bourgeoisie can dispose of the economic surplus entirely through waste (in the form of advertising, high salaries, public relations work and so on), the responsibility for fullish employment and for maintaining effective demand must fall on the state.

At home this means that the state is increasingly involved in the provision of collective goods like education and health, in under-writing infrastructural programmes, and in fuelling the arms race (the one sure way to equate supply and demand) – all of which buys time, literally. In a brilliant critique of this 'domestic Keynesianism' Baran charges that it is the new economics of the madhouse.[6] It is little more than a license for printing money, he says, anticipating Mrs Thatcher by twenty years. It is an inflationary discourse which assumes that society is indifferent to the way its purse is spent. A pound on hamburgers, a pound to dig and fill holes, a pound towards the upkeep of an old peoples' home, there is really no difference. Except in one respect. Paying people to dig and fill holes creates 'employment' and thus boosts the bargaining power and wages of the working class. Naturally this is not to the liking of capitalists. Indeed, Keynesian techniques *per se* are not really to their liking, but they accept them grudgingly as a set of necessary political sops or bribes. What the capitalist would prefer

is a 'solution' to the malaise of monopoly capitalism which pre-
serves the domestic peace without threatening profits.

It is at this point that we are get our most direct pointers to the
work of Frank and Wallerstein. Baran now suggests that the
logical second 'safety valve' for monopoly capitalism is to be found
in the imperialistic exploitation of the Third World. He further
argues that this exploitation will not foster the long-run development of the periphery (as classical Marxism taught), but will
ensure its continuing underdevelopment. Finally, Baran offers
some thoughts on why it is that Western Europe and North
America have for so long been the imperialist powers.

Consider first the safety-valve thesis. Baran's comments on this
issue are not always clear, and they are certainly not easy to
summarise. We have to draw on anecdotes here and there to form
any sort of coherent picture. Even so, he is precise on at least two
points: that 'spending on imperialist policy . . . is the one form of
[government spending] that is fully acceptable to monopoly capital' (Baran, 1973, pp. 246–7), and that it is for this reason that
'economic development in underdeveloped countries is pro-
foundly inimical to the dominant interests in the advanced capitalist countries' (ibid, p. 120).

This conjunction needs emphasising. For Baran (unlike Frank,
who later reversed the causal arrow) the exploitation of the Third
World is not the primum mobile of metropolitan development. Of
course one can find passages which seem to contradict this interpretation. Early on in *The Political Economy of Growth*, Baran
maintains that 'the backward world has always represented the
indispensable hinterland of the highly developed capitalist West'
(ibid, p. 120),[7] and he is not slow to criticise that multinational
exploitation of the periphery which supplies 'many important raw
materials to the industrialised countries [and provides] their corporations with vast profits [as well as] investment outlets' (ibid), but
it is surely the investment outlets which are critical. Unless I have
misread Baran, the logic runs firmly from under-consumptionism
in the core to the exploitation of the Third World. It is because of
the contradictions of metropolitan monopoly capitalism that large
firms are driven to invest in the periphery. It is because they
cannot push their home workers too far that the super-exploitation
of foreign workers becomes necessary, and it is because government spending at home is so problematical that spending on

imperialism is so desirable. From Baran's perspective, the increase in income and employment that an imperialist country may gain from trade and foreign investment is not of primary concern (though it is with Frank). What matters is that imperialism offers an ideologically sound outlet for the overflowing economic surplus. As Baran puts it:

> the continuation or even expansion of imperialist policies and of military outlays related to them obtain the support not merely of their direct beneficiaries: the corporations collecting vast profits from their government-backed dealings abroad, the firms whose business is to supply the government with military equipment, the generals and admirals anxious not to be relieved of their none-too-arduous responsibilities, the intellectuals who find ample application for their talents in various organisations that owe their existence to those policies, and the 'labour aristocracy' gathering the crumbs from the monopolistic tables. Large-scale spending on military purposes appears essential to society as a whole, to all its classes, groups, and strata whose jobs and incomes depend on the resulting maintenance of high levels of business activity (Baran, 1973, p. 247; see also Figure 2.1).

This could not be much plainer, and it is in this fashion that Baran provides neo-Marxism with its distinctive under-consumptionism, even as he pulls back from Frank's later apophthegm that capitalism *per se* creates the development of underdevelopment. (In *The Political Economy of Growth* it is monopoly capitalism that is charged with this crime.) Nevertheless, the similarities between Baran and the later neo-Marxists far outweigh any differences. Baran's discussion of a labour aristocracy, for instance, sits cosily with the idea that the South as a whole must throw off the chains of the North as a whole. (See in particular Emmanuel's unequal exchange thesis.)[8] Similarly, Baran is in accord with later neo-Marxists in his appreciation of imperialism's effects on the Third World. Just as firmly as Frank, he maintains that 'the ruling class in the United States (and elsewhere) is bitterly opposed to the industrialisation of the so-called "source countries" and to the emergence of integrated processing economies in the colonial and semi-colonial areas' (Baran, 1973, p. 120.

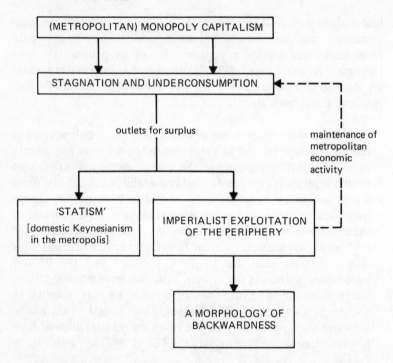

FIGURE 2.1   *Baran: monopoly capitalism and underdevelopment*

Chapter 4 will take up this claim at greater length). He believes
too that this must mark the periphery with a peculiar morphology
of backwardness. Baran suggests that a typical Third World country will be dependent upon a large agricultural sector, itself dominated by large export-oriented plantations. It will also be staffed
by sizeable stratum of merchants and money-lenders and other
'parasites', just as it will be topped off by various unhealthy
regimes – be they colonies, comprador elites or self-deluding
New-Deal-style governments.

Finally, Baran foreshadows the future in what he has to say
about the past, about the origins of development and underdevelopment, or at least he does so some of the time. In the first half of
The Political Economy of Growth Baran seems to subscribe to a
rather rose-tinted view of metropolitan competitive capitalism.

The dynamic for this is located firmly within Europe and North America, with its entrepreneurs and with its class structures. Towards the end of the book, however, more Frankian perspectives emerge which emphasise plunder, rapine and the geographical transfer of a surplus as a [the?] crucial boost to Euro-American development. Here we are told that [seventeenth or eighteenth century?] pre-capitalist systems were everywhere entering a period of disintegration and decay (Baran, 1973, p. 268). The only difference between Europe, Asia and Africa is that mercantile accumulations were especially large in Europe (in part because natural resources were so poor) and this, plus an early lead in navigation, allowed the ascendency of Western Europe. Even then Baran draws back from a bluntly zero-sum conception of world affairs, noting that 'Western Europe's large leap forward need not necessarily have prevented growth in other countries' (Baran, 1973, p. 271). Reverting to his distinction between competitive and monopoly capitalism, Baran suggests that in the early years of modern capitalism:

> the expanding contact with the scientifically and technologically leading Western European nations might have been expected to facilitate the forward movement of the countries with which Western Europe came into contact [and] so it actually appeared during the later seventeenth and eighteenth centuries (ibid, p. 272).

Only later did things change and did it become obvious that the country which is more developed industrially was not showing to the less developed the image of its own future.

A certain ambiguity, then, marks *The Political Economy of Growth* (or, if you prefer, a proper respect for the enormously 'complex effects of Western European capitalist penetration of the outside world', Baran, 1973, p. 273). Nevertheless, it is clear that Baran does anticipate most of what was to become neo-Marxism. Though his starting-point is some way removed from Frank's, Baran does link the development of some few countries with the underdevelopment of the many, and he does set in train a straightforwardly quantitative model of capitalist economic growth (based on the transfer of a physical surplus). He also begins to suggest that a precondition for Third World development involves the severing of its links with international capitalism.

Frank and Wallerstein

None of this is meant to decry the significance of Gunder Frank and Immanuel Wallerstein, the two remembered heroes of radical development geography.[9] Both these authors added to Paul Baran's work in ways which were at once attractive to geographers and which removed neo-Marxism still further from its classical roots.

Frank   Let us begin with the work of Gunder Frank. Frank is the first to acknowledge his debt to Baran, and he has written rather touchingly of the latter as a 'pioneer who inspired'.[10] More substantively, it is clear that Frank has taken from Baran a rigid underconsumptionism and a contempt for the supposed stagnationism induced by metropolitan monopoly capital. Following on from Baran, Frank is quite unable to conceive of the possibility of autocentric and qualitative development in the core. Instead he is led to present Baran's quantitative model of economic development and underdevelopment in a more explicitly spatial guise. In Frank's early work we are faced with an account of underdevelopment cast in terms of a chain of exploitative metropolis–satellite relationships wherein:

> at each stage along the way the relatively few capitalists above exercise monopoly power over the many below, expropriating some or all of their economic surplus and, to the extent that they are not expropriated in turn by the still fewer above, appropriating it for their own use . . . at each point the international, national and local capitalist system generates economic development for the few and underdevelopment for the many (Frank, 1969, pp. 7–8; see also Figure 2.2).

Frank moved beyond Baran, however, when he declared that these monopolistic surplus transfers had been characteristic of capitalism since the time of its birth; that they were not just a product of an unhappy later stage. For Frank these unequal global exchange relations become the very essence of capitalism, and in

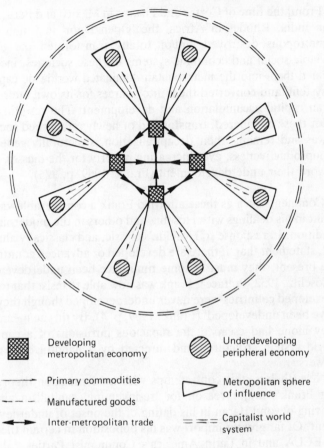

SOURCE   Adapted from Gore (1984), Figure 21.

FIGURE 2.2   *Frank: core, periphery and the capitalist world-system*

his account they quite displace the old Marxist emphasis upon the conjugation of particular forces and relations of production as the defining feature of a mode of production. (This is an area of some ambiguity in *The Political Economy of Growth*.) Most importantly, this new definition allowed Frank to argue that development and underdevelopment have been produced as two sides of the same capitalist coin since the inception of this global system in the later fifteenth century. As he put it in 1969:

[From] the time of Cortez and Pizarro in Mexico and Peru, Clive in India, Rhodes in Africa, the 'Open Door' in China – the metropolis destroyed and/or totally transformed the earlier viable social and economic systems of these societies, incorporated them into the metropolitan dominated worldwide capitalist system, and converted them into sources for its own metropolitan capital accumulation and development. The resulting fate for these conquered, transformed or newly established societies was and remains their decapitalization, structurally generated unproductiveness, ever-increasing poverty for the masses – in a word their underdevelopment (Frank, 1969, p. 225).

Comments such as these afforded Frank a considerable vantage point in his dealings with Hoselitz and others in the modernisation tradition. In response to Hoselitz's classic, and classically ahistorical, statement that 'if there are developed or advanced countries in the present, they must at some time have been underdeveloped' (Hoselitz, 1952, Preface), Frank was now able to insist that today's 'developed countries were never underdeveloped though they may have been undeveloped' (Frank, 1969, p. 4). By this he meant that they alone had escaped the rapacious intrusions of a capitalist world system structured and directed by a handful of external powers.

Nevertheless, this contretemps with modernisation theory was not Frank's major reason for 're-inventing' capitalism and for moving beyond Baran in his dating of the onset of underdevelopment. Of far greater import was his opposition to certain theorists in ECLA and in Latin America's Communist Parties.[11] In the early 1960s these two groups were arguing that Latin America could not hope to become socialist in the foreseeable future. Radical activists had to devote their energies, instead, to working for the victory of a progressive national bourgeoisie over the feudal– imperialist alliance.[12] Frank was quite opposed to this advice. Looking to Cuba he saw concrete evidence of the possibilities of socialist advance, and it is significant that one collection of his essays is dedicated to 'the Latin American Revolution and the inspiration it finds in the Cuban Revolution, whose tenth glorious anniversary we celebrate while writing these lines' (Frank, 1969, p. ix). Nevertheless, Frank was aware that the Cuban example could be dismissed as the exception that proved the rule. A less vulnerable case for socialist politics would have to be made in wider, possibly theoretical, terms. It is for this reason, I think, that Frank sought to characterise Latin America as a long-established capitalist society. Once the idea was implanted that Latin America had been capitalist since 1492 Frank could go on to portray its apparently different labour systems (latifundia, minifundia, even slavery) as essentially capitalist labour systems describing essentially capitalist class relations of production. More pertinently, Frank could insist that it was absurd to look to a capitalist bourgeoisie to develop Latin America. According to Frank's account this bourgeoisie had actually been an accomplice to the process of underdevelopment. It remained a comprador element introduced into Latin America by the imperialists to part-supervise the transfer of a surplus from satellite to metropolis. As a result the real political choice facing Latin America lay between barbarism and socialism.

Now critics might argue that this is a case of the tail wagging the dog, and before long I shall want to comment on the circularity of Frank's logic here. As Brewer points out, Frank has to define capitalism in the way that he does to square the circle of his previous assertions: that capitalism always creates underdevelopment, and that Latin America has been underdeveloping since 1492. Apart from global exchange relations, 'What other characteristics of the economic system could [Frank] point to that have been operating in Latin America over such a long span?' (Brewer, 1980, p. 160).

For all that, Frank's significance cannot be gainsaid. Rightly or wrongly (perhaps rightly and wrongly) he has alerted politicians to the 'perils of collaborationism' in an unequally interdependent world. More so than Baran he has drawn attention to impulses and demands operating at a global or systemic scale. At the same time Frank has put revolutionary socialism back on the agenda, confirming a whole host of academics in a belief that 'short of liberation from this capitalist structure, or the dissolution of the world capitalist system as a whole, the capitalist satellite countries, regions, localities and sectors are condemned to underdevelopment' (Frank, 1967, p. 11). In geography this is evident in Blaut's suggestion that 'there is no real foreign aid (save Green Berets and guns), and there is no population problem' (Blaut, 1973, p. 23). It is also apparent in Browett's claim that 'a benevolent capitalism . . . does not, never will, constitute a panacea which provides a middle route between barbarism and socialism' (Browett, 1981, p. 160). Many other examples also exist.

Wallerstein   These claims have since been taken up by Immanuel Wallerstein, who has become the latest guru to radical development geography. In outline terms the account that he has offered of *The Modern World System* is little removed from that of Frank. Once more we are told:

1. that metropolitan capitalist social formations penetrate natural (pre-capitalist) economies and appropriate their economic surplus;
2. that this is the direct result of under-consumptionist contradictions in the core;
3. that this penetration leads almost immediately to the capitalist transformation of the periphery, and to a process of underdevelopment which is not only economic, but also political and social.[13]

Nevertheless, Wallerstein has added to the neo-Marxist pantheon in three clear respects. First, Wallerstein has offered a more precise delineation of both pre-capitalist and capitalist social systems. Like Frank before him, Wallerstein insists that it is the social system that it is of prime importance, and that external factors must take precedence over internal factors in accounts of underdevelopment. Wallerstein believes that modern nation–states bow to the logic of social systems whose chief defining characteristic is the existence within them 'of a division of labour, such that the various sectors or areas within are dependent upon economic exchange with others for the smooth and continuous provisioning of the needs of the area' (Wallerstein, 1979, p. 5). Wallerstein moves beyond Frank, however, when he suggests that there have been three such social systems and not just one, or one and a bit. Where Frank sees capitalism and 'natural economies' Wallerstein sees mini-systems (closed local economies), world-empires (defined by the extraction of tribute by a central authority) and world economies.[14] This last system is clearly capitalist, says Wallerstein, because its 'essential feature is production for sale in a market in which the object is to realise the maximum profit' (ibid, p. 15). It is also a world system because it comprises a unit with a single division of labour and multiple cultural systems. It follows that 'Capitalism and a world economy (that is, a single division of labour but multiple polities and cultures) are obverse sides of the same coin. One does not cause the other. We are merely defining the same indivisible phenomenon by different characteristics' (ibid, p. 6).

Second, Wallerstein further refined Frank's work when he looked at the geographical divisions of this capitalist world system. Wallerstein argues that there are not two, but three, tiers of states: those of the core, the periphery and the semi-periphery. 'The essential difference between these is the strength of the state machine in different areas' (Brewer, 1980, p. 165), and it is this which cranks the handle of Wallerstein's model of surplus transfer. Actors in the core (the capitalists) are able to call on their state machines to manipulate an economic system which is otherwise geared to the geographical equalisation of profits. In effect they use state power deliberately and persistently to weaken (underdevelop) the periphery; by conquest, by monopoly, by protectionism and so on. But not the semi-periphery. Wallerstein implies that it suits the core states to preserve a (variable) semi-periphery as a sort of buffer between themselves and the periphery.[15] Brewer likens this to a kind of labour aristocracy of states or geographical areas, and this just about captures it. Certainly the semi-periphery is vital to Wallerstein's divide-and-rule account of the failures of peripheral politicisation.

Third, there is the matter of Wallerstein's class analysis. Again this is in the Frankian mould, with any number of 'modes of labour control' (wage labour, serfdom, share-cropping, slavery, etc) held to be capitalist so long as they take shape within a capitalist world market. However there are some subtle differences. Wallerstein is more explicit than Frank in rejecting the classically Marxian view of capitalism as a system based on the production and reproduction of free wage labour. He argues that:

the relations of production that define a system are the 'relations of production' of the whole system and the system at this point

in time is the European world economy. Free labour is indeed a
defining feature of capitalism, but not free labour throughout
the productive enterprises (Wallerstein, 1974, p. 127).[16]

More crucially, it is Wallerstein who points up the true functionalism of the neo-Marxist project. In this same paragraph he suggests
that 'free labour is the form of labour control used [he might have
said chosen] for skilled work in core countries whereas coerced
labour is used for less skilled work in peripheral areas. The
combination thereof is the essence of capitalism. When labour is
everywhere free, we shall have socialism' (ibid). It would be hard
to find a more concise statement of the belief that class systems, or
modes of labour control, are but the secondary results of the
functioning of a world system.

2.2 A critique of neo-Marxism

It must be emphasised that this view is not Wallerstein's alone.
Wallerstein is merely codifying what is already implicit in the work
of Frank and many others (Dos Santos, for example, and Amin)
whose work we have not space to consider here. What matters is
that a strong tradition has grown up around Baran, Frank and now
Wallerstein, which challenges the 'progressive' view of capitalism
in the Third World, and which has begun to reshape disciplines
such as geography.

Frank had been especially influential in this last respect. It is
now clear that it was Frank's attack on the linear evolutionism of
Rostow's stages of growth model which pushed McGee to denounce a geography of modernisation which 'reasserts the primacy of the American–European experience and [which] assumes
a repetitive process in the LDCs' (McGee, 1974, p. 31). Likewise
it was Frank's success in challenging the absurdities which, he said,
comprised the sociology of development – a perspective that spoke
of consensus and convergence even as Saigon burned and the
development gap widened–which encouraged Slater to repudiate
those geographies granting 'no history to the so-called traditional
sector of the underdeveloped economy' (Slater, 1973, p. 22).
Frank's work has also been called upon to banish the evils of
Eurocentrism and ethnocentrism (see McGee, 1978; Browett,

1981); to turn on its head the spatial logic of core–periphery and regional planning models (Friedmann and Wulff, 1976; Blaikie, 1978; Gore, 1984); and to make the case for a committed, revolutionary geography (Santos, 1974). Now it is Wallerstein's turn to come to the fore. His insistence upon the epistemological primacy of a world systems perspective has been warmly welcomed by Taylor, who believes that the 'modern world capitalist economy [may be] the ultimate solution to the geographer's problem of object of study' (Taylor, 1981, p. 162). It has also been lauded by those anxious to 'sociologise the geographical imagination'.[17]

The question which we now have to ask is whether or not this enthusiasm is justified. In some respects it is tempting to agree that it is. The views of the neo-Marxists were clearly instrumental in the reinvigoration of theoretical development geography in the 1970s, and they helped the discipline to retheorise a number of contentious issues. Above all, the neo-Marxists helped to steer geography away from an often unconsidered empiricism and towards an account of national and regional geographies which took note [perhaps too much note] of systemic impulses and transnational factors. (In this context see Ron Johnston's article, 'The World is Our Oyster' [1984]. Johnston argues passionately that geography must give up an encroaching parochialism and that it must focus on an 'economic system which links all parts of the world into a single functioning unit and which contains the dynamo for all societal activity' [Johnston, 1984, p. 443]. Elsewhere, Johnston has spoken of the impact upon him 'of the structuralist argument; that there are underlying forces creating a differentiated world and one has to see this differentiation in the context of the structural whole' [in Gold and Shepherd, 1983, p. 121].)

Nevertheless, we must be wary of assuming that the validity of any perspective is guaranteed by one prescient observation, or by an ability to punch holes in the argument of a poorly defended opponent: in this case modernisation theory and the geography of modernisation. Still less should we assume that neo-Marxism has brought geography to some sort of 'scientific' nirvana where we can at last escape those spells of bourgeois ideology which previously stopped 'development geography from effectively analysing the spatial patterns and structures of underdevelopment' (Slater, 1973, p. 30). (See also Peet, 1978, and Blaut, 1976, for further misuse of the science/ideology division.) This is not only a *non sequitur*, it also happens to be quite false in this instance, for whilst many radical geographers busied themselves with re-runs of the modernisation–underdevelopment debate (see Browett, 1981, 1982; Ettama, 1979, 1983; McGee, 1978; Peet, 1978; Riddell, 1981; Taylor, 1981) a growing number of radicals from economics and sociology were coming to question the very terms of this confrontation, and the very relevance of the new 'scientific' Marxism. Specifically, they started to challenge the one assumption which both neo-Marxists and modernisers take for granted: that the post-1492 expansion of a world market has been the primum mobile behind world development and underdevelopment.

Brenner   In my judgement Robert Brenner has presented this challenge most forcibly (Brenner, 1977; but see also the penetrating accounts of Palma, 1978; Bernstein, 1979; Wolf, 1982; and the articles by Bath and James, 1976; Cardoso, 1977; Laclau, 1979; Lall, 1975, Smith, S, 1980, and Slater, 1977). He recognises, of course, that the neo-Marxist interpretation of the consequences of an expanding world market (the development of underdevelopment) is far removed from the moderniser's account. Not for Frank and Wallerstein a simple tale of light and joy whereby the rationality of a market mentality is progressively introduced into the darkest corners of the globe. Yet Brenner considers this difference of interpretation to be less important than the refusal of neo-Marxism to break with the underlying 'individualistic-mechanistic' presuppositions of its opponent's model.[18] Frank and Wallerstein are still committed to the neo-Smithian conception of capitalism that first surfaces in the latter reaches of Baran's *The Political Economy of Growth*.[19] In this quantitative vision of the modern world system the growth of the core is made to depend upon the workings of an ever more efficient world division of labour.

To be fair, Baran, Frank and Wallerstein have all tried to give this definition a radical gloss. All make abundant reference to Marx in their work and Frank, especially, is careful to insist that the capitalist world system is structured by an 'essential internal contradiction between the exploiting and exploited [which] appears within nations no less than between them' (Frank, 1969, p. 227).

However, this insistence is far from convincing. At the end of the day, Frank, no less than his neo-Smithian opponents, conceives of such 'changing class relations as emerging more or less directly from the (changing) requirements for the generation of surplus and development of production, under the pressures and opportunities engendered by a growing world market' (Brenner, 1977, p. 27). Brenner takes this to be the fundamental flaw of neo-Marxism, and not unreasonably. For having once displaced 'class relations from the centre of their analyses of economic development and underdevelopment' (ibid), Frank *et al.* are unable to grasp the true uniqueness of capitalism as a system of qualitatively expanding commodity production based upon the prior separation of the workers from their means of production and of enterprise from enterprise. Lacking this insight they are instead condemned to present no more than a mirror-image of the 'progressist' thesis they wish to surpass – historical foibles and all.

Some of these foibles are worth looking at because they expose very clearly the political and empirical limitations of a neo-Marxist geography.

Consider, first, the inconsistencies in the neo-Marxist account of the origins of capitalism. Frank and Wallerstein (more so than Baran) claim to be able to trace this back to the fifteenth and sixteenth centuries – well before the traditional Marxist starting-point. They are able to do so because they believe that capitalism exists wherever direct producers assign their produce to the market whilst being deprived of the economic surplus which they helped to create. In their own words:

> a common network spread out from the Italian cities such as Venice, and later Iberian and North-western European towns to incorporate the Mediterranean world and sub-Saharan Africa and the adjacent Atlantic islands in the fifteenth century [and continued] until the entire face of the globe has been incorporated into a single organic mercantilist or mercantile capitalist, and later also industrial and financial, system (Frank, 1972, p. 9).

> with the emergence of the modern world economy in sixteenth century Europe . . . we saw the full development and economic predominance of market trade. This was the system called capitalism (Wallerstein), 1974. p. 67).

However, there are problems with this account. Specifically, it raises the question of why capitalism began as *late* as the fifteenth century. After all, if capitalism is no more than a system of exploitative production for the market, it surely also shaped the lives of 'the slave on a Roman latifundium or the gleb serf of the European Middle Ages, at least in those cases – the overwhelming majority – where the lord assigned part of the economic surplus extracted from the serf for sale' (Laclau, 1979, p. 23). Indeed by this logic 'we could conclude that from the neolithic onwards there has never been anything but capitalism' (ibid). By inventing a definition of capitalism for their own political reasons, Baran and Frank have ensured that modern neo-Marxism is bereft of historical and spatial sensitivity.[20]

Even less convincing is the neo-Marxist account of capitalist development in the core countries. Rather too quickly this asks us to move from the following three propositions:

1. that up to 1492 the world is much of a muchness. (In Blaut's words, Europe at this time is 'traditional and unprogressive; it is . . . a thoroughly medieval culture, indistinguishable in level or trend from a dozen other mercantile, maritime cultures of Africa and Asia' (Blaut, 1973, p. 24);
2. that the voyages of Columbus changed all this. (Themselves the product of geographical good fortune [Blaut] or a limited technological superiority [Wallerstein] they gave the Europeans access to the wealth of the New World);
3. that this wealth has been continually appropriated by the metropolitan nations,

to the conclusion that the West's undoubted ability to control and extend this trade-based division of labour has been, and is, a necessary and a sufficient condition of its economic development. But there are reasons for mistrusting this neo-Smithian logic. As Brenner points out (see Figure 2.3), an inflow of wealth from the periphery will stimulate a systematic development of the core's productive forces:

> only when it expresses certain specific social relations of production, namely a system of free wage labour where labour-power is a commodity. Only where labour has been separated from possession of the means of production, and where labourers

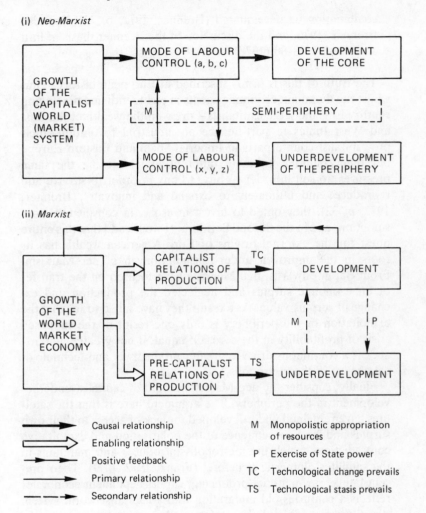

(i) *Neo-Marxist*

(ii) *Marxist*

➡️	Causal relationship
⇨	Enabling relationship
▸▸	Positive feedback
→	Primary relationship
– – ▸	Secondary relationship

M   Monopolistic appropriation of resources
P   Exercise of State power
TC   Technological change prevails
TS   Technological stasis prevails

FIGURE 2.3 *Brenner: the origins of capitalist development*

have been emancipated from any direct relation of domination (such as slavery or serfdom), are both capital and labour-power 'free' to make *possible* their combination at the highest level of technology. Only where they are free, will such combination appear *feasible* and *desirable*. Only where they are free will such combination be necessitated (Brenner, 1977, p. 32). See also Brenner, 1976, and the discussion of the Brenner thesis in *Past and Present* 78–80 (1978).

The truth of this is firmly inscribed in European history. Thus whilst the dominant economic agents in eighteenth and nineteenth century England – the capitalists – drew on the wealth of the East and West Indies to part-finance an industrial revolution, their pre-capitalist counterparts in Imperial Spain and Eastern Europe put their 'plunder' to quite different uses. Lacking the same pressures 'to sell in order to buy, to buy in order to survive and reproduce, and ultimately to expand and innovate' (Brenner, 1977, p. 32), they opted to invest in usury, in conspicuous consumption, and in the Second Serfdom. (I would add that this entire quest for the external origins of Euro-American wealth has its roots in the unproven under-consumptionism of neo-Marxism. From Baran onwards, neo-Marxists have focused on the transfer of an economic surplus and neglected the production and exchange of surplus-value. As a result they have failed to see that the exploitation of the periphery is only one result of the supposed crisis of profitability in the core. Of equal, if not greater, importance is a continuous drive to greater productivity and technological change in the metropolis.)

Finally, consider the neo-Marxist account of capitalist underdevelopment in the periphery. The argument here is that the satellites have remained underdeveloped for lack of access to their own surplus and 'as a consequence of the polarisation and exploitative contradictions which the metropolis introduces and maintains in the satellites' domestic structure' (Frank, 1972, p. 9). Their present fate as raw-material-producing, export-dependent economies reflects a centuries-old integration into a capitalist world system structured by such a plethora of spatially uneven exchange mechanisms – from pillage to debt-financing – that all talk of development within the system can be dismissed as so much wishful thinking. Indeed it is one of Frank's strongest claims that Third World development presupposes a disengagement from the world system,[21] and to this end he cites not only the experience of Meiji Japan (see also Moulder, 1977), but also the historical experience of Latin America since 1914. As he puts it:

It is clearly established and generally recognised that the most important recent industrial development – especially of Argentina, Brazil and Mexico, but also of other countries such as Chile – has taken place during the period of the two World Wars and the intervening depression. Thanks to the consequent loosening of trade and investment ties during these periods the satellites initiated marked autonomous industrialisation and growth (Frank, 1969, p. 10).

Now this may indeed be the case [though see Chapter 4], but think what Frank misses here. To begin with he misses the 1950s, and the 1960s, both decidedly integrationist decades which coincided with a marked upturn in the rates of growth of GNP and industry in Brazil, Mexico and Argentina. More fundamentally, he neglects the past. No less than his modernising opponents, Frank allows no history to the so-called traditional sectors of the underdeveloped economy: precisely the charge that Slater once put to modernisation theory. When Frank looks to Japan he looks not to that country's long struggle to capitalism (so ably documented by T. C. Smith and others),[22] but to the absence of colonialism and metropolitan exploitation from its shores. Development occurs because certain 'systemic' factors are missing. When he looks to Latin America the reverse happens. The fact that 'balanced' development may not have come to Mexico or Brazil because of the dynamics of their *particular* class structures and allied conditions of existence is all but ignored. These factors are mere residuals in an account obsessed by the global level, and the world system. Instead, Frank presents us with an unbelievable picture of a Latin America on the verge of take-off but wickedly foiled by the incoming Spanish and Portugese who imposed their own 'class/labour' systems unopposed.

In short, neither history nor geography is the muse that the neo-Marxists would like it to be. But what lessons are we to draw from all this? Frank and Wallerstein, and their geographical camp-followers, will doubtless insist that nothing has really changed. As far as they are concerned this sort of 'Warrenite' attention to regional industrialisation rates and the like can be dismissed as a bourgeois predilection for empiricism.[23] Indeed Petras, Peet, Slater and Blaut (amongst others) have all at one time denounced it as a mistaken preference for the ideological realm of appearances over the truly scientific, and curiously unchanging, sphere of essences. (In this case the essence of the capitalist world system is the existence of an unequal flow of surplus from the satellite to the metropolis. What is incidental to it is the precise form in which these transfers take place, and the mediating factors that might affect their effectiveness in time and space.)

Others will find this perverse. There is much to value in neo-Marxism, but not this Churchillian tendency to shout where the argument is weakest. This merely highlights an arrogant delight in the epistemological one-two; in that science–ideology word-play which Koestler once likened to 'a kind of Wonderland croquet played with mobile hoops' (Koestler, 1980, p. 63). Worse still, it points up the fatal flaw of neo-Marxism: its ahistoricism. Ironically, it is this which cripples it politically. At the end of the day all that is left is a radical typology, [24] which trumpets not a rigorous concern for history or geography – or for the politics of the possible – but an abstract emphasis upon the ubiquity and continuity of economic development and underdevelopment throughout the expansion and development of the capitalist system at all times and places. As Anne Phillips sums it up, we are heirs to an underdevelopment theory which has successfully 'established that ideal development cannot occur under capitalism [but which] in pursuit of this objective . . . cannot perceive or fully analyse what *is* occurring' (Phillips, 1977, p. 19. Emphasis in the original). Precisely.

2.3 Classical Marxism rediscovered

In the wake of these criticisms it is not surprising that radical scholars began to rethink the links binding capitalism to development and underdevelopment. Simplifying greatly, we might say that from the mid-1970s in economics and sociology, and from the late 1970s in parts of geography, a quest has been on for a Marxism more attuned to the spatial and temporal specificity demanded of Third World studies, and less inclined to the nationalism that is the obvious conclusion of neo-Marxism. Production, not exchange, was to be the new God. Henceforth the emphasis would be on the production of surplus value and not on the transfer of a physical surplus.

In geography this trek away from neo-Marxism was led by David Slater and whilst I do not want to labour his comments here it will be apparent that the following discussion owes much to Slater's 1977 article in *Antipode*. Slater's article also leads us, rather neatly, to the more recent concern with the articulation of modes of production.

The quest for a more classical 'productionist' Marxism began with a review of the ideas of Marx himself. Now at one level Marx's texts were not thought to be especially helpful. Slater reminds his readers (as others reminded theirs) that Marx was not really a theorist of imperialism or of underdevelopment at all. Marx's master work deals with capitalism as a closed system and most of the references that Marx made to the colonies were but 'footnotes' to this major thesis or 'mere' journalistic efforts for the *New York Daily Tribune*.

Nevertheless, closer inspection revealed that *Das Kapital* had indeed proposed a *model* of capitalist accumulation which had the most insistent, and quite un-Frankian, development implications. The details of this thesis have been considered elsewhere (see Dunford and Perrons, 1983). For our purposes we might sum up Marx's model in terms of five linked propositions:

1. Marx defines capitalism as a 'historically specific form of economic and social organisation in which the direct producer is separated from both the means of production he operates and the objects he produces, and where this separation is effected through the transformation of his labour into a commodity to be bought and sold through a wage-labour market regulated by price signals' (after Gregory, 1983, p. 26). This definition immediately confirms Marx's central concern with the relations of production and with the labour process.
2. Marx argues that the labour process under the rule of capital is inherently exploitative. Capitalism is a system which demands the privileged production of exchange values over use values, and though these exchange values express prices equivalent to average socially necessary labour times there is nonetheless a lack of equivalence between the value produced by *labour* in a given time period and the price paid for it (the *labour-power*). This price or wage is no more than the average socially necessary labour time required to produce and reproduce the labourer and

his family; a subsistence wage. The value it produces, however, is equal to the value/price of the goods that the capitalist is able to obtain from their sale. The difference between labour and labour-power is then surplus labour, or surplus value, and the rate of exploitation, e, can be written as

$$e = \frac{s}{v}$$

(where s = surplus value, and v = variable capital, or labour power).

3. Marx maintains that the fact of competition under capitalism forces the capitalist continually to seek ways of maximising his profits so that he might maintain a rate of profit, p, defined as

$$p = \frac{s}{c + v}$$

(where c = constant capital, or the 'dead' past labour embodied in the means of production. Remember that only labour-power can be exploited in the Marxian schema).

4. Marx sees this perpetual search for high profit rates leading to higher and higher organic compositions of capital, q, where

$$q = \frac{c}{c + v}$$

The reason for this is simple. The capitalist can only hope to maximise his profits in one of two ways: by decreasing v, that is, by decreasing the wages paid to the workers, or by increasing s, the surplus value appropriated from the workers. Given that the former soon runs up against the 'facts' of biology – starvation wages will not guarantee the reproduction of a labour force – it follows that most attention is paid to expanding s. Again, this may be done in two ways: by extending the working day, and/or by increasing the productivity of labour. Since the former quickly runs up against another set of physical limitations – notably the twenty-four hour day – it follows that capitalism is inevitably characterised by a tendency to substitute capital for labour. This is the one sure way to increase productivity, exploitation and profits.

5. Marx concludes that these competing but complementary tendencies to lower and lower wages and to higher and higher levels

of 'capital intensity' generate inevitable, and ultimately destructive, contradictions for capitalism as a whole. On the one hand if wages are too low there may be a realisation crisis. (This is the under-consumptionist crisis so beloved of Baran. We should be wary, however, of reading the same intentions into Kapital itself. Brewer [1980] argues convincingly that Marx was not an under-consumptionist and that in Marx's analysis shortfalls in demand for consumption goods can always be made good by increased demand for Department II – or capital – goods from other capitalists. More positively, Marx argues that the real crisis engendered by low wages is a political one. Lower wages reveal to the working class a basic truth about capitalism; namely that, unchallenged, it is a force for the ever more private appropriation of the products of an increasingly social process of production).[25] On the other hand there is a tendency – an 'iron law' says Marx [Marx, 1976, p. 91] – to a declining rate of profitability. A quick look at the equation for the rate of profit shows that as c increases (that is, as individual capitalists fall over themselves to copy each others' labour-saving innovations), so profits must fall (so long as s and v are unchanged).[26] Again, this will generate unwelcome, if inevitable, political consequences. As capital seeks to restructure its relations with labour by throwing more and more workers out of work and into the industrial reserve army, so labour will fight back and will seek to overthrow the entire capitalist system. At this point the capitalists have to think of new ways of restructuring capitalism, and this may involve the export of capital to the colonies: see Figure 2.4, which occupies *all* of page 48.

When these five points are added together it is clear that Marx's work is at a far remove from that of the modern neo-Marxist (see also Chapter 4). Doubtless this proved a comforting finding. At the same time, however, these five points told tales of an unexpected endorsement of 'colonial capitalism' on the part of Marx. To those scholars returning to the master for guidance on the development of underdevelopment, it appeared that Marx took a rather too optimistic view of the possibilities of peripheral capitalist development. Marx seemed to look upon capital exports as a motor behind a process whereby metropolitan capitalism would reveal to the periphery an image of its own (developed) future.[27]

48

1. Labour is the source of all value.
2. The difference between *labour* [what a worker produces in terms of value] and *labour-power* [the value of labour as a commodity] is *surplus labour-value*.
3. Capitalists obtain profit, and thus accumulate capital, by not returning to the labourer the full value of his or her labour.
4. Struggles over the length and the productivity of a 'working day' are thus endemic to capitalism:

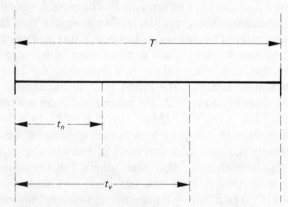

T = total working day
t_n = 'necessary' labour time (or labour-power)
t_v = total productive time
$T-t_v$ = idle time
$(t_v-t_n)/t_n$ = rate of surplus value (or rate of exploitation)

5. To increase the rate of surplus value, a capitalist can:
   a. *Reduce* $T-t$ by piece-work, by conveyor belts, by specialisation, etc.
   b. *Extend* T by shift-working, by overtime etc [often in the Third World?]
   b. *Reduce* t_n by increasing productivity
      by increasing mechanisation
      by lowering wages
      by lowering wages through the export of capital to the Third World

SOURCE   Adapted from Dunford and Perrons (1983), chapter 9.

FIGURE 2.4   *Marx: the labour theory of value and the export of capital*

On a happier note, Marx's ambivalent attitudes towards the colonies, and to colonial policy, could always be discounted on the grounds that he was not, after all, really interested in underdevelopment. Not a few radicals reasoned that Marx would have come to quite different conclusions had he lived on to see the dawning of the era of monopoly capitalism – an era so adroitly dealt with by Lenin and Luxemburg. As a consequence their attention (and Slater's attention) begins to switch to these two later theorists. (A close interest in the work of Lenin and Luxemburg still continues: see Harvey, 1982, and Smith, N., 1984.)

Lenin's work proved less encouraging than many had been led to expect. Although his theory of imperialism has a number of pressing spatial implications, a close reading of his work reveals that imperialism is to be considered in essentially non-spatial terms: it is the highest stage of capitalism. Moreover the essence of imperialism, for Lenin, embraced five characteristics, the third of which, in particular, was clearly in line with the 'progressive' thesis argued by Marx. To recapitulate, imperialism exists where:

1. the concentration of production and capital has developed to such a high stage that it has created monopolies which play a decisive part in economic life;
2. the merging of bank capital with industrial capital has secured a coalescence of interests between fractions of capital;
3. the export of capital acquires exceptional importance;
4. international monopolist combines are formed to share the world among themselves;
5. the territorial division of the whole world among the biggest capitalist powers is completed (based on Slater, 1977, p. 6).

Only the fourth and fifth of these characteristics seem to hint at the deliberate spatial exploitation which is the very stuff of neo-Marxism, and which most radical scholars still wish to emphasise.

If Lenin's work was something of a disappointment, however, some compensation was to be found in the work of Rosa Luxemburg; the one classical Marxist who really was concerned with core–periphery relations. Here at last was a Marxist theoretician who drew attention not only to the inherent expansionary drive of metropolitan capitalism (as per Marx and Lenin) but who recognised also the attendant violence of this process, and the hiccups in the process of capital export. If we briefly restate Luxemburg's thesis we find that she was the first to theorise capitalism and underdevelopment in terms of a dynamic capitalism facing certain barriers to its diffusion in the periphery.

There seem to be three main points to Luxemburg's work and they are all touched upon by Slater. Luxemburg begins by contending that capitalism can only survive by invading the non-capitalist world. Now this might sound very reminiscent of Frank and Wallerstein but in fact it owes more to Marx and Lenin. Luxemburg is not suggesting that the extraction of a 'surplus' is a precondition for capitalist development in the metropolis. Rather, she is maintaining that in its later life capitalism is driven to the continuous penetration and assimilation of pre-capitalist economies because the internal market of what is now called Northern capitalism is not in itself capable of realising an expanded surplus.[28] At a certain point in its development metropolitan capitalism runs up against the bar of under-consumptionism at home, and is forced to secure an external market for its products. This is point one.

Point two concerns the struggle that develops between the metropolitan powers for these export markets, and here Luxemburg distinguishes three phases: (i) the struggle against natural economy; (ii) the struggle against commodity economy; and (iii) the competitive struggle of capital on the international stage for the remaining conditions of accumulation (see Luxemburg, 1972; Geras, 1977).

Let us take them in turn. With respect to phase (i) Luxemburg argues that wherever natural economies prevail the expansion of capitalism is everywhere confronted with barriers to its mode of production. Land, for instance, might be owned collectively (or at least the tiller might not be separated from it) and there may be little in the way of demand for domestic, let alone foreign, goods. Where this is the case capitalism will have to destroy such economies if its own conditions of existence are to be fulfilled, and it is thus a mark of Luxemburg's work that she attributes to capitalism in this struggle the generalised quality of violence. Because the internal disintegration of natural society is so slow, she argues, the urgent accumulation needs of capital will have to be secured by a combination of measures, including:

military force, oppressive taxation by the colonial state, and the importation of cheap goods. Overall, capital in its struggle against societies with a natural economy pursues the following ends – the appropriation of natural wealth; the liberation of labour power and its coercion into the service of capital; the introduction of a commoditised economy . . . and the elimination of rural industry (as summarised by Slater, 1977, p. 9).

Perhaps the most important of these battles is the battle for the land of the peasant. Luxemburg maintains that it is in capitalism's interest to drive the peasants from the land to provide labour in the mines and the plantations, and to 'inspire' them to buy foreign goods in the market place. 'By limiting peasant production to agriculture' says Luxemburg, 'the self-sufficiency of the natural economy is broken down, thus opening a market for the products of European capital' (Slater, 1977, p. 9). However, this is still only the first stage of capitalist penetration. Once a system of commodity exchange has been introduced the battle is then on for the organisation of agricultural production itself, with the colonial government pressing for the capitalist transformation of the native farming systems. Again this takes many forms, but the aim is always to subject the peasant to the 'unfair competition' of a government-aided 'technical' agriculture and to expel him or her to the nascent industrial sector. Once this is under way the stage is then set for the third stage of pre-capitalist transformation: the industrialisation of the hinterland which had formerly purchased the output of the metropolis. To secure this:

> Metropolitan capital is allocated, at a rate of interest, to the satellite country and this capital is then used to buy machinery and materials from the advanced industrial countries, with sales by these newly created industries taking place within the satellite. In addition metropolitan loans are utilised in the laying out of cash-crop plantations and the building up of the satellite's social overhead capital (roads, railways, docks, dams and irrigation systems) (Slater, 1977, p. 10).

Naturally, this closure or capitalisation of the periphery is not without its implications for capitalism generally, and in the third and final part of her thesis Luxemburg argues that once the pre-capitalist social formations have been assimilated into the capitalist world economy, that world economy is itself doomed to collapse. Once capitalism is denied its external escape route it has no choice but to face up to the full weight of its internal contradictions and to perish in the mires of over-production. In Lee's telling summary, 'capitalism engulfs the world before the proletarian revolution destroys it' (Lee, 1971, p. 855).

Thus summarised, it is clear that Luxemburg's legacy is a valuable one and that she does base the 'laws of motion' of capitalism in the historically changing demands of its accumulation dynamic, just as she directs our attention to the stinging embrace of capitalist and pre-capitalist social formations. Unlike Frank she *is* able to stress the task that capitalism faces in overcoming its precapitalist peripheries. Indeed her emphasis upon the violence of this process puts her at a considerable remove from Frank's Medusa-like interpretation of capitalist expansion. (For Frank the mere glance of Cortez and Pizarro on the shores of Latin America seems enough to secure the advent of capitalism.) By the same token Luxemburg takes us beyond the naive and rather 'technicist' interpretations of transport developments in, say, Africa. As she points out, the provision of roads and railways was hardly an act of colonial goodwill or geographical common sense. Rather, it was part and parcel of capitalism's disruption of both natural and commodity economies.

Yet, for all this, it is not possible to see Luxemburg as a pioneer of the sort of work later to be done by the likes of Claude Meillassoux and Henrico Cardoso. The reason for this is that Luxemburg's sole concern remains with the logic of metropolitan capital. At no point does she show an 'awareness that capitalism's destruction and assimilation of other modes could be influenced by anything other than the immediate needs of capitalism' (Bradby, 1980, p. 108). Nor is it Luxemburg's intention to interrogate the particular problems posed to capital by particular pre-capitalist social formations.

Luxemburg's work actually brings us to the limits of what classical Marxism has to teach us about underdevelopment. Since her day events have shown us that capitalism has not promoted the quick and even industrialisation of the Third World; nor has it even demanded the systematic erosion of natural economy of which Luxemburg spoke, and its replacement by capitalistic farming systems. If I might draw on Bradby again, 'the traditional modes are not destroyed so thoroughly, or dominated so power-fully, as at the parallel stage in the metropolis'. Indeed, because a complete expulsion of the peasant from his land is so difficult where 'men can pass from one mode to another and back again [capitalism tends] not to bother itself with developing agriculture and integrating it into the market' (Bradby, 1980, p. 114).

Of course this is exaggerated, but one sees her point. For Bradby, unlike Luxemburg, the recent history of the Third World points up the need to theorise its continuing underdevelopment in the face of metropolitan capitalist expansion. Naturally this de-mands that close attention is paid to the 'laws of motion' of the capitalist world system, but it also demands a conceptualisation of capitalist and pre-capitalist *articulation* which pays rather more attention to the internal dynamics of the latter, and to the vari-egated nature of First World–Third World interaction.

2.4 Structural Marxism and the articulation of modes of production

To date the vast bulk of this theorising has been outside the realms of geography and at this point we have to take our leave of David Slater and his admirable guide to early post-Frankian development studies. From now on we will have to plough our own path, turning our gaze to those authors towards whom Slater nods at the end of his 1977 article: authors such as Meillassoux (1964, 1971, 1972); Terray (1972); Rey (1971, 1973) and Dupré (with Rey, 1973). Even then we are only scratching the surface, of course, for a concern with the articulation of modes of production is by no means confined to the 'Althusserian' school of French anthropol-ogists. It is present, too, in the Indian agricultural debates, in the debates on African capitalism, and in the work of certain Latin American '*dependencias*' (notably Cardoso, 1977; Cardoso and Faletto, 1979; and Laclau, 1979). But their voice will have to be raised elsewhere.[29] For the moment let us concentrate on some of the changing themes of this new approach as they have emerged from the work of the Althusserians.

An obvious starting-point for this analysis is the work of Pierre-Philippe Rey (see Foster-Carter, 1978, for such a view). Rey follows Luxemburg in insisting that capitalism is a force for devel-opment, and that it should not be reproached:

with the one crime that it has not committed, that it could not think of committing, constrained as it is by its own laws to enlarge the scale of production. Let us keep firmly in mind that all the bourgeoisies of the world burn with desire to develop the 'underdeveloped countries (Rey, 1973, p. 16).

Nevertheless, Rey recognises that underdevelopment is with us yet awhile. His task is thus to explain the preservation of pre-capitalist modes of production, and it is to this end that he makes use of Althusser's famous distinction between a mode of production and a social formation. (To recapitulate: a mode of production is an abstract, timeless, theoretical entity, precisely identified by particular relations between classes. A social formation is also a theoretical entity, but in practice it approximates a 'real' society and it may contain within it more than one mode of production.) However Rey introduces a twist. The early Althusserians suggested that if a social formation was a combination of modes of production, it was normal for one mode of production and its laws of motion (usually capitalism) to dominate its partner, except in brief periods of transition. Rey stands this on its head. He argues that in the Third World the normal state of affairs is transition. He agrees that there is a persistent contradiction between the logic of capitalism and the logic of its pre-capitalist partner(s), but seems to suggest that transition lingers on because the reproduction of each mode of production is dependent upon the reproduction of the other. (I should qualify this by saying that there is another, more evolutionary, strand to Rey's work, which brings him closer to Luxemburg. I will come back to this.)

The one exception to this rule of extended transition is the transition from feudalism to capitalism. Rey argues that the conditions for the expanded reproduction of capital continue to be met by feudal systems because 'feudal landlords acting in their own interest simultaneously serve the interests of the emerging capitalist class, so that an alliance between the old and new ruling classes is possible' (see Brewer, 1980, p. 186 for further elaboration). In non-feudal pre-capitalist modes of production, however, there is no such meeting of minds. The productive and reproductive needs of metropolitan *merchant* capital may be met in these societies, says Rey, but the effects of such interaction through exchange strengthens rather than dissolves [*pace* Frank] the productive relations of the pre-capitalist mode. In such circumstances capitalist relations of production can only be instilled by force. Like Luxemburg, Rey sees the essence of colonialism as systematic state violence.

It was in these rather abstruse terms that Rey established much of the conceptual architecture of the present articulation paradigm. To his great credit, however, Rey did not rest content with theoretical labour alone. Rey developed this vocabulary to help him to understand the class alignments created by the articulation of foreign capitalism and one particular pre-capitalist society: the slave-based, lineage society of Congo-Brazzaville. Sadly I cannot hope to do justice to the breadth of this work here. (Rey's two major texts on *Les Alliances des Classes*, 1973, and *Colonialisme, Neo-Colonialisme et Transition au Capitalism*, 1971, are both over 500 pages long). Nevertheless, if we follow through the two major scenarios etched into these texts we will get some insight into the empirical 'workings' of articulation theory.

The first stage of these scenarios opens with Rey's account of the characteristics of a lineage mode of production prior to the history of its interaction with metropolitan capitalism. At this time three features command attention, says Rey:

1. A lineage mode of production is not classless. It is defined by two classes – the chiefs (elders) and their dependents (juniors) – who are in conflict over the control and use of a surplus product.[30]
2. This lineage mode of production is already well capable of generating slaves for export. Chiefs and dependents are grouped together in networks of exchange co-ordinated by the former. These exchanges at once establish the class power of the chiefs and ensure that prestige goods – produced by the surplus labour of the dependents – are exchanged for other exchange goods, for brides or, crucially, for slaves.[31] Slavery and slave-exchange are thus part of this economic system and the circulation of men (and their wives) which it promotes allows for a redistribution of population from over-populated to underpopulated groups and areas.
3. A lineage mode of production is incapable of effectively producing 'other goods' for export, given the subsistence nature of its production system.

These points established, Rey then probes the history of the interaction of this system with foreign capitalism. Not surprisingly he sees this as falling into two parts or eras. Initially there is a period of commodity exchange in which European merchant capital seeks to integrate Congo-Brazzaville into an international trading system. In keeping with his theoretical comments Rey suggests that this is not unduly destructive of lineage societies. Because the slaves can be supplied from an existing system there is no need for the merchant capitalists to redefine the relations of production of the area. Instead they can rest content with playing the part of 'super-chiefs'.

However all this changes when the slave trade declines. Merchant capital is now forced to maintain its profits by moving into the export of such goods as ivory and rubber. The problem it faces is that a lineage society is not geared to the efficient production of these commodities, and any intensification of its techniques of production (shifting cultivation, hunting and gathering) threatens ecological destruction. As a result a struggle begins to establish rational (that is, capitalist) relations of production. Rey documents this at some length, and for the most part he paints a depressing picture of French colonial failures – of the fiasco of the concessionary Companies, and of the forced recruitment of labour for the Congo-Ocean railway. Late in his account, however, Rey argues that a colonial, or proto-capitalist, mode of production is finally established in the early 1930s.[32] This owes its origins to the monetisation of the bride-price and to sheer military conquest, and it is further extended in the post-war era when metropolitan finance capital assumes the ascendancy.

This sudden success of capitalism is a significant aspect of Rey's work and it has confused a number of his readers. In fact it is quite in keeping with a wider ambivalence that marks his texts. Thus, on the one hand, Rey has given us a concise and innovative rendition of articulation theory. His explanation of 'dualism' is a convincing one which suggests that this morphology is imposed, not within sectors of capitalism (as per neo-Marxism), but as a result of capitalism's interaction with peripheral pre-capitalist modes of production. At the same time, Rey's politics are not as discursive as these sentiments would lead one to expect. Indeed they are oddly akin to Frank's, since for Rey 'the revolutionary struggle must confront capitalism head on and must not compromise itself by limiting its assault either to pre-capitalist abuses or to foreign capital alone' (Brewer, 1980, p. 198). With this suggestion Rey reveals his other self; the Luxemburg-ish self which I mentioned earlier. In this guise Rey points to the inevitable slow victory of capitalism over pre-capitalist modes of production, and he sets forth the sort of model we have met before, where: (i) an initial link is forged in the realm of exchange, where interaction with capitalism reinforces the pre-capitalist mode; (ii) capitalism takes root, subordinating the pre-capitalist mode but still making use of it, and (iii) there follows the total disappearance of the pre-capitalist mode, even in agriculture.

In this guise, too, Rey turns his back on the concerns of certain other articulation theorists (who eschew 'necessary' progressions of this type) and on those who would argue that 'capital created underdevelopment not because it exploited the underdeveloped world, but because it did not exploit it enough' (Kay, 1975, p. x). From Rey's perspective this smacks of an uncalled-for voluntarism since it contradicts the 'fundamental law of capitalism, as true today as on the day when Marx discovered it: [that] capitalism has as its final goal the destruction at every point on the globe of antecedent modes of production and relations of production, in order to substitute for them its own mode of production and its own relations of production'. If this were not so, he continues, we would instead have to exhort our capitalists to 'Invest in Africa or Asia! Extort surplus labour from blacks, from yellows, from reds at the same rate as you extort it from whites' (Rey, 1973, pp. 10–11) – a ridiculous notion indeed.

In short, Rey has not yet abandoned the classical model of imperialism. He still endows metropolitan capitalism with a quest, or a motive; with a quality of 'homoficence' (Foster-Carter, 1978, p. 58) which detracts from the empirical soundness of his case. However, not all theorists of the articulation of modes of production fall into this trap, and it would be wrong to close this section without first mentioning the work of Claude Meillassoux and Harold Wolpe, just two of the authors who have moved beyond Rey in suggesting that the preservation of pre-capitalist modes of production can indeed be in the interest of metropolitan capital. (Do note, though, that their logic holds to the same starting-point: what is good for metropolitan capital.)

Their argument is really quite simple and in some respects it parallels Rey's ideas on 'subsidisation'. Both Meillassoux (in West

Africa) and Wolpe (in South Africa) maintain that it is in the interest of certain sectors of the metropolitan bourgeoisie (notably mine- and plantation-owners) to preserve, and indeed perpetuate, the existence of domestic forms of subsistence production. By acting in this manner they can avoid the necessity of providing the level of wages required to secure the reproduction of a fully proletarianised labour force (Figure 2.5). Instead, some of these costs can be offset to the domestic sector where a small cash wage is but a supplement to the traditional social wage of the villager. In this way the village secures the reproduction of capitalism's labour force itself. It ensures that there is 'a process of transfer of labour value to the capitalist sector through the maintenance of self-sustaining domestic agriculture' (Hoogvelt, 1982, p. 179).

Apartheid is a particularly clear example of this. Under the apartheid system black South Africans are given the 'opportunity' to live in their own 'homelands' on condition that they secure the reproduction of a black labour force which can be exploited in the townships and cities of white South Africa (see Wolpe, 1972; see also Bundy, 1979 and Smith, D. M. *et al.*, 1976). However it is not the only example. Meillassoux has detected a similar form of subsidisation in French West Africa, where it was:

> convenient for the Europeans to make cash wages only a sort of target wage for the worker: a target for three things, to pay the colonial taxes, to have a little extra to buy European commodities, and to pay the bride-price. Since the elders in the community controlled the bride-price and the brides this was in their interest as well: monetisation of the bride-price meant that they could buy fancy European commodities and become richer all the time (Meillassoux, 1972; as summarised by Hoogvelt, 1982, p. 179).

As Hoogvelt notes, this is indeed a literal form of articulation – but the underlying contract remains the same. From the point of view of the capitalist his cash-wage bill is nothing like what it would need to be to pay for the reproduction of his wage labour in other circumstances. The burden of reproducing a labour force is once more firmly with the domestic economy.

Again, these are not the only examples. Many more could be rehearsed (and not just from Africa: see Corbridge, 1982a, on the

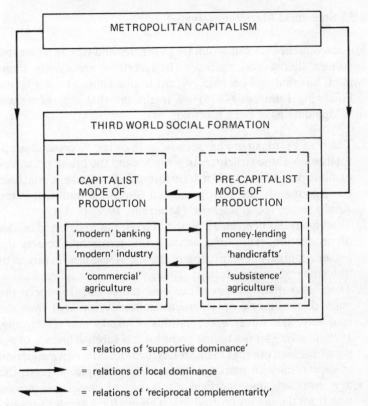

= relations of 'supportive dominance'

= relations of local dominance

= relations of 'reciprocal complementarity'

FIGURE 2.5 *The articulation of modes of production: a simple schema*

recruitment of an iron ore mining labour force in India), just as many more variants of the articulation thesis could be outlined. (We have yet to mention Ken Post, for example, and his scrupulous work on the history of the Jamaican working class [Post, 1978], or Norman Long's attempt [1975] to operationalise these concepts locally, under an analysis of 'brokerage'). But this is really not the place to trace the history of an idea *ad infinitum*.[33] Instead, the time has now come to take stock of some of the themes that have emerged from this hurried run through the post-Frankian years of development studies. We also need to examine their relevance for a future radical development geography.

2.5   Structural Marxism evaluated

For convenience we can group these themes and trends under two headings: theory and practice. (In fact they are closely intertwined, but that will become evident in due course.)

Following Mouzelis (1978) we might say that the theoretical developments have been fourfold:

1. The post-Frankian era has seen 'a more or less rigorous conceptualisation of the structures of societies and the broad principles of their persistence and/or transformation'. Mouzelis contrasts this rigour with 'the narrow-minded empiricism rampant in the Anglo-Saxon social sciences' (Mouzelis, 1978, p. 44).
2. This rigour has been aided by the Marxist theorisation of modes of production. This theorisation 'cuts across and rejects the present compartmentalisation of the social sciences' in favour of 'the study of a social totality' (ibid).[34]
3. These two qualities direct the new radicalism 'to where the main dimension of development–underdevelopment lies: the economy, the forces and relations of production' (Mouzelis, 1978, p. 44). This is a telling point for it is surely a feature of the post-Frankian era that the Left has abandoned a naive equation of capitalism with market exchange. In principle, at least, the new emphasis upon particular relations of possession-separation from the means of production allows for a greater sensitivity to the spatial and temporal diversity of the colonial-development experience.
4. This emphasis upon production 'provides a much clearer and more rigorous conceptualisation of underdevelopment as well as pointing to the type of dependence that Third World countries are experiencing' (ibid, p. 45). By focusing on the articulation of modes of production the Althusserian approach can point up a more precise picture of 'dependent' or 'deformed' capitalism. Mouzelis presents the case of Greece (defined by the World Bank as a 'middle income country') as an example. In this country, he says, 'the imprecision of the modern–traditional dichotomy can be overcome if Greek underdevelopment is considered as a special type of articulation between two different modes of production: the capitalist mode of production (CMP) which prevails in 'big' industry, and the simple

commodity production (SCP) prevalent in agriculture and 'small' industry . . . Underdevelopment persists because, contrary to the Western pattern, the CMP has neither expanded far enough into the economy (it has failed to destroy the SCP), nor has it organically integrated the SCP into itself. [That is to say] (a) the links between the two modes are such that there is a one-sided, systematic transfer of resources from the simple commodity to the capitalist sector; and (b) the capitalist sector has more numerous and positive connections with the economies of the 'metropolitan' centres, so that its dynamism and productivity gains are transferred abroad' (Mouzelis, 1978, p. 45).

Rigour and specificity, then, seem to be the hallmarks of a return to the productionist concerns of classical Marxism. But there is more to it than this, for these apparently theoretical breakthroughs have also counselled (or imposed) a rather different political praxis, with:

> those writers who now focus on imperialist-induced class structures inside Third World countries perceiving great scope for local struggles [and] for articulating defensive class alliances which may redefine and 'improve' the links of dependency with the world capitalist system and which can 'construct paths to Socialism' (Hoogvelt, 1982, p. 172).

In Hoogvelt's eyes this is all rather nebulous, being an argument 'that has a voluntarist emphasis [and] an almost Gramscian inspiration' (ibid), but Gramscian or not, it is difficult to see how a 'productionist conception of exploitation' (Hoogvelt, 1982) could lead to anything but a politics sensitive to local opportunities and struggles. In any case, this is surely to be preferred to the political logic of the 'circulationist' position, where writers such as Frank and Wallerstein deny the very possibility of meaningful political action in Third World countries (see also Chapter 5). As far as they are concerned the people of the South are little more than prisoners, bound by the logic of capital accumulation in the core countries and awaiting that happy day when the entire world capitalist system falls to its knees under the weight of its internal contradictions. At least the new radicalism allows them a role in making their own history.

The question is whether it goes far enough. It is tempting to say that it does, of course; to maintain that this is the latest in development thinking and that it strikes a balance between the sort of ultra-determinism which makes men and women captives of external forces, and the extreme voluntarism of the New Right which finds no place for Marx's famous dictum that people make history, but not under conditions of their own choosing. This seems to be Mouzelis's point when he praises 'Althusser's insistence on the relative autonomy of the political and ideological instances because it warns the student away from a mere reduction of political and cultural structures to the economic bases' (Mouzelis, 1978, p. 44).

But is this not rather illusory? To be sure the concept of relative autonomy allows a certain friction to appear between the economic imperatives of a mode of production and the political and social policies necessary to secure its reproduction. As such it might be used to 'explain' the different state policies of two such clearly capitalist countries as Brazil and Argentina, but beyond that what sort of autonomy is really being conferred? Indeed is there any at all, given that in Althusserian parlance relative autonomy is always subordinate to the economy's ability to 'determine in the last instance'?

These are far from idle questions, though in raising them I am not suggesting that some empirical notion of relative autonomy cannot be salvaged.[35] Nor am I suggesting that the potential for political action in any one Third World country is unconstrained by the exegeses of the world capitalist system. That would be absurd, but then this is not really Althusser's contention. What he has advocated, and what is now creeping into the development literature, is the rationalist contention that:

1. there is something called a capitalist mode of production, which is an appropriation of the concrete in thought;
2. this CMP is structured by an articulated combination of relations and forces of production, in which the relations are dominant and set in train a particular form of 'structural causality'. (Very roughly, this is the laws of motion idea, and it involves the claim that capitalism suffers from certain inevitable long-run tendencies: notably a declining rate of profit);
3. this CMP is itself articulated with other modes of production in

a social formation, though in such a way that 'in the last instance' its economic motor is the overriding force;
4. (thus) the relative autonomy for economic or political action within particular peripheral PCMPs is always subordinate to the accumulation 'needs' of metropolitan capitalism and to the reproduction of capitalist relations of production.

Now such a contention might seem to allow for the matrix of interaction of which we spoke earlier, but on reflection it is clear that these are controversial and highly restrictive claims.

First, there is the question of the rationalism of the whole Althusserian enterprise. There can be little doubt that what we are now being offered in development studies is an interpretation of social transformation in which the production and elaboration of abstract theory is made the guarantee of 'concrete' events and processes. In this way the obstacles to a socialist politics in, say, India or Latin America, are not derived from a close analysis of the situation there, but from a theoretical exposition which demands that, in the last instance, capitalist relations of production are reproduced. In other words, the barriers to a more-than-nominal political praxis are set in advance. As with neo-Marxism they are an *a priori* specified by the internal logic of a theoretical system.

Second, there is the structural causality of the Althusserian discourse. This certainly lends the new radicalism a pleasing symmetry, in so far as it suggests that 'institutions, roles, structures are what they are because they constitute effects of a fundamental cause – the reproduction needs of the productive system' (Mouzelis, 1978, p. 51), but if these reproduction needs are held to be sacrosanct and determinant in the last instance, it is hard to see how this structuralism is so different from the functionalism so often berated on the Left (see Taylor, 1978, ch. 1). The end-product is an explanation devoid of real change, and dependent upon a degree of 'teleological compatibility' (Mouzelis) wherein the existence and preservation of peripheral PCMPs (or not, as the case may be) is simply read off from the needs of metropolitan capital. If the PCMP survives (as in the Bantustans) then that is evidence of its functionality for capitalism; and if it does not (as in the plantations of Latin America) then that too is evidence of capitalism's functional requirements. In each case the possibility that the particular peripheral social formation might be the result of an unhappy compromise between two 'modes of production' is swept away beneath the structural causality of capitalism's laws of motion.

Third and last, there is the matter of economism. Here I can be brief because it is clear that the Althusserians have not escaped the sins of economic determinism; Mouzelis notwithstanding. All they have done is put it back one stage. By inventing the notion of relative autonomy, the economy is supposed to be subject to the feedback of other instances in the social formation, but only to a degree. Closer inspection reveals that the economy is still determinant in the last instance, thus giving the lie to the claim that we have escaped the clutches of teleology. At no point do the Althusserians conceive of the possibility that the (economic and non-economic) conditions of existence of capitalism's relations of production will *not* be secured in the face of hostile political, cultural or environmental action. In their curiously changeless theories, capitalism is endowed with an endless and ageless capacity to secure its own perpetuation. Indeed it is given in its theoretical specifications – a point which brings us full circle back to rationalism.

2.6   Relations of production and their conditions of existence

The one question which remains to be asked concerns the future. Is it possible to conceive of capitalist development and underdevelopment in terms that deny the different teleologies apparent in both structural and neo-Marxism? Or is it too soon to be thinking of new ground rules for radical development geography? My answer to this is yes and no, in that order. It surely is the case that a less deterministic 'Marxism' exists which might provide the theoretical backdrop for future development geographies.[36] Empirically it is already evident in the work of Henrico Cardoso (and Faletto), the *dependencia* theorist so rightly praised by Palma at the end of his magisterial review of underdevelopment theories. (I see parallels too in the work of Gavin Kitching [1980] and Colin Leys [1975] in Africa, and in Fitzpatrick's analysis [1980] of law and society in Papua New Guinea.)

Cardoso explicitly rejects Frankian underdevelopment theory for basing itself on five interconnected and erroneous theses:

1. that capitalist development in Latin America is impossible;
2. that dependent capitalism is based on the extensive exploitation of labour and tied to the necessity of underpaying labour;
3. that local bourgeoisies no longer exist as an active social force;
4. that penetration by multinational firms leads local states to pursue an expansionist policy that is typically sub-imperialist;
5. that the political path of the sub-continent is at the crossroads, with the only conceivable options being socialism or fascism (after Palma, 1978, p. 903).

Moreover, Cardoso judges such stagnationist theories to be static, ahistorical and politically unhelpful – not to mention circular. By measuring all forms of capitalist advance against the forms *assumed* to have existed in nineteenth-century Britain or Germany, or twentieth-century North America, the neo-Marxists inevitably mistake the necessary unevenness of capitalist development in the periphery for no development at all.

Cardoso also shows how current development theories can be improved upon by an analysis sensitive to the 'unity in diversity' of what he calls capitalist associated development. His own work bases itself upon a central proposition of neo-Marxism – that Latin American (and Asian and African) economies are integral parts of a world capitalist system, the central dynamic of which lies outside their borders – but enters the caveat that the logic and demands of this world economy are in a state of continual re-constitution. In other words Cardoso finds it necessary to theorise core–periphery relationships in a more contemporary manner than either the Frank or Rey models allow (in their different ways). Space must be found for the fact of decolonialisation, and for the post-war rise of the USA, for the challenge of the Soviet bloc and for the new strategies of foreign multinational capital. Most crucially of all, Cardoso recognises the partiality of any account which confines itself to the analysis of metropolis–satellite relationships, or which attempts to theorise the 'dialectical' interplay of internal and external factors in such a way that the former are considered as mere 'concrete effects produced by the latter' (after Palma, 1978, p. 910). It is necessary to move beyond this, he says, to break not only with the Frankian analysis (which classifies different forms of social production and organisation under the one heading of mercantile capitalist expansion), but also with those articulation theorists who see the preservation of pre-capitalist modes of production (and their political 'agents') as part of capitalism's grand – dare I say functional? – plan. Space must be found for the fact of struggle and for the fact that in Latin American history different sectors 'of local classes allied or clashed with foreign interests and organised different forms of state, sustained distinct ideologies or tried to implement alternative strategies to cope with imperialist challenges in diverse moments of history' (Cardoso and Faletto, 1979, p. 12).[37] Similarly, space must be found for the realities of different resource endowments and climatic variation – in other words for those conditions of existence of capitalist and non-capitalist relations of production that are either ignored or assumed away in so many Marxist accounts of underdevelopment.

I shall come back to these concerns in Chapter 3. For the moment, let me re-emphasise that in Cardoso's work we do have the makings of a radical theory of development–underdevelopment which comes close to meeting the criteria of adequacy which I have been developing throughout this chapter. Cardoso's work is sensitive to asymmetries of power and wealth, but it also finds a place for human agency and for a 'possible politics'. Furthermore, it is a contribution which attends to the concrete and to the particular: to relations of production and their conditions of existence, rather than to self-reproducing totalities or modes of production.

It is also a theory which finds (unwitting) support in the writings of the team of 'post-Marxists' associated with Barry Hindess and Paul Hirst. Though ritually abused on the Left, theirs is a contribution which attends directly to the economism, rationalism and teleology of the structuralists. It also lends theoretical support to Cardoso's work in at least two respects. First, it gives us good grounds for believing that modes of production can *only* be theorised in the rationalist format we are trying to reject:

> *either* the articulation of relations and forces of production is conceived in terms of the connection between social relations and the forms in which their conditions of existence are realised, *or* it must be conceived in terms of some kind of necessity in which the character in one object of discourse, the 'relations' or the 'forces', is deducible from the concept of the other. The first alternative means that there is no reason to posit 'modes of

production' as distinctive objects of analysis in Marxist theory, while the second idea leads directly into the quagmire of rationalist conceptions of the relations between distinct objects of discourse (Hindess and Hirst, 1977, p. 55. Emphasis in the original).

Second, the Hindess and Hirst team argue a distinctive case for focusing on the relations of production and their conditions of existence. Echoing Cardoso again, they insist that these conditions of existence *cannot* be supposed to be secured in advance:

> while specific social relations and practices always presuppose definite social conditions of existence, they neither secure those conditions through their own action nor do they determine the form in which they will be secured (Cutler, Hindess, Hirst and Hussain, 1977, p. 336).

This last point is of the utmost significance. The work of the Hindess and Hirst team has established, to my mind, that there is nothing in the concept of capitalism itself which should lead us to expect that it must have X, Y or Z development (or underdevelopment) effects. Such contingencies are not forged at this macro-theoretical scale. The reproduction of capitalist relations of production clearly presupposes the existence of definite conditions of existence (private property relations, for example, and free wage labour), but it tells us nothing about whether they will be secured, or about the all-important forms in which they are made flesh. There is nothing in the concept of capitalism, for example, which demands that high population growth rates must obtain in the periphery to secure a cheap labour force, nor is there anything in the concept of capitalism which suggests that democracies must exist, or must exist in a particular form, or that a significant and 'developmental' industrialisation cannot occur in the periphery. Whether or not these events and processes are secured or are fulfilled is a matter for empirical investigation and of political significance. The thrust of this 'third approach' is to the empirical and to the particular: to what Wolpe misleadingly describes as 'a mere inventory of relations and conditions' without social 'effectivity' (Wolpe, 1980, p. 25).

More than this, though, our third approach opens the way for a much needed dialogue between Marxist and non-Marxist development geographers. Once it is accepted that there are no privileged concepts or 'facts' which need to be defended on epistemological grounds, then the 'need' for a ritual purging of bourgeois ideologies disappears. I hope that the next three chapters will bear the imprint of this conclusion and will point to the gains that are to be made from a spirit of open and critical engagement.

Part II

Capitalism and Development: Space, Time and Conditions of Existence

3
Capitalism, Determinism and Development

Introduction

Chapter 2 was concerned with the logic of the various theories of the relationship between capitalism and underdevelopment that still occupy the minds of radical development geographers. In the remaining chapters I shall explore the political and empirical implications of these theories as they surface in particular debates: on the scale and significance of Third World industrialisation, on the scope for national development action in North and South, and on the proper role of environmental and demographic 'factors' in explanations of differential development.

The basic argument I wish to make is common to all three chapters and concerns the Janus-like quality of many radical interventions. Thus in the determinism debate I can well understand that geographers must be on their guard against arguments which assume a necessary, general and causal relationship between either the environment and development, or between population growth and underdevelopment. Radicals are quite justified in their insistence that these relationships are always mediated by particular economic, social and political structures, and they have rightly steered geography to an understanding that, in the majority of Third World countries, environmental and demographic 'problems' cannot be divorced from the wider calculations and constraints of capitalism. At the same time I am concerned that some radical geographers are now closing as many doors as they once opened, and that by adding a degree of epistemological dogmatism to an already deterministic reading of capitalism and its effects, they are promoting that very dialogue of the deaf against which Professor Chisholm has warned us.

In particular, it seems that two riders are being attached to the relatively uncontroversial propositions established above, *vis-à-vis* demographic and environmental determinism. The first of these holds that population and environmental problems are merely the epiphenomena of an irrational and contradictory capitalist world system. In this vein it is suggested that capitalism not only conditions and shapes the scale and effectivity of environmental and demographic 'disasters', but that it also fully determines (and so explains) them. It follows that environmental and demographic factors can have no real place in the syllabuses of radical development geography, a suggestion borne out by the simplest of literature searches. The second rider argues that a failure to recognise this 'fact', which is established by the true relational method of Marx's dialectical materialism (see Harvey, 1974 [reprinted, 1978]), necessarily places one in the camp of the determinists. There is no intermediate position. (The most recent variant of this rider can be found in Neil Smith's book, *Uneven Development*. Although excellent in many respects, Smith's central argument is based on a sharp division between bourgeois and Marxist theories of nature. According to Smith, the great failing of the bourgeois theories is that they rest upon a Kantian dualism of society and nature in which nature is externalised for the purpose of subjugating society. Marxism alone is able to see through this ideology, and to emphasise the continual transformation and production of nature and space [see Smith, N., 1984, pp. 15–18]).

I will argue here that there are good reasons for rejecting these claims and for reopening the debate on determinism and development (albeit under a different title). The argument falls into three parts. Section 3.1 examines the way in which radical development geographers have tended to polarise work on population and development issues into two camps: the Marxist and the Malthusian. I argue that this division has lent a certain weight to the radical critique of Malthusian and neo-Malthusian geographies, but that it is too often used to occlude the distinctions which exist between Malthusian and more simply modernising perspectives on population and development. The result is that these latter viewpoints are unjustifiably ignored. This point emerges most clearly from an extensive engagement with David Harvey's influential 1974 paper on 'Population, Resources and The Ideology of Science'. Harvey spoils an incisive critique of Malthusianism by retreating under the covers of an unnecessary dogmatism, and by using epistemology to guard Marxism against all competing, non-Malthusian, perspectives on the population – development issue. Above all, Harvey fails to consider the views of what might be called the 'savings-loss' and 'structural transformation' theorists. He also refuses to engage with the practical problems of population planning and control. The same cannot be said of the more recent and more sophisticated Marxist demography which is associated with the likes of Meillassoux (1981, 1983) and Rapp (1983), and with which this section concludes. Such 'Marxism' urges that population growth in no sense causes underdevelopment, but it recognises that it may be a decidedly contradictory condition of existence of capitalist development in the Third World. As such it does not rule out a progressive role for population planning.

Section 3.2 repeats the pattern of section 3.1, but this time the focus of attention is on the relationship between the environment and development. Once more the work of certain radical development geographers is favourably contrasted with the efforts of the environmental determinists, but readers are warned against seeing the debate in such dichotomous terms. Three further accounts of the possible impact of environmental factors upon development are thus considered, and conclusions drawn from them. Particular attention is paid to the work of Michael Chisholm.

Section 3.3 offers some thoughts on the whys and wherefores of radical geography's reluctance to admit any role for environmental and demographic factors in explanations of differential development; that is, it considers the bases of the current stand-off. Our focus here is upon what might be called the 'socialist Utopia syndrome', or the fact that many radicals believe that environmental and demographic problems cannot be real obstacles to development because they could not occur under socialism. Socialism, by definition, is a society of perfect, and perfectly co-operative, men and women, untrammelled by mere genetics and quite unsullied by the ruderies of opportunity-cost. This view is quickly shown to be idealistic at best and untenable at worst, but it remains a powerful force for division. Along with epistemology and with the determinisms of both Left and Right, it must be rated a major barrier to intellectual exchange.

3.1   Population growth and economic development

Malthus, the neo-Malthusians and radical development geography

It is perhaps unfortunate that radical development geography came of age in the early 1970s. Had it surfaced it in the 1950s or early 1960s it is doubtful whether its limiting preoccupation with Malthusian ideas would ever have materialised. In those halcyon days economic development seemed assured and there was little or no market for the theses of Malthus. Certainly, few geographers believed that because populations grow geometrically, so they must outstrip the food supplies available to them, which grow only arithmetically; nor was there wide support for the view that famine, pestilence and wars are the inevitable products of a population imbalance. In the 1950s and 1960s most academics accepted that if 'overpopulation' did threaten it could be accommodated by those very marital and contraceptive 'arrangements' which Malthus had regarded as 'unnatural and therefore unthinkable'.[1]

Nevertheless radical development geography did make its entrance in the early 1970s, and the implications of this are still with us. For it was at this time also that Malthusian ideas were making their academic comeback. Borrowing heavily from the 'scientific' language of systems theory, and with prescriptions of family planning lushly abundant, a neo-Malthusian paradigm emerged which seemed to confirm men and women as prisoners of the long-run laws of nature. It also proposed that the earth itself was approaching its finite limits to growth.

Leading this onslaught was the Club of Rome team associated with Meadows *et al.* (1972). Spurred on by their mentor Jay Forrester (1971), and in tandem with Paul Erhlich (1972), the Club of Rome team set up a model of the world system structured by the positive (and more rarely negative) interactions of five variables: population growth, food output, industrial output, pollution and resources.

In theory this model was meant to distance the Club of Rome from Malthus. Malthus, after all, had suggested that but 'two *postulata*' are needed to fashion a coherent world view: 'that food is necessary to the existence of man [and] that the passion between the sexes is necessary and will remain nearly in its present state'

(Malthus, 1970, p. 70). By contrast the Meadows team had five variables in their model and they accepted that world food production had grown exponentially since 1870, and that it could continue to do so up to a point.

These proved to be mere qualifications, however. As radical geographers were quick to point out, the basic outlook of *Limits to Growth* is recognisably Malthusian. For all its talk of positive feedback loops in and between each of the five variables, the exponential growth which the Report charts in pollution, in food production and in industrial production, remains a by-product of the exponential growth of population and the exponential decline of resources. The Report's major computer simulation, the World Model Standard Run (see Figure 3.1), bluntly predicts that a Malthusian threshold will be reached some time around AD 2040. Beyond that date Armageddon threatens: 'the industrial base collapses, taking with it the service and agricultural systems [and] population finally decreases when the death rate is driven upward by lack of food and health services' (Meadows *et al.*, 1972, p. 125).

Similar sentiments were expressed by Paul Ehrlich. Readers of his book, *The Population Bomb*, are told that they are the inhabitants of a non-renewable planet which, if present trends continue, will be populated by some 20 billion people in the year 2040. Suitably frightened, they are then consoled with the thought that these are neo-Malthusian and not Malthusian times. That is to say, there is now not one 'but two kinds of solutions to the population problem. One is a birth-rate solution in which we find ways to lower the birth-rate. The other is a death-rate solution in which ways to raise the death-rate – wars, famine, pestilence – find us' (Ehrlich, 1972, pp. 13–14). In this fashion Ehrlich defines neo-Malthusianism as Malthus with the options open. Neo-Malthusianism becomes a discourse which accepts that underdevelopment is the result of the independent operation of a law of nature (the exponential rate of growth of population), but allows that this law can be offset by man. In practice, indeed, it commands that man offsets this trend to exponential growth. Neo-Malthusianism attaches itself to, and soon becomes, the ideology of the birth control movement. Henceforth it is contraception, and not Marx, Lenin or Mao, that is to be held up as a saviour of the Third World.

It is against this background that radical development geogra-

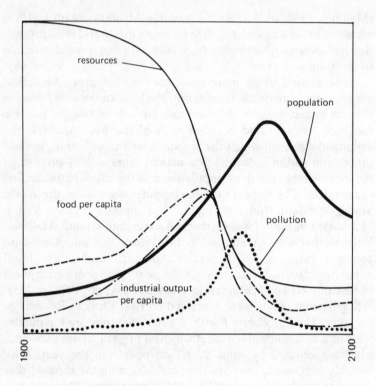

The 'standard' world model run assumes no major change in the physical, economic or social relationships that have historically governed the development of the world system. All variables plotted here follow historical values from 1900 to 1970. Food, industrial output, and population grow exponentially until the rapidly diminishing resource base forces a slowdown in industrial growth. Because of natural delays in the system, both population and pollution continue to increase for some time after the peak of industrialisation. Population growth is finally halted by a rise in the death rate resulting from decreased food and medical services.

SOURCE   *The Limits to Growth* (Meadows *et al.*, 1972)

FIGURE 3.1   *World model standard run*

phy's obsession with Malthusian demography became inevitable. Anxious to proclaim that the lot of men and women can be improved by socialist political action, many radicals saw the need to counterpose the naturalism and the determinism of Malthus with a critique of capitalism *per se*. For some this meant going back to Marx. With some pleasure it was recalled that when Marx crossed swords with Malthus he had reviled the latter's *Essay on the Principle of Population* as 'nothing more than a schoolboyish, superficial plagiarism . . . declaimed in the manner of a sermon' (Marx, 1976, p. 766). For many others, though, the time was ripe for a direct assault upon the neo-Malthusians. Thus it is that from the early 1970s a distinctively radical demography begins to emerge in geography. At first its ideas are rather hazy. Keith Buchanan (1973) simply warns his colleagues against an account of underdevelopment which abstracts so totally from institutional contexts. Like many others he is worried that the apparent precision of the neo-Malthusian case – its use of systems theory and computers, its 'untainted' policy relevance – might find a welcome in a discipline then chasing the goal of scientific objectivity.[2] More menacingly Darden (1974) accuses the Malthusian thesis of being little more than a justification for genocide.[3] Before long, though, this critique matures, and with the publication of an article by David Harvey in 1974 (and reprinted in 1978) the Malthusian and neo-Malthusian case is put firmly under the Marxist microscope.

David Harvey: 'Population, Resources and the Ideology of Science'

Harvey's article is a landmark in the discipline's discussion of Malthusian arguments and it is worth considering at some length. I shall argue later that it is not an unqualified success, and that it even highlights the epistemological dogmatism that is too often characteristic of the radical account of population and development. This is one reason for giving it such an extended coverage. For the moment, though, let us consider the three positive interventions that Harvey is able to make in the Marxian – Malthusian clash.

The first of these concerns what Harvey calls the 'ethical neutrality assumption' and it sets his article off on a sound methodological footing. Harvey's target is the notion that the scientific method 'guarantees the objectivity of factual statements, as well as the conclusions drawn from them' (Harvey, 1978, pp. 213–14). It is an important target because Malthusians are prone to make just such a claim in the population–resources–development debate. Malthus himself speaks of his sorrow that disasters are inevitable, but reminds his readers that his conclusions are the result of systematically processing a wealth of empirical facts.[4] Had he been prepared to speculate, he continues, he might well have arrived at more optimistic results but they would no longer have been scientific. Similar sentiments are today expressed by the neo-Malthusians. The authors of *The Limits to Growth* talk pointedly of their use of 'the scientific method, systems analysis and the modern computer' (Meadows *et al.*, 1972, p. 21). Like Malthus they might regret their conclusions but they would defend them as the inevitable results of working in a scientific, which is to say ethically neutral, manner. To ignore these conclusions is to opt for mere ideology or propaganda.[5]

Harvey is right to reject these claims on the grounds that they cannot be demonstrated. Indeed the assertion that scientific knowledge is only to be gained by the direct experience of empirical facts can only be 'validated by appeal to something external to science itself' (Harvey, 1978, p. 214), perhaps religion or metaphysics, or simply convention (see also Hindess and Hirst, 1977, ch. 1). The irony then is that the claims made on behalf of the scientific method are themselves unscientific, and it is for this reason that Harvey concludes that any attempt to privilege one's argument under the banner of science, and in opposition to ideology, is unacceptable. In a sense we are all ideologues now.[6]

Once this is established Harvey sets about a more specific critique of Malthusian politics. The roots of this second intervention are to be found in Harvey's contention that Malthus's support for 'the existing order of things' is an inevitable result of his 'use of the logical empiricist method' (Harvey, 1978, p. 217), but we can postpone consideration of this for the moment. The substance of his critique is that Malthusian arguments have always been related to quite definite political concerns, and that geographers must be aware of this.

Of course these concerns have varied. For Malthus they were made clear in the full title of his famous work: *An Essay on the Principle of Population, as it Affects the Future Improvement of*

Society, With Remarks on the Speculations of Mr Godwin, M. Condorcet and Other Writers. What agitated him was the belief of the cited authors that society was perfectable, and that the state might catalyse this perfectability by relieving the stark poverty of the lower orders. Malthus would have none of it. This was pure speculation, he asserted, and speculation quite in the face of the evidence that he, Malthus, had collected. That evidence supported the view that misery and vice were the inevitable lot of the labouring classes, because of the operation of the natural laws of population (see Malthus, 1970, p. 72). The tendency of population growth to outstrip the growth of the food supply meant that the perfectability of man could never be generalised. Moreover it made state intervention on behalf of the poor not just fruitless but positively harmful. In the short-run this was because such poor relief would raise the price of labour above its true market value, an argument we hear often enough today. In the longer run such relief was deemed harmful because it encouraged the poor to indulge their uncontrollable sexual passions and to breed. This would set off the whole vicious circle again, said Malthus. An increase in population would put excess pressure on resources and set in train a dire series of disasters and 'positive checks'.

For the modern Malthusian this attack on harmful poor relief has been updated into an attack on needless foreign aid and on social engineering generally. Thus Lord Peter Bauer is (in)famous for attacking all ideas of a 'widening gap' and of any 'external culpability' for underdevelopment, yet he happily disparages the 'humanitarian' aid lobby for throwing away money on fast breeding, fecund, populations of the ill-adapted, and on those without the 'human aptitudes and attitudes' for development (Bauer, 1976, p. 41).[7] Meanwhile, a member of the British government that Bauer once advised, the late Sir Ronald Bell, made population growth one of his reasons for opposing the Brandt Commission's call for more foreign aid. Why, he asked, 'should the most advanced peoples in the world . . . have the moral duty of supporting an increase of 2000 million in the equatorial and tropical regions of the world, where family limitation does not exist?' (in Hansard, 17 June 1980).[8] Malthus, Bauer or Bell, Harvey's conclusion would doubtless be the same: Malthusians have never intended their 'scientific' arguments to support apolitical conclusions. Geographers should remember this.

However, they must also combat Malthusianism. This is the message of Harvey's third and most telling intervention which focuses on the internal contradictions of the Malthusian argument. Harvey argues that the Malthusian discourse is flawed in its very conception (*sic*). This is because it mixes a '"natural" law of population [which] asserts a doctrine of inevitable misery for the mass of mankind [with] a theory of effective demand [which] points to social controls to the employment of both capital and labour' (Harvey, 1978, p. 220).

Again, this is especially clear in Malthus's own work, which is the focus of Harvey's attention. Malthus's natural law of population depends entirely on social, and thus historically transient, conditions of existence: that society comprises upper and lower orders, that the upper orders control the employment opportunities of the lower orders, and that only the upper orders are capable of regulating the size of their families. Nevertheless, a similar fallacy is present in the work of most modern neo-Malthusians. Their penchant for making the poverty of India, say, a simple function of the number of Indians divided by that country's (fixed) resources, once more enshrines the social and historical as natural and eternal. It simply takes as given the present global division of resources and its apparent tendency to depletion. Likewise it assumes that the reproductive behaviour of poor Indians is but a natural corollary of a lack of family planning education. There is no suggestion that it might have a rational social basis.

Harvey is right to argue that this will not do. Indeed there is merit in all three elements of his critique of Malthusianism: that its claims to objectivity are spurious, that it is supportive of a reactionary and elitist politics, and that it is riddled with logical contradictions. Were Harvey to end his article at this point we could have no quibbles with it.

The problem is that he does not. Throughout his paper Harvey strives to make two further, and more controversial, propositions. The first of these amounts to a defence of the 'early Maoist' line on population,[9] or the belief that there is no such thing as a population problem, just as there is no need for a population control programme in a properly organised, socialist, society. (Implicit in this defence is Harvey's support for what might be called the Mamdani thesis [see Mamdani, 1972]: the belief that effective fertility regulation will only follow a significant redistribution of

wealth from rich to poor; it cannot be sponsored by family planning programmes.) The second proposition is rather different.
Harvey suggests that 'the only kind of method capable of dealing
with the complexities of the population/resources relation in an
integrated and truly dynamic way is that founded in a properly
constituted version of dialectical materialism' (Harvey, 1978, p.
241). By contrast, but by definition, 'the method of logical empiricism invariably produces [the] Malthusian or neo-Malthusian
results' (ibid, p. 215) which we have already seen to be deeply
flawed. We can consider these propositions in turn.

Harvey's support for the Mao–Mamdani line on population is a
product of his distinctive reading of the Marxist perspective on the
population–resources–development issue. This perspective, he
tells us, has its roots in a critique of precisely those conditions
which Malthusians accept as given: the property arrangements of
late eighteenth-century England, for example, or the present
global distribution of resources. For Marx and for Harvey they are
anything but natural. These givens are the specific creations of the
capitalist system, just as the Malthusian's inevitable law of over-
population is really the tendency of capitalism to produce a relative surplus population, or an industrial reserve army. For Marx it
is the accumulation process under capitalism which renders segments of the labouring population superfluous, first nationally and
now globally, as capital replaces labour. Equally it is capitalism
which demands that a relative surplus population should exist to
permit a further accumulation. Since the production of surplus
value depends on the exploitation of variable capital (labour) it is
essential that wages are depressed to subsistence levels (see section 2.3). It follows, too, that it is quite wrong to speak of The
Limits to Growth, whether these are held to be arithmetical or
exponential. Such a notion is based on an ill-founded technological
pessimism, says Harvey, and upon a resolutely finite view of
resources. From Marx's more relational perspective no such abstract constraints are seen to exist. Rather, it is then clear that it is
capitalism's relations of production which are holding back the
development of the forces of production. The real constraint on
agricultural or industrial production is thus the operation of the
law of value and the need to make a profit. It is far from a
straightforwardly demographic (or environmental) obstacle.

Roughly paraphrased, this is Harvey's account of the Marxist perspective on population–resources and development, and (again) we can have few objections to it as an account. I am less convinced than Harvey, however, that this account supports the radical, Mao–Mamdani, line on population and development. There seems to me to be a significant difference between the three basic propositions of Marx:

1. that laws of population dynamics cannot be phrased abstractly – they must be specific to particular modes of production;
2. that there can thus be no question of population growth causing underdevelopment – it is never an unmediated variable;
3. that there are no absolute natural or technical barriers to the construction of a socialist society,

and the three propositions which radical social theorists are often wont to prosecute in his name:

1. that population growth and over-population are the simple, unmediated products of capitalism;
2. that population growth thus has no role to play in explanations of the differential pace and pattern of world development – its effects can be referred back to the laws of motion of capitalism;
3. that it is a myth to believe that population control could be successful under capitalism, or necessary under socialism.

Moreover, the effects of this disparity are important. By moving so determinedly away from the Malthusian perspective that population growth causes underdevelopment to the notion that the relationship between population growth and development is to be explained entirely by other factors, radicals of this persuasion are ignoring a series of more subtle viewpoints on this issue. In particular they are forgetting the arguments of certain modernisation theorists: that a faster pace of population growth retards not the possibility but the pace of economic growth (certainly within capitalist societies); that excessive population growth retards technological innovation adoption; and that changes in fertility are dependent on far more than simply economic variables.

These are important claims and it is right and proper that they are given a critical hearing. (Apart from eroding an unhealthy stand-off, such an analysis might throw some light upon the more deterministic readings of Marxist demography: see also Seccombe, 1983.) For the moment, though, let us try to clear up two outstanding questions. Why is it that Harvey, amongst other radicals, is so keen to avoid the arguments of mainstream (non-Malthusian) economic demography? Why are these arguments dismissed in advance?

The simple answer is that it is beyond Harvey's brief, and in a sense this is legitimate. First and foremost Harvey's article is a critique of Malthusianism, but it goes deeper than this. Harvey's restricted brief is itself encouraged by the strong streak of epistemological dogmatism that runs throughout his article. This dogmatism first raises its head in the article's introduction where Harvey alerts us to his belief that 'The adoption of certain kinds of scientific methods inevitably leads to certain kinds of substantive conclusions which, in turn, can have profound political implications' (Harvey, 1978, p. 213). It assumes a more aggressive stance, however, in those later statements where Harvey suggests that 'the method of logical empiricism inevitably produces Malthusian or neo-Malthusian results' (ibid, p. 215), and that 'the only kind of method capable of dealing with the complexities of the population–resources relation in an integrated and truly dynamic way is that founded in a properly constituted version of dialectical materialism' (ibid, p. 241).

There can be no doubting what Harvey is claiming here. In simple language he is saying that any perspective on the population–resources–development issue which fails to adopt a 'proper' Marxist methodology is predestined to repeat the errors of Malthus. It is for this reason that the arguments of modernisation theory can be ignored.

There can be no doubting, too, that this is as dangerous and ironic as it is misleading. It is misleading because the successful prosecution of a logical empiricist method can itself be shown to be impossible,[10] and it is dangerous because in practice Harvey equates logical empiricism with little more than the patient collection of empirical facts. To make such an activity grounds for dismissing an argument is frightening; indeed, it is rationalism run wild.[11] Finally, it is ironic because Harvey's dogmatic privileging of a 'properly constituted version of dialectical materialism' contradicts his earlier advice that we are all ideologues now. Apparently Harvey wants it both ways. We may all be ideologues, but some of us (the proper Marxists) are more scientific than others.

Such doubletalk, and the dogmatic message which it cloaks,

must be resisted. A Marxian perspective on population and development may well be the most appropriate one, but any triumph of Marxism must be achieved by persuasion and not by assertion. Specifically, it must persuade some of the theorists to whose arguments we are now coming.

The moderniser's perspective

Modernising perspectives on population and development are distinctive in at least two respects. On the one hand they reject the catastrophism that is inherent in Malthusian accounts. Rapid population growth is held to be an obstacle to rapid economic development and to the uplifting of the poorest – no more. It is not an inevitable portent of disaster. On the other hand these perspectives leave unproblematic the supposition that capitalist economic growth and Third World development are one and the same thing.

Naturally these general parameters set important limitations to the moderniser's discourse, and it is not my purpose to conceal this. Even so, it would be tedious to interrupt this account with continual references to the moderniser's fallacious tendency to equate capitalist growth with economic development. It would also be unnecessary. In this section our major concern is to evaluate the claim that rapid population growth at times exerts a secular influence upon economic growth. If this can be demonstrated it clearly has important implications for planning capitalist, or for that matter socialist, economic development. One final point: the general parameters of the modernisation perspective also conceal considerable variations of emphasis in the accounts of particular modernisers. As ever, this variation does not preclude overlap, but three major areas of emphasis do seem to merit special attention. They are: (i) the population-growth–savings-loss controversy; (ii) the relationship between population growth and technological change, and (iii) the debate concerning economic development and population control.

Population growth and savings   The notion that population growth in some sense diverts an individual's and/or a nation's savings from more properly developmental initiatives is a common theme in the literature of modernisation theory.

In geography it tends to be stated fairly vaguely. Zelinsky claims only 'that a programme of general economic development cannot be pursued in any of the current underdeveloped countries without also encouraging a retardation of population growth' (Zelinsky, 1970, p. 5). In economics, though, a more precise formulation exists, one which bases itself firmly with the Harrod–Domar tradition of making development a direct function of the savings rate (mediated only by the capital output ratio). Since this savings-led development is invariably fashioned by the twin processes of capital accumulation and capital deepening, it follows that rapid population growth can only be conceived as a check. As Enke puts it:

> The economic danger of rapid population growth lies in the consequent inability of a country both to increase its stock of capital and to improve its state of art rapidly enough for its per capità income not to be less than it otherwise would be. If the rate of technological innovation cannot be forced, and is not advanced by faster population growth, a rapid proportional growth in population can cause an actual reduction in per capita income. Rapid population growth inhibits an increase in capital per worker (Enke, 1971, p. 800).

Much the same point is made by Johnston and Kilby, who focus on the young 'dependents' of the Third World as a specific class of dissavers. They believe that:

> Rates of population growth ranging from 2 to 3.5 per cent, are perhaps the single greatest handicap that latecomers face in their efforts to achieve economic modernisation. The problems of expanding food supplies, educational facilities, housing and other goods and services, are obviously much more severe when a country's population is doubling every 23 years rather than every 70 years. [Moreover] . . . the higher rate of population growth imposes an additional burden in the form of a higher dependency ratio. High birth-rates mean a young population: in Africa 44 per cent of the population is under the age of 15, in Latin America 42 per cent, and in Asia 40 per cent; in contrast, for Europe and America the figures are 25 and 29 per cent respectively. Savings that otherwise could have been directed toward raising the human and material stock at the disposal of a given sized labor force must instead be expended to combat

decreasing returns in agriculture and to provide for the consumption needs of additional children (Johnston and Kilby, 1975, p. 82).

On the face of it such arguments do not seem unreasonable. They certainly embody a number of moral and conceptual judgements which we might wish to challenge: that additional children are an undesirable alternative to growth; that investment in education can be the subject of an essentially static cost–benefit analysis; that capital–output ratios are a practical guide to economic planning, and so on. But within the framework that these authorities have adopted are not their conclusions as unimpeachable as they are un-Malthusian?

Actually this is not the case. Any radical prepared to make the effort could point up a number of straightforwardly empirical ambiguities in this modernising account. The most important of these are as follows:

1. Enke and others like him are ignoring the findings in some countries that 'increases in capital per worker account for only a small proportion of increases in output per worker, and that the major part of increases in output per worker appear to be due to increases in output per unit of total inputs' (Thirlwall, 1978, p. 144). In particular, they are overlooking the possibility that population growth can go hand-in-hand with an improved productivity of labour. Yet in China and Sri Lanka there is evidence to suggest that just this has happened, albeit for different reasons. In China it reflected the more efficient use of labour after the 1949 revolution (see Buchanan, 1970; Rawski, 1979 and Chesneaux, 1979). In Sri Lanka it followed, less directly, from the better health of an increased labouring population in the wake of the malaria eradication programmes of the 1950s (see Gray, 1974).

2. Enke *et al.* support their arguments, including their claim that the opportunity cost of birth control is minimal, by effectively setting the marginal productivity of child labour in the Third World to zero, thereby making them consumers only. This is unrealistic. Whilst it seems likely that dependency rates and savings rates do vary inversely (Neff, 1969) they do not do so to the extent that Enke implies. Anyone who has been to the

Third World knows that the contribution of child labour is far from minimal. (Quite how much they contribute is difficult to say, but preliminary assessments can be found in White, 1976; Cain, 1977, and Lindert, 1980. Vlassoff, 1979; 1982, is more sceptical of the 'economic value of children', and both he and Cassen, 1976, rightly draw our attention to the problems of allowing for true discounting techniques and opportunity costings. Nevertheless, there are grounds for believing that Vlassoff's 'negative' findings are themselves partly a product of poor methodology [Cain, 1982], and partly a product of the peculiar ecology of his study area [Corbridge and Watson, forthcoming]).

3. The moderniser's argument ignores the existence of another set of 'dissavers': the old and the retired. As a result their correlation between an aggregate savings ratio and a dependency ratio must be partial, and may well be misleading. As Thirlwall notes, 'if the propensity to dissave of the retired was greater than that of the inactive young, the aggregate savings ratio might fall with a reduction in the birth-rate as the retired dependency ratio rose' (Thirlwall, 1978, p. 144). Again, more empirical research is needed.

4. The moderniser's argument is characteristically insensitive to basic geography. To argue that the rapid growth of young populations is an impediment to economic growth in land- and job-starved South Asia might be thought to have some limited validity, but to argue the same for parts of sub-Saharan Africa is stretching belief (see Table 3.1). It is possible that such countries might gain from the economies of scale that larger populations, and higher population densities, can bring.

Taken together, these objections seriously weaken the first of our moderniser's arguments. Even allowing for the fact that a 'savings effect' is weakened in the Third World by inefficiencies in local credit and banking systems, there is still 'only minor support' (World Bank, 1984, p. 82) for the view that per capita savings vary inversely with household dependency ratios. Indeed there are some grounds for believing that in aggregate terms – if not at the margin – higher rates of population growth are weakly but positively associated with higher rates of per capita income growth (see Thirlwall, 1978, Table 6.1; and Table 3.2 in this text). If a negative

TABLE 3.1 *Population densities of selected Asian and African countries (per square kilometre, 1982)*

China	105
India	249
Bangladesh	645
Pakistan	108
Sri Lanka	230
Thailand	94
Sudan	8
Zaire	13
Zambia	8
Niger	5
Angola	6
Zimbabwe	19

SOURCE *World Bank Development Report*, 1984, Table 1

TABLE 3.2 *Population growth and increases in income per head, 1960–79 (%)*

	Annual Average Population Growth	PCI Growth
Argentina	1.5	2.4
Brazil	2.55	4.8
Burma	2.2	1.1
Chile	1.9	1.2
Colombia	2.65	3.0
Cyprus	–	–
Dominican Republic	2.9	3.4
Ecuador	3.2	4.3
Greece	0.55	5.9
Guatemala	2.85	2.9
Honduras	3.2	1.1
India	2.2	1.4
Ireland	0.75	3.2
Israel	3.05	4.0
Jamaica	1.5	1.7
Korea, South	2.15	7.1

Mexico	3.05	2.7
Morocco	2.7	2.6
Nicaragua	3.1	1.6
Nigeria	2.5	3.7
Pakistan	2.95	2.9
Paraguay	2.75	2.8
Peru	2.75	1.7
Philippines	2.8	2.6
Portugal	0.6	5.5
Puerto Rico	–	–
Syria	3.4	4.0
Turkey	2.5	3.8
Taiwan	–	–
Uruguay	0.7	0.9
Venezuela	3.35	2.7
Zambia	2.9	0.8
Australia	1.75	2.8
Austria	0.85	4.1
Belgium	0.35	3.9
Canada	1.45	3.5
Denmark	0.55	3.4
Finland	0.45	4.1
France	0.8	4.0
Germany, West	1.0	3.3
Iceland	–	–
Italy	0.6	3.6
Netherlands	1.05	3.4
Norway	0.65	3.5
South Africa	–	–
Sweden	0.5	2.4
Switzerland	0.95	2.1
UK	0.3	2.2
USA	1.15	2.4

Spearman Rank Correlation Coefficient = +0.18 (All countries)
                                          +0.01 (Third World only)
                                          (both insignificant)

NB. Based on a similar exercise, for similar countries (1950–66), in
    Thirlwall (1978) Table 6. 1. (His coefficients also insignificant.)
SOURCE *World Bank Development Report*, 1981, Tables 1 & 17

general relationship between rapid population growth and under-development is to be sought, it follows that it must be looked for elsewhere – perhaps in the realm of qualitative changes.

Population growth, structural transformation and equilibrium traps   A concern for the adverse qualitative impact of population growth on economic development is precisely what distinguishes a second strand of non-Marxist demography. This deals with the issue of structural transformation, and advances various equilibrium trap models.

Again this shared concern takes many forms. In its simplest guise it manifests itself in a reaction against the more aggregated claims of Enke and his followers. Thus Robert Cassen rejects the argument that population growth in independent India has diverted savings in general away from development, but he does insist that India's rapid population growth has induced a less than optimal investment mix. Simply to keep pace with the growth of rural India, he says, and to feed it, resources have had to be transferred to the agricultural sector. Unfortunately this transfer has not been conducive to the structural transformation that is demanded of India's agriculture. Thus overall 'the potency of population growth as a negative factor in India's economic performance is clear' (Cassen, 1978, p. 228). Simon Kuznets would probably agree. Like Cassen he is sceptical of those arguments which assume that 'material capital is the sole agent of increases in per capita product' (Kuznets, 1974, p. 17). However, he does believe that an increase in material capital is essential for the development of the 'A' sector (agriculture, forestry and fisheries) of the Third World, and that this presupposes a decline in the 'A' sector's share of world population.

Johnston and Kilby take this argument a stage further. They also believe that it is axiomatic that the development process, or structural transformation as they call it, should consist of a 'transfer [of] investable resources from agriculture to the faster growing non-farm sectors' (Johnston and Kilby, 1975, p. xvi). However they are more explicit than either Cassen or Kuznets in detailing why this process should be held back by rapid population growth.

Briefly, their argument is that a rise in the natural rate of population increase will slow down the change in the occupational composition of the work force. In more detail:

the time it takes to transfer the bulk of the labor force from agriculture to higher productivity sectors depends upon three magnitudes – the initial weight of non-farm agricultural sectors in the total labor force (Ln/Lt), the rate of growth of the total labor force ($L't$), and the rate of growth of non-farm employment ($L'n$) . . . The rate of structural transformation may then be defined as the absolute increase per year in the non-farm labor force ratio: $RST = Ln/Lt. (L'n - L't)$ (Johnston and Kilby, 1975, p. 83).

This model clearly places an enormous emphasis upon $L'n - L't$ and thereby assigns population growth a vital role in the development process. It is a matter of simple definition that 'the impact of a high rate of population growth ($L't$) is . . . to diminish the value of $L'n - L't$ (ibid, p. 84), and thus the rate of structural transformation. Indeed where $L't$ equals or surpasses $L'n$, structural transformation will either cease or be reversed. Johnston and Kilby suggest that this has happened in Ceylon, Egypt and Indonesia in recent decades.

Johnston and Kilby's model can also be used to predict the number of years it will take to reach the turning point where the absolute size of the farm labour force begins to decline. A glance at Table 3.3 reveals that the timing of this happy event will be greatly delayed by a high rate of growth of the total labour force, $L't$. In Johnston and Kilby's mythical country, Earlyphasia, the initial weight of the non-farm agricultural sectors is 20 per cent. If this 'early developing' country continues to register an increase in its total labour force of 2 per cent a year, whilst providing for industrial growth of 3 per cent a year, it will take 123 years to reach its turning-point. By contrast, if this same country could cut its rate of growth of total labour force to 1 per cent, whilst maintaining annual industrial growth of 3 per cent, it would reach its turning point in twenty six years. In the case of Middlephasia the same 'moral' applies. The only difference is that in Middlephasia the time-periods are greatly truncated because of its more favourable (more 'developed') Ln/Lt ratio. Table 3.3 also underpins Johnston and Kilby's major conclusion that:

a reduction in the birth-rate is a potent lever for compressing by 20 to 50 years (or even more) the interval required by these

TABLE 3.3 *The structural transformation model: years required to reach the turning-point when absolute size of farm labour force begins to decline*

Earlyphasia ($Ln/Lt = 0.2$)			Middlephasia ($Ln/Lt = 0.5$)		
$L't$ (per cent): 3	2	1	$L't$ (per cent): 3	2	1
[years required]			[years required]		
$L'n = 3\%$ n	123	26	$L'n = 3\%$ n	29	1
$L'n = 4.5\%$ 83	33	3	$L'n = 4.5\%$ 20	a	a

n = never;
a = already reached

SOURCE Johnston and Kilby (1975) p. 86

countries to transfer at least half of their labor force into non-farm pursuits. Attention to factors that bear most directly on family limitation . . . should thus command first place in the development effort (Johnston and Kilby, 1975, pp. 86–7).

Similar conclusions would no doubt be drawn by Kuznets and by Cassen, indeed by anyone who subscribes to some version of the demographic logic first developed by Nelson in 1958, and more recently deployed by Mark Elvin (1973). Their studies focus quite directly on an assumed trade-off between population growth and technological change, and it is as well to run through their equilibrium trap models before bringing this section to a close.

Elvin's model is the less formal of the two, but it scores highly on empirical content so we will consider it first. His basic argument is that Imperial China in the eighteenth and nineteenth centuries paid the price for its great era of technical invention and innovation between 800 and 1300 AD. It paid this price in two ways. First, the agricultural breakthroughs of that time (especially the introduction of Champa rices and new irrigation technologies) encouraged an early extension of the cultivated area in China. By the late eighteenth century there was really very little land left to colonise. Meantime, these same agricultural advances dramatically increased China's short-run food-production capabilities, and this encouraged an upward trend in the population growth rate that was particularly marked under the Ch'ing regime (1618–1911) (see Ho, 1959). These two phenomena could not long coexist. By the early nineteenth century population pressure on cultivable land was immense and Elvin argues that it could only be accommodated by a generalised 'agricultural involution' in the wet-rice areas.[12] The effects of this were disastrous. On the one hand it reduced the agricultural surplus to a minimum and diffused what surplus there was amongst millions of 'petty' cultivators. On the other hand, it denied the possibility of further technological advances (chemical fertilisers, electrification and so on) by making the opportunity cost of capital in a labour-intensive eco-system inordinately high (see Perkins, 1967, for a similar argument). A trap was thus sprung. Nineteenth-century China was condemned to see its productivity increases minimised for lack of technological, not social, change, and eaten away by still greater increases in its population. For want of population controls it begins to underdevelop.

Elvin calls this a high-level equilibrium trap for obvious reasons, but the formal model on which it rests is clearly Nelson's more contemporary model of a low-level equilibrium trap. Nelson's basic contention is that the underdeveloped countries of today are trapped at a low-level equilibrium point where per capita income is permanently depressed: see Figure 3.2. The low-level equilibrium point is represented here by $S = X$ (the subsistence point), and Nelson argues that in the early stages of development any rise in per capita incomes (between $S = X$ and Oa) will call forth an even greater rise of population. This excess population in turn eats into the nation's surplus or savings, so preventing technological change and thus ensuring that per capita incomes are once more forced down towards $S = X$.

The one real difference between Nelson's work and that of Elvin is that Nelson's model is meant to be prescriptive. Indeed it suggests that if a country can develop to a point beyond Oa it will escape the trap in which it finds itself. To do this it must do at least one of two things. Either it must raise per capita incomes to Oa in one fell swoop (which is the big-push idea of the 1950s, and which implies a heavy dependence upon foreign aid) or it must act to curb its birth-rate until a drop in the dp/p curve brings Oa closer to $S = X$.

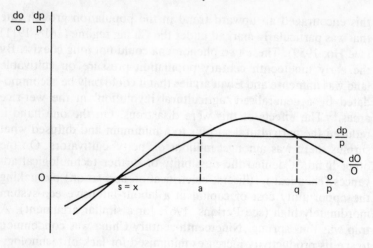

SOURCE   Thirlwall (1978, p. 162)

FIGURE 3.2   *Nelson's low level equilibrium trap*

Today the latter option would be favoured by most equilibrium trap theorists. The five authorities we have been considering may present their arguments in different ways, and more or less formally, but they are united in the belief that rapid population growth either restricts and/or distorts technological change, and thus structural transformation, in the Third World. The question is what should we make of this common call and this common belief? Clearly there is a case to answer and it will not do to denounce such work as yet more empiricist, and thus Malthusian, twaddle. It is not. Nevertheless, this does not mean that the equilibrium trap case is watertight, or that it should not be modified. Even in its own terms there are a number of possible counter arguments that can be made. Chief amongst these is what might be called 'Boserup's objection', or the belief that population growth, far from hindering agricultural transformations, actually sponsors them (Boserup, 1965, 1967, 1981). With every new mouth comes a new pair of hands and new ideas. (For a judicious review of the Boserup thesis see Grigg, 1979).

Another set of objections emerges once we relax our earlier strictures and challenge the assumption that forms of economic development can be abstracted from particular social relations of production and their conditions of existence. Consider nineteenth-century China again, as an example. Elvin argues that the stagnation of China at this time reflected an inability to generate a surplus for technological change; the pressure of population growth simply dissipated any surplus that emerged.[13] However, this account fails to render problematic the role of social structures in nineteenth- and early twentieth-century China. A more convincing account is that of Riskin (1975). He demonstrates that late-Imperial and Republican China generated a sizeable economic surplus,[14] particularly in the agricultural sector. Indeed he suggests that it would have amounted to something like 37 per cent of China's GDP in 1933 (Riskin, 1975, p. 74). What prevented this surplus being used for investment in technology, or even in basic infrastructure, was the manner of its appropriation. The bimodal and exploitative structure of rural China meant that just a fraction of the surplus remained with the vast mass of cultivators; too little for many to innovate on their own behalf. The bulk of the surplus found its way into the pockets of a parasitic class of absentee landlords, merchants and moneylenders who, says Riskin, preferred not to invest on behalf of their tenants and clients. Instead, they chose to invest abroad or to squander their wealth on conspicuous consumption. China's failure to develop was thus very definitely not a result of population pressure *per se*. Nor is it population pressure which directly inhibits a structural transformation in, say, modern India. Radical development geographers would be quite right to reject modernisation theory when it is presented in this rather crude and unmediated form.

But can it not be reformulated, and must we move from a critique of these ideas to the proposition that rapid population growth is entirely incidental to the development prospects of the Third World's poor? This is less obvious. It is perfectly proper to argue that scarcity (of jobs, housing and the like) is socially created under capitalism, whilst noting at the same time that it may be exacerbated by population pressure. This seems to me to be one of the strengths of the 'new Marxist demography' associated with Meillassoux (1981, 1983) and others, and in a rather different way with Rayna Rapp (1983). Both these authors are concerned with the interplay of production and reproduction and with the way in which capitalist relations of production may be reproduced within or by non-capitalist 'domestic' communities. However, Rapp is also concerned to combat the 'lurking functionalism' of any Marxism which assumes that 'families of proletarians and peasants must be reproduced for cheap labour to be available' (Rapp, 1983, p. 34). To this end she points up the way in which peasant and proletarian households have organised their sexual, familial and reproductive strategies not just to accede to the demands of capitalism, but also to resist them. She argues that 'Entrance into labour relations is organised not only by capital's need for a changing labour force, but by the struggles which people organised within households wage for survival, using and changing their family forms' (Rapp, 1983, p. 37).

In this fashion Rapp draws our attention to one contradictory aspect of the relationship between production and reproduction under capitalism. To this I would add one more: the contradiction between private and social rationality which is at the heart of Cassen's demography (his 'isolation paradox'), and which Marx himself long ago took to be characteristic of capitalism generally.[15] Perhaps an example will make this clear. Consider the case of a poor Indian family who seek to accommodate themselves to, or contest, the logic of an increasingly capitalist agricultural and industrial system by having a third, fourth or fifth child. This decision may well make sense at the household level, but if every other household is coming to the same decision it may have the effect of further intensifying the very capitalist relations of production which these families are seeking to challenge (and which radical development geography holds responsible for underdevelopment). At the most obvious level this is because the child itself will come of age in a society of not 700 million, but 900 million people, and in the absence of fundamental reforms it is likely that he or she will then find it harder, not easier, to find housing and remunerative employment. But that is not all, for this greater incidence of poverty may in turn be no catalyst to economic development and structural transformation.[16] It is more likely that it will depress the level of real wages still further, and thus delay any qualitative changes that may otherwise have taken place in agricultural and industrial relations and technologies. In this way the generalisation of individually rational fertility decisions can actually provide one of the conditions of existence for the most primitive forms of capitalism and capital accumulation: the exploitation of absolute surplus value (see also Chapter 2).

Again, I must emphasise that this reformulation is not meant to imply that the answer to Third World poverty and unemployment is population control. Clearly a more equitable restructuring of society is the real answer. All I am suggesting is that if restructuring is not forthcoming – and in many places it may not be for some time – population growth is hardly a friend to the poor in general, as distinct from selected poor households. It is for this reason that I would urge radical geographers to pay more (serious) attention to non-Malthusian demography, and to face up to a third question which this paradigm has raised: is it possible (and/or desirable) to curb population growth in advance of a wider restructuring of social and economic relationships?

Population control and economic development   It is hardly surprising that radical geographers have tended to steer clear of this question, or to answer it with a blunt negative. Given an attachment to epistemology, and to a rather cut-and-dried vision of capitalism versus socialism, it is to be expected that capitalism will be equated with a necessary push to relative over-population and that the possibility of a sizeable decline in the Third World's fertility is made the preserve of socialism. There are, however, problems with such a view. For one thing it is not clear how capitalism can be blamed at one and the same time for causing over-population and for sponsoring genocide through population control programmes (though Darden, 1974, has tried to square this circle). Nor is it clear how this view can be set against the evidence which has emerged from China, where Mao's early disavowal of a link between rapid population growth and slow economic development quickly gave way to the fiercest forms of population planning (see Croll, 1983; Yuan-Tien, 1980). To say that China /is no longer socialist because of this concern is no answer at all, as I shall show in the section 3.3. Finally, it is not clear how this more deterministic Marxism can deal with the evidence of declining population growth rates which is now emerging from certain capitalist Third World countries. (The 'flexible response' Marxism of Rapp is another matter entirely.) Of course this evidence is not cast iron, and much depends on the definitions employed which are always open to more than one interpretation. There is also a lot of it, which makes it difficult for me to provide a comprehensive review here. Nevertheless there is a case to answer.

Those taking a positive stance on the question of fertility decline in the Third World tend to cast their work within the general framework of demographic transition theory; that is to say, they have in mind a rough timetable of demographic developments (Figure 3.3) whereby a period of high birth and high death rates progressively gives way to a regime based on low birth and low death rates as modernisation proceeds. It is this latter phase which is now under way in the Third World, they say, and especially in Latin America and East Asia (Table 3.4). Moreover the transition itself, the movement towards lower fertility rates, has been largely independent of the income distributions of particular countries. Modernisers find this worth emphasising because:

> Early work concerned with income distribution and fertility showed that nations which had relatively low GNPs, like Sri Lanka, China, Taiwan and South Korea, had been able to reduce fertility as income distribution became more equal, while nations like Mexico, Brazil and Philippines, which had relatively high income levels and growth rates, and relatively unequal income distributions, showed little sign of fertility decline (Eberstadt, 1980, p. 49)

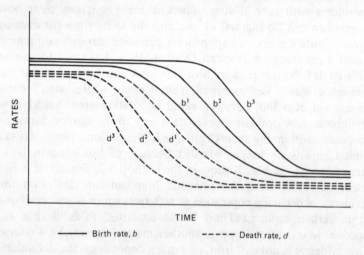

SOURCE   Woods (1982)

FIGURE 3.3   *A variable model of the demographic transition*

TABLE 3.4 *Changes in world vital rates by region, 1950 – 82*

	1950	1960	1970	1982
Crude birth rates				
(per 1000 popn)				
Developed countries	23	21	18	14
China	40	37	30	19
Other LDCs	44	43	42	36
African LDCs	48	48	47	46
Other Asian LDCs	44	43	41	35
Latin American LDCs	42	41	39	33
Crude death rates				
(per 1000 popn)				
Developed countries	10	9	9	9
China	23	16	11	7
Other LDCs	26	19	17	15
African LDCs	28	24	20	17
Other Asian LDCs	27	20	18	14
Latin American LDCs	15	12	10	8

SOURCE *World Bank Development Report*, 1984; after Eberstadt, 1980.

Today no such clear-cut picture emerges. As more evidence has accumulated it has become clear that fertility has sometimes dropped significantly in countries with increasing income differentials (Brazil and Mexico of late), and that it has failed to decrease in some countries where income equalisation has been secured (Burma for example). Eberstadt, who holds no brief for modernisation theory, is thus forced to accept the conclusion that: 'Equalising income distribution . . . is neither a necessary nor a sufficient condition for reducing fertility' (Eberstadt, 1980, p. 49).

But if fertility is declining and is doing so in the absence of a major redistribution of wealth and power, what can be causing it? At this point our modernisers take different paths and the debate becomes more complicated. For some it will be the result of family planning campaigns pure and simple, though not for many. (See Anker, 1978, for a critical review of this hypothesis, and compare

World Bank, 1984, ch. 6.) The majority have recognised that the success or otherwise of family planning campaigns must itself be explained, and they have therefore turned to a series of less proximate explanations.

One such explanation focuses on the recent decline in infant mortality rates in the Third World, the argument being that there is now less need for high fertility levels to ensure a particular family size. The classic study here is Heer and Smith's (1968) analysis of Indian birth and death rates. These two authors calculated that an average Indian couple in the mid-1960s had to have 6.5 children to be 95 per cent certain that at least one male child would still be alive when the parents reached the age of 65. Today the figure may be somewhat less, given a slight fall in Indian infant mortality rates in the interim. Another explanation emphasises the increased educational opportunities open to women in the Third World. Education is held to predispose women to use modern contraceptive techniques (see Lal, 1968; Knodel and Pichit, 1973; and Khalifa, 1976, amongst others. For an excellent critical overview, which is sensitive to the many dangers of autocorrelation in such studies, see Cochrane, 1979). Still another account dwells on the changing occupational status of women, particularly in the wake of industrialisation. It is claimed that a steady job and a cash wage is a disincentive to child-bearing (see Stycos and Weller, 1967; Snyder, 1974; and, for nineteenth-century Britain, Anderson, 1980. An equivocal reading of the 'new household economics' implicit in such studies can be found in Mueller, 1982). A fourth account, which really brings the other three together, argues that the recent uptake of modern family planning practices in the Third World has followed a reversal of the traditional inter-generational flow of wealth from the child to the parent (see Caldwell, 1977, 1978; and Easterlin, 1975).

Taken together these accounts leave us in little doubt that a decline in fertility can be secured in advance of radical structural changes, as the moderniser claims. But whether this amounts to a sizeable fertility decline is still disputed. Some radicals doubt that an active fertility transition is under way – believing that much of what we are seeing is a decline in birth rates consequent upon past rapid population growth (which led to a shrinkage in the proportion of women of child-bearing ages) – and many more cling to the belief that fertility rates remain high in rural areas. Noting that a good deal of the moderniser's case depends upon urban fertility trends, these radical continue to support Mamdani's thesis concerning the economic utility of children in poor rural households. For communities or households divorced from land and capital, says Mamdani, the labour of children is both a source of immediate wealth and a form of old-age insurance. It follows that 'people are not poor because they have large families. Quite the contrary: they have large families because they are poor' (Mamdani, 1972, p. 14).

Recent research, however, suggests that even this aspect of the radical case must now be suspect. John Caldwell and his team in South India is slowly corroding the conclusions that Caldwell himself once reached in West Africa, where he noted that 'fertility remains high and is declining slowly or not at all' (Caldwell, 1977, p. 6). He now believes that this conclusion was either premature and/or specific to the poorly commercialised, and still basically communal, societies of Nigeria's rural Yorubaland. (For areas with similar characteristics: see Cain, 1977, on Bangladesh, and Corbridge and Watson, forthcoming, on South Bihar, India). In South India's Karnataka State there is evidence that rural fertility has declined by some 30 per cent over the past twenty years, and that it has done so in the absence of significant economic advance or an improvement in 'social justice'.[17]

The Caldwell team account for this fertility transition in terms of a change in local inter-generational flows of wealth. More specifically they attribute it to the progressive secularisation, commercialisation and urbanisation of Karnatakan rural life since independence. As basically capitalist relations of production and exchange have penetrated the countryside, so the power of the family patriarch has been eroded, and so too has the position of women generally, and daughters-in-law specifically, been enhanced (Caldwell *et al.*, 1984). The upshot of this, and of the decline in farm-holding sizes that has paralleled previous population growth, is that couples are now more willing and able to opt for smaller and better educated families. The increased importance of non-farm employment, together with a greater availability of family planning advice and technologies has prompted a reduction in household parity levels even as general levels of economic well-being, and of equity, have remained substantially unchanged. This transition has been further hastened by the recent local take-up of Western medicines, by the recent gradual fall in infant mortality rates, and by a growing reluctance on the part of young men to accept long periods of sexual abstinence.

It is this conclusion that the Left must now come to terms with. Far from capitalism being necessarily supportive of over-population, it appears that an extension of capitalist relations of production and exchange can actually provoke that very trend to anti-natalism that is central to demographic transition theory. Of course one can still argue that a redistribution of economic wealth may be the catalyst of this transition (Repetto, 1979), and that it is beneficial in its own right. It is not, however, integral to the process of fertility decline. The evidence now accumulating suggests that even in rural areas of the Third World changes are afoot which are making the adoption of the most efficient contraceptive technologies more, not less, likely. It is in the areas which are marginal to the modernisation process – to Westernisation generally – that high fertility rates continue to make sense: in land-abundant communal societies like Yorubaland, and in relatively isolated economic and ecological zones such as South'Bihar.

Conclusion: population growth and economic development

To sum up: the moderniser's perspective on population and development is ultimately flawed because it refuses to render problematic the supposition that capitalist economic growth and economic development are one and the same thing. By assuming capitalism to be a constant, and thus in some sense given, modernisers fail to recognise its role in shaping the influence of an apparently malevolent population growth factor. This is evident not only in Elvin's work on China, but in Johnston and Kilby's (largely admirable) work on structural transformation, in Kuznet's work on capital deepening and so on. They all fail to see capitalist relations of production as a condition of existence of over-population: what Harvey calls 'relative over-population'.

Nevertheless, it would be a mistake to jump from the conclusion that the modernising perspective is signally flawed, to the conclusion that it is Malthusian, or that it has nothing to teach us. One can still accept Marx's central proposition that it is capitalism not population growth *per se*, which creates a relative surplus population and yet accept the following three points. First, increases and decreases in fertility are not fully determined by the economy. Once under way population growth curves have a tendency to fuel themselves. (This has implications for planning because even if population growth rates could be reduced to replacement levels in the next decade, an absolute increase in population will continue for something like the next eighty years). Second, within a capitalist framework, population growth can exacerbate a number of problems even where it does not cause them. Unemployment, lack of housing and a lack of industrialisation are obvious examples. Third, and again within a capitalist framework, there is clearly the possibility of checking population growth in advance of major societal changes, and certainly in advance of socialism (which in itself is no guarantee of lower birth rates).

The sum total of this is a far less deterministic reading of Marx: one which accepts that capitalism tends to promote a relative surplus population, but which accepts also that population has an absolute dimension which in turn has implications for the accumulation and distribution of capital. Population growth is thus a decidedly contradictory condition of existence of capitalist development. In many countries it may be of no great benefit to the poor, and it may be that we should support non-authoritarian action to check it. Of course this is at odds with the more fundamentalist line advanced by Harvey and others, but then it would be. Our conclusion emerges from an engagement with the work of a number of non-Marxist scholars. Harvey's is based on the epistemological premise that the work of non-Marxists need not be considered.

3.2 Environmental resources and economic development

A similar tale of missed opportunities is evident in the debate on the 'environmental factor' in differential development. Once again the radical critique is at its most effective when it is contrasting Marx's theory of nature with the views of the environmental determinists. It is less effective in dealing with a number of more sophisticated perspectives on environment–development relations, and with any perspective which offers a more mediated account of capitalism's culpability for the world's environmental problems. In particular it has little to say on one of Michael

Chisholm's current *cause célèbres* – the role of climatic change – or on possible human-induced bio-geophysical feedback systems, or on the likely developmental significance of the spatially uneven distribution of the world's non-renewable resources.

Environmental determinism and radical geography

This reluctance is not easily explained. After all if Malthusianism is a minority interest amongst modern geographers, there can be still fewer colleagues who take seriously the sorts of claims which we have come to associate with environmental determinism; for example Ellen Semple's suggestion that 'the earth has set [man] tasks . . . directed his thoughts' (Semple, 1911, p. 2), or Victor Cousin's proud boast: 'Give me a map of a country, its configuration, its climate, its waters, its winds and all its physical geography . . . and I pledge myself to tell you . . . what the man of this country will be, and what part this country will play in history, not by accident, but of necessity' (source unknown). Still less is there any support for the frankly racist geography that was the stock in trade of Fairgreave (1932) and others well versed in the ways of social Darwinism.

But whilst all this is true, the case for studying the tenets and pitfalls of environmental determinism is made almost daily outside geography, in the speeches of certain right-wing politicians and in the writings of a growing band of academics. One thinks again of the late Sir Ronald Bell, and of Enoch Powell, two politicians who have made regular use of the floor of the House of Commons to argue that giving aid to poor countries like India is a waste of time because of the climatic, cultural and genetic make-up of South Asia.[18] This view they assume to have the support of a number of development economists (especially Peter Bauer), and is clearly supported by the cruder versions of sociobiology now being challenged in both the natural and the social sciences.[19] (If I might digress for a moment, it is interesting to see that a biologist has recently had cause to call upon our own Prince Kropotkin to defeat the sociobiological view that 'developing man/woman' is a necessarily aggressive and competitive individual, who is most at home in the aggressive and competitive environment of Western capitalism. According to Lynda Birke this is not so, and was long ago disproved by Kropotkin's researches amongst the animal populations of Siberia.[20] Kropotkin's observations led him to believe that co-operation, not competition, is the guiding nature of both human and beast, a view which led him also to his political credo of decentralised small-scale socialism, or mutual aid. I shall come back to this in section 3.3.) Perhaps the most worrying example of the new determinism, however, is that displayed in Andrew Kamarck's book, *The Tropics and Economic Development: A Provocative Inquiry into The Poverty of Nations*. I say this because Kamarck is a World Bank staff member (a Director of its Economic Development Institute no less) and he has chosen to use the auspices of that organisation to argue that 'tropicality' is the determining factor in underdevelopment. To support this thesis he devotes some eight chapters, and some 30 000 words, to 'proving' not just that soils and climate and health and minerals are important elements in the development mosaic, but that the tropics are uniquely and unhappily burdened by the world's worst soils ('largely laterites' p. 25), by the world's worst climates ('extreme to the point of absurdity', p. 16), by the world's worst health problems ('bilharzia, malaria, river-blindness, worms and leprosy', pp. 62–78) and by 'the world's worst share in mineral deposits' (Kamarack, 1976, ch. 6).

Chisholm (1982) has already called these ideas 'naive' (and I would add, quite dangerous), but he chooses not to spell out just why this is the case, nor to offer an alternative explanation of the role of such environmental factors in development. It is here, I think, that the radical critique comes into its own. Being well versed in the woes and wrongs of geography's past determinism, radical scholars are well placed to point up the specious logic which joins Semple to Kamarck – they both believe in guilt by association – and to point out that 'environmentalism' only works in so far as it refuses to ask certain questions and to consider certain alternative hypotheses. For example, where in Kamarck is there any consideration of the benefits that tropical soils and climates bring to agriculture? Has he forgotten that it is the 'absurdly heavy' rainfall of Zaire that allows it to produce more organic material per square acre than any other country in the world (Eyre, 1978), or that double cropping (even triple cropping) is the norm in South-east Asia, but not in the Shetlands? Where, too, is Kamarck's sense of contrast or of the counter-factual method? Are we to suppose that because bilharzia and malaria are impediments to tropical development now, that one could not, two or three centuries ago, find similar, and since much reduced, problems of influenza, cholera and plague in Britain and the rest of 'developed' Western Europe? Finally, where is Kamarck's sense of human agency and of spatial variation? How does he explain the differential impact of the Sahelian drought, say, and how does he account for the radically different patterns of development that can be found in Kenya, Uganda and Tanzania, three neighbouring countries sharing a similar environment? (Like Kamarck I am ignoring micro-climatic variations and the national geography of soils!) The blunt answer is that he does not and that he cannot. Questions such as these – and there are many more – comprise the missing agenda of environmentalism, and stand in stark contrast to the theory of nature in Marx (as it is called)[21] which most radical development geographers now choose to prosecute.

Let me say something about this theory before offering some qualifications about its use and misuse by certain radical development geographers. The essence of the theory is quite simple. We have seen before that for Marx a mode of production is an articulated combination of the forces and relations of production. In other words 'nature' provides men and women with certain of their conditions of existence. At the same time these 'objects' only become resources when they are transformed by human labour. It therefore follows that the manner in which they become resources is conditional upon the specific relations of production that govern man's use of nature.

Let us consider the Sahelian disaster as a case in point. Most 'bourgeois' scientists can see the fallacy of a deterministic explanation of the drought that has afflicted Africa's sub-Saharan belt over the last fifteen years or so. Indeed it is a feature of the work of geographers like Hare *et al.* (1977), Johnson (1977) and Goudie (1981) that they account for desertification in terms of a 'combination of man's activities with occasional runs of dry years' (Goudie, 1981, p. 46). What they fail to elaborate upon, however, is the precise structure of these social relationships, and why it is that our activities should provoke Africa's 'environmental' crisis. By contrast the work of the better radical geographers takes us straight to the heart of these relationships and activities. Michael Watts's recent article (1983) is a good example. He argues that the roots of the Sahelian crisis must be located in the uneven penetration of capitalist commodity relationships into areas like northern Nigeria. In more detail he talks about the way in which colonial systems of agriculture and taxation were imposed upon the Sahelian peasantry, effectively destroying the 'network of horizontal and vertical relationships and reciprocities which were [once] embedded in [their] social relations of production' and which secured 'peasant reproduction in the face of a hazardous climatic environment' (Watts, 1983, pp. 27–8). It was the disappearance of these traditional mechanisms and safeguards at a time of deepening 'dependence upon volatile world commodity prices (for coffee and groundnuts) . . . [which left] households increasingly vulnerable to environmental perturbations such as drought or harvest shortfalls' (Watts, 1983, p. 30).

Watts's is a convincing article, so far as it goes, but there are a few questions which even Watts chooses not to put, and thus not to answer: for example, on the reasons for the timing of the disaster (did commodity relations only come of age in the early 1970s?) and on the reasons for its absence from other areas in similar latitudes, and with not dissimilar colonial pasts (the Indian Deccan comes to mind). In less sophisticated articles this second missing agenda becomes more yawning still. Indeed there is a tendency for some radical geographers to assume *a priori* (and as with population) that environmental problems are entirely the fault of capitalist commodity relations, and that an explanation of them can be divorced from any serious consideration of the geography of climates or of soils, and with no thought for the possibility that sheer scale, technology, or management problems might be involved somewhere along the line (in which case it would be a problem for socialist countries too). This seems to be Neil Smith's perspective when he berates the revisionism and the fetishism of two members of the Frankfurt School. Jurgen Habermas and Alfred Schmidt are both accused of 'dwelling on the abstract philosophical necessity of technology for mediating human/natural relations' (Smith, N., 1984, p. 28). Apparently this is very un-Marxist. Similar, if less opaque, statements can be found in Mumy (1979) and Cannon (1977).

It strikes me that such views are a long way from Marx's own thoughts on these matters, and much closer to the Utopian views of Stalin and Mao, of whom more later. More to the point, they provide yet further evidence of the preference for epistemology over debate which I have already argued is radical geography's bugbear. Of course it may indeed be the case that men and women are free agents when it comes to socialist development, and that they really can shape the earth in their own image and for their own purposes. But this must be demonstrated. In the meantime radical development geography has everything to gain from examining its own assumptions and prejudices, and from re-engaging with the proponents of competing views on the man–environment interface. It is in this spirit that I offer the following critical remarks on three such areas of debate: on the role and significance of long-run climatic change; on the role and impact of man-induced climatic and environmental changes; and on the developmental significance of the geography of non-renewable resources.

Betwixt Marxism and environmental determinism

Climatic change   Not so long ago the orthodox view of climate in the historical period was that 'the contemporary pattern of climates had become more or less established before the last ice retreat began' (Sauer, 1956, p. 53; quoted in Chisholm, 1982, p. 166). Over the past twenty or thirty years, however, and certainly since the publication of Charlesworth's classic survey (1957) of post-glacial sea-level changes, most disciplines have swung to the view that change and not stasis is the motif of our recent climatic past. The work of Lamb (1966, 1977) and Goudie (1977, 1981), amongst others, has strengthened the view that 'North-western Europe experienced a "little optimum" in the period from AD 750–1300' (Chisholm, 1982, p. 171), and a little ice age from then until sometime in the nineteenth century. They have also drawn attention to the global evidence which now exists for climatic change (albeit change at different rates and in different directions in different regions). This can be seen in such things as the variable thickness of tree rings, in the higher strand lines that bound certain inland lakes, in varves, in lines of glacial advance and retreat, and so on. Finally, the mechanics of long-run climatic change are now better understood. Textbooks by Lamb, Goudie and others deal non-technically with the role of such things as differential sun-spot activity, and an increase in atmospheric aerosols.

For all this, it has fallen to Michael Chisholm to argue that these changes have been significant for past and future global development, and for global development planning. He it is who spells out what the implications for Britain and Japan would be of a decrease of between one and two degrees Celsius in the average annual temperature: a loss of no more than 0.002 per cent of GDP, he says, through increased fuel consumption. It is Chisholm, too, who takes up Slicher van Bath and Parry's work on agricultural marginalisation in pre-twentieth-century Europe to argue that climatic changes which are now of minor significance to developed and continental areas can be 'sufficient to have an impact on the wealth of nations in at least some parts of the world – and especially those which are climatically marginal' (Chisholm, 1982, p. 185). Chisholm takes these to be the hot (and cold) arid areas where precipitation and temperature thresholds are already critical, and which include 'some 290 million people [living] in countries which are entirely arid [and] some 2460 million, or 60 per cent of all mankind [living] in countries which contain substantial areas of aridity' (Chisholm, 1982, p. 185). He suggests that these areas are not best fitted for economic development.

There are problems with Chisholm's account, however, and with others of this ilk. For one thing, Chisholm's definition of arid areas – this 60 per cent of all humankind – rests on the rather dubious tactic of assuming that all of India's [then] 638.4 million people, and all of China's 975.2 millions, plus many others, live in areas of 'substantial aridity'. But this is really by the by. A more telling criticism is that Chisholm does not tell us what adverse effects are presumed to be associated with climatic change. Far less does he indicate the orders of magnitude of these presumed climatic shifts and their impacts. Chisholm is rightly wary of suggesting that a 5 per cent drop in rainfall in arid areas will lead to X, Y or Z effects, because these relationships are unlikely to be linear, and will usually be subject to a host of intervening variables and 'adjustments'.

The most important objection to Chisholm's work, however, is that it is too concerned with questions of climatic change *per se*, as opposed to climatic stability, and that this concern reflects a disguised attempt to smuggle a modified environmentalism back into geography. If this sounds more than a little paradoxical, not to say conspiratorial, consider the wider structures that govern *Modern World Development*. The logic of the book is clearly expressed in its diagrammatic representation of the relationship of time,

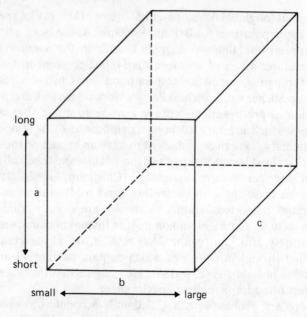

a — Time period of study

b — Size of geographical area

c — Relevant factors/model specification

FIGURE 3.4   *The relationship of time, space and explanatory
system (after Chisholm)*

space and explanatory systems (reproduced here as Figure 3.4).
On the face of it this is an attempt to show that different forms of
explanation may be appropriate at different spatial and temporal
scales – an innocuous enough claim, and one popularised in
physical geography by Schumm and Lichty (1965). In practice,
though, Chisholm is claiming more than this, for he tends to
restrict economic and political explanations of differential development to the bottom left-hand corner of the cube. At wider
spatial and temporal scales it is cultural, and then environmental,
factors that are supposed to play the key roles, and it is this that
has induced fears in some quarters (Gore, 1983) that Chisholm is
paving the way for a return to a modified form of environmentalism in geography: what Lewthwaite (1966) once called a 'diluted

determinism'. (No doubt these fears have also been fuelled by Chisholm's choice of Ellsworth Huntington as his 'hero' in *Modern World Development*, and by his own admission that an emphasis upon cultural and environmental differences runs the 'risk of being labelled "racist"' [Chisholm, 1982, p. 155]). The one way to allay these fears is to write a chapter on environmental change in the way that Chisholm has done, camouflaging any environmentalist sentiments beneath a learned emphasis upon climatic change and the perils of long-run carbon dioxide build-ups.

But this also creates certain problems, for it limits Chisholm to a discussion of climatic change alone, and thus to a discussion of its developmental impact at the margin. The question of environmental influences upon the core areas (areas of climatic stability we might call them) is all but overlooked. It is for this reason that Chisholm's account of the environmental factor is so different from that evident in another recent book by a Cambridge geographer – Farmer's *An Introduction to South Asia* (1983) – or which is apparent in Chambers *et al.*'s edited volume, *Seasonal Dimensions to Rural Poverty* (1981). Both these texts illustrate the importance of environmental influences upon development (*contra* cruder radical development geographies), but they do so in a manner that is a long way removed from either Kamarck's determinism or Chisholm's rather forced emphasis upon climatic changes. For Farmer it is the tripartite division of South Asia into 'plateau, plain and mountain' (Farmer, 1983, p. 5) that is important, and the fact that in their day-to-day lives most South Asians are faced by the 'seasonal rhythm . . . of a wet south-west and a dry north-east monsoon, which determines the two crop seasons, kharif and rabi, respectively' (ibid, p. 9). Although he does not say so it is evident that Farmer regards these relationships as essentially fixed and conditioning in the short-run, with the result that both capitalist and communist governments in South Asia (let us say Bihar and West Bengal) are faced by a number of problems in common; for example, a lack of suitable aquifers for tubewell irrigation, or the fact that every one year in four the monsoon will fail, involving costly adjustments for peasants of all manner of political persuasions.[22] A similar perspective emerges from the Chambers collection. The authors of this text are all keenly opposed to determinism and they point out that a number of different social organisations are compatible with any given environment.

Equally, a number of different adjustment mechanisms are possible in the face of most short-run climatic fluctuations. Nevertheless, they are sensitive to the developmental role that climatic seasonality can play, and to the implications it holds for such things as the provision of public works (see also Clay, 1981), for the provision of health care facilities, and for population planning (see Figure 3.5). In a wider sense they draw attention to the way in which 'seasonality presents contexts which bring poverty to periodic crises' (Chambers *et al.* 1982, p. 223), and thus to ways in which a very starkly seasonal climate, such as that in monsoon Asia, can set a very different policy agenda to that appropriate to similarly non-socialist countries lying in the 'flatter' precipitation and temperature regimes which one finds in equatorial Africa. In this way they emphasise the geographically variable nature of the environment as a condition of existence of development planning, and thus of the variable problems and responses that different governments face. This is some way from either environmental determinism or Utopianism.

Biogeophysical feedback mechanisms   A rather different approach to environment–development relations is to be found in the recent physical geography and environmental physics literature where two complementary theses have been advanced: (i) that human-induced environmental changes can trigger off a set of secondary, and more far-reaching, climatic changes, and (ii) that short- and long-run ecological setbacks might now be in the making not so much because of specifically capitalist patterns of environmental misuse, as by the sheer scale and organisation of a given technology. To examine these ideas I shall review two particular areas of controversy. The first concerns the possibility that Sahelian droughts are now being perpetuated, and indeed made worse, by biogeophysical feedback mechanisms. The second centres on the way in which certain Green Revolution technologies are creating future agricultural problems for South Asian peasants by lowering water-tables. (Other topics such as deforestation and its links to soil erosion could make this point just as well: see Redclift, 1984, ch. 2; World Bank, 1984, pp. 95–6.)

Consider the question of drought first. We have already seen that there is substantial agreement between natural and social scientists on the reasons for the current Sahelian disasters. Most

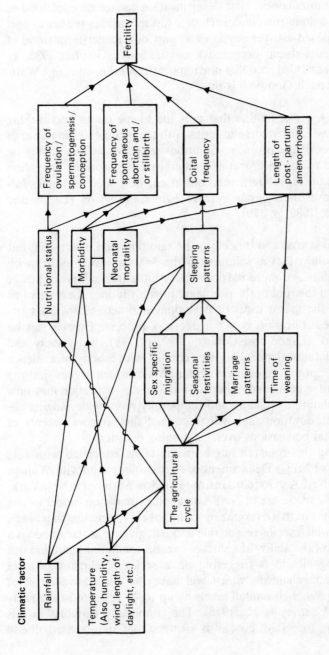

FIGURE 3.5 A simplified diagram of some of the main interrelationships likely to bring about a seasonal fluctuations in births (after Dyson and Crook)

commentators concur that desertification cannot be explained in terms of a 'long-run climatic change towards aridity (either as part of a supposed 200-year cycle or as part of a longer-term trend of alleged post-glacial progressive dessication)' (Goudie, 1983, p. 77). We have also seen that one implication of this – through Watts if not through Goudie – is that:

> An analysis of famine that puts the blame on an encroaching desert will never come to terms with the inequalities in power at the root of the problem. Solutions proposed will inevitably be limited to the technical and administrative aspects – irrigation programmes, modern mechanisation, new seed varieties, foreign investment, grain reserve banks and so on (Lappé and Collins, 1982, p. 179).

All this is true and it needs to be said time and time again, but does it follow that a 'solution' to the Sahelian problem lies with society alone, or more particularly with the inequalities of power that are at the root of the problem? Possibly it does. Certainly this must be the major locus of developmental action, not least because 'desertification is not a one-way process. Deserts can be reclaimed' (Lappé and Collins, 1982, p. 179). But society and social relations alone? This may conflict with a body of evidence now emerging from environmental physics which argues that the past twenty years or so of human-induced desertification may now be stimulating a spatially and temporally more wide-ranging climatic deterioration that will threaten Sahelian governments of all political persuasions over the coming decades.

Leading this research has been the team associated with Jule Charney at MIT's Department of Meteorology, and with William Quirk at NASA's Goddard Institute for Space Studies in New York. They have made use of NASA's general circulation model to test the hypothesis that overgrazing in the Sahel is increasing that area's albedo (which seems reasonable enough, given that the albedo is a measure of the ability of a surface to reflect radiation) and that this increasing albedo is triggering off a series of climatic positive feedback mechanisms which will have the cumulative effect of lowering Sahelian rainfall levels by up to 40 per cent in the rainy season (Charney *et al.*, 1975). The connecting variables in this model are threefold. First, it is assumed that an increased albedo will lead to a decrease in net incoming radiation, and thus to a radiative cooling of the air. (It is argued that the albedo for a vegetated Sahara is roughly 0.14 or 14 per cent, and that it rises to 0.35 as desertification occurs.) Second, it is assumed that this will cause 'the air to sink to maintain thermal equilibrium by adiabatic compression' with the result that 'cumulus convection and its associated rainfall would be suppressed' (as summarised by Goudie, 1981, p. 250; see also the discussion in Bach, 1979). Third, the Charney team assume that a positive feedback mechanism will then appear, for the lower rainfall must in turn have an adverse impact on plant life and lead to a further decrease in plant cover. They try to show that this is already happening by plotting a series of recent July rainfall rates for locations at different latitudes and with different albedos in North Africa. In their judgement these results 'do indicate a decrease of rainfall immediately south of the latitude at which an increase in vegetation causes an increase of rainfall [and thus support] the observation that the recent drought in the Sahel was accompanied by increased rainfall just to the South' (Charney *et al.*, 1976, p. 101, and see Figure 3.6).

Now if this is true then it is clearly reasonable to assume that Sahelian governments will soon be living with a more serious drought than is currently the case, and that their room for developmental action will be correspondingly diminished: droughts can certainly be combatted but only at a cost. It also suggests that the cruder versions of radical development geography are simply not credible, and that a 'cure for capitalism' is not quite the same thing as a cure for the environmental maladies that are not fully determined by capitalism's social relations of production.

But is it true? Before turning tack it is worth pointing out that a number of criticisms have been levelled at the Charney team's model. At the level of pure meteorology Ripley has argued that although the Charney team 'have taken account of the vegetation's effect on albedo, they have completely ignored its effects on evapotranspiration' (Ripley, 1976, p. 100). This is unacceptable, he continues, because research in Uganda and elsewhere has shown that whilst 'vegetated surfaces often absorb more radiation than bare ground, they are usually cooler because much of the absorbed energy is used to evaporate water' (Ripley , 1976, p. 100). This being so, the second and third assumptions of the Charney team's own model imply that 'protection from overgraz-

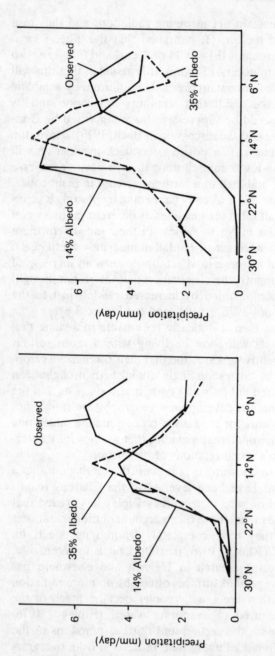

FIGURE 3.6 *Biogeophysical feedback in North Africa (after Charney)*

a. Latitudinal distribution of zonally averaged mean rainfall during July in North Africa for the case of variable ground wetness and negligible evaporation.

b. Latitudinal distribution of zonally averaged mean rainfall during July in North Africa: a case of fixed ground wetness and excessive evaporation.

ing [should] be expected to reduce convection and precipitation rather than to increase them' (ibid, p. 100). *Pari passu*, overgrazing should stimulate an increase in rainfall, not a decrease.

At a more general level Ripley disputes the notion that 'localised land and vegetation management can have a significant effect on rainfall climate' (ibid, p. 100), and this seems to be a most telling point. For whilst one can find proponents for each of the two views on the albedo–rainfall relationship[23], there are few takers for the Charney team's assumption of a significant rainfall effect. Until there are, and until more work has been done, it is probably right to regard the work of Charney *et al.* as still being at a preliminary stage. At best it is an interesting hypothesis which should make development geographers think long and hard about the possible developmental significance of positive feedback sequences in man–environment relationships.

A less controversial example of a biogeophysical feedback system, if one might call it that, is to be found in some of the areas of South and South-east Asia that have recently undergone a Green Revolution. The locus of concern this time is with the water table.

The Green Revolution is essentially a technocratic attempt to solve the world's food problem, and in rice areas it involves the application of fertilisers, pesticides and water to genetically improved grains such as IR8 and IR42.[24] Of these inputs water is the most critical. Without it the application of fertilisers is worse than useless; it actually burns up the plant. The problem is that in many areas of South and South-east Asia surface water is often scarce, and some of the old 'co-operatively' managed canal systems have fallen into disrepair. To adopt the Green Revolution technology, therefore, it is rational for the richer farmers to invest in deep tubewells powered by either diesel or electric pumpsets, even though this can have some unwelcome and unexpected side-effects. Worst of all, it can induce a long-term lowering of the water-table, and a very early and marked drying-up of the more traditional technologies involved in tapping ground-water supplies (see Farmer, 1983, p. 183; Edwards *et al.*, 1978). Now it might be argued that this has nothing to do with 'nature's revenge' (Chisholm, 1982, p. 194), and that the whole phenomenon is simply the result of the inegalitarian and hierarchical social and economic relations that are characteristic of, say, South India or Gangetic Bihar. After all, there is plenty of evidence to suggest that these same relationships have discouraged the necessary post-colonial maintenance of canal irrigation schemes in India (Sengupta, 1982; Wade, 1981) – for want of a common interest – just as they shaped the particular conditions (including times) of access to irrigation water (see Carlstein, 1982, ch. 7). But this is not the whole story, for whilst it is true that a lowering of the water tables is not the be-all and end-all of development, and that it might be restored to former glories by more provident water management, it is nonetheless instructive to note that social inequalities are not a sufficient explanation of such a phenomenon. One has only to look to China to see the same unexpected consequences of a Green Revolution (Kuo, 1972; Smil, 1984) together with a host of more or less serious environmental setbacks (see Westoby, 1979, on the afforestation fiasco of the 1950s, or Komarov, 1980, on the Soviet Union's ecological disasters). Taken together these environmental similarities in dissimilar social structures suggest that we must find a role in our explanations for the sheer scale of developmental technologies. It may be that some few technologies have environmental and/or organisational implications which largely transcend their usage in particular economic and social contexts, and that, as a result, some radical geographers are deluding themselves in looking forward to a socialist society with a perfect environment. That the future may be better under socialism is a reasonable contention. One must be wary, however, of setting up an *a priori* and Utopian conception of [a necessarily small-scale?] socialism. Again, this is something to which we shall return at the end of the chapter.

The geography of resources   A third area of concern which radical development geographers have tended to evade involves the developmental significance of the 'regional distribution of resources' (Chisholm, 1982, p. 114), or the fact that non-renewable resources are not evenly distributed on a country-by-country basis.

This is not to be confused with the issue of long-run global resource depletion. Any radical worth his salt (and any neo-classicist for that matter) can destroy the arguments of those who would maintain that the world is heading for an early collapse because world gold supplies will be exhausted by the end of the 1980s (Eyre, 1978), or because the world's oil wells might be dry by the turn of the century. We have already seen how David

Harvey deals with views like this by insisting that all resources are 'relational', and we can find a similar perspective in the work of non-Marxists like Burton, Kates and White when they define a resource (and a hazard, which is a negative resource) as the product of both natural and social systems (Burton *et al.*, 1978, p. 19). Similarly whilst it is fair to credit Marx (after Plato!) with the aphorism that necessity is the mother of invention, the idea that declining oil reserves will call forth new energy sources and or technologies is made just as forcefully by those neo-classical economists who argue that 'the unit costs and relative prices of mineral materials tend to fall through time as increasing supplies of lower-grade materials become available through technological advance and improved industrial organisation' (as summarised by Manners, 1981, p. 3).

None of these points, however, deals with Chisholm's complaint or with Ken Swindell's charge that 'One of the problems for Marxian geographers is how to treat the role of the environment in the distribution of resources and population' (Swindell, 1979, p. 254). Chisholm does not dispute the view that new and old re-sources remain to be discovered. Like Manners he settles for 'a guarded optimism that supplies will remain available but at a price' (Chisholm, 1982, p. 111). At the same time he is concerned that current debates are overlooking the 'geographical implications of relative scarcity and higher prices for fuels and minerals' and the fact that 'for a very large number of non-renewable resources the presently known reserves will last no more than three decades' (Chisholm, 1982, p. 112).

Let us consider the specifically geographical implications of resource depletion in more detail. Chisholm points out that a very high proportion of the known reserves currently used to fuel industrial development is to be found in just five countries: the USSR, the USA, Canada, South Africa and Australia. This being the case Chisholm draws two conclusions. First, he notes the 'impossibility' of the less advanced nations (as a whole) 'replicat-ing the patterns of production and consumption of the more advanced states for the want of necessary fuels and materials' (Chisholm, 1982, p. 114). Global development in this sense is out of the question. Second, Chisholm suggests that if scarcity dogs the future, then this very uneven distribution of the world's non-renewable resources guarantees that at least some countries 'will be given an opportunity to embark on development on the basis of revenues [rent] from mining ventures' (Chisholm, 1982, p. 114). In particular, Chisholm foresees a bright future for countries such as Chile, New Caledonia, Peru, Zambia and Zaire, providing their governments are willing to work with foreign mining multinationals to seize this 'once-only chance' (ibid) they are about to be offered. (Chisholm has no truck with the view that multinational corporations will create anti-developmental export enclaves in these mineral economies. He tends to see such dualism as a necessary by-product of the high-risk, short-life technology characteristic of the mining industry *per se*, and not of its multinational organisation in particular. He also believes that a new upswing in the 'Kondratieff cycle, superimposed on a secular trend towards resource scarcity' [Chisholm, 1982, p. 140] will improve the bargaining position of the resource-owners over the next generation or so. Provided governments are sensible they will 'be able to effect a transfer, probably a sizeable transfer, of resources in their direction. Exploration licenses, production royalties, profit taxes, etc., all provide the means whereby substantial revenue to government funds can be obtained' [Chisholm, 1982, p. 141])

Now what are we to make of this? It would be easy to fall back on a number of off-the-peg responses at this point, attacking Chisholm on three fronts. For example, we might begin by noting that Chisholm's case is poorly constructed in its own terms. Most of the quotations I have taken from Chisholm come in the opening or closing paragraphs of chapter 4 of *Modern World Development*. The bulk of that chapter is concerned with elaborations upon the Canadian and Australian experiences in resource-based development, courtesy of export base theory, and with a rediscovery of the main principles of Weberian location theory. As a result, the theme that Chisholm wishes to prosecute is clear enough, but the evidence called in support is fragmentary to say the least. Moreover Chisholm is rather curt in the way in which he deals with contrary evidence and unwelcome opinions. For a scholar who is impressed by the 'apparent dialogue of the deaf which seems to characterise much [current] writing' (Chisholm, 1982, p. 11), it is a little puzzling to find Chisholm rejecting Stuart Holland's well-known views on the national and regional implications of multinational activities (Holland, 1976, 1981) on the grounds that they take 'little account of the overall realities of the situation'

(Chisholm, 1982, p. 141). Where, too, is any mention of Girvan's pioneering work on the multinational mineral corporations and underdevelopment? This may have its critics (see Auty, 1983, for an estimable review) but Girvan's notion of *Corporate Imperialism* (1976) remains a challenging riposte to those who would set up an unmediated relationship between the mere availability of resources between a nation's borders, and the future development of that country. At the very least this thesis backs up Harvey's claim that resources are only resources – for someone – under determinate social relations of ownership and control.

A second rejoinder to Chisholm would point out that many countries have developed, or are developing, without the benefit of large quantities of natural resources. Denmark and Switzerland are two examples that come to mind when one thinks of Western Europe, and the much vaunted successes of Taiwan and South Korea bear equal testimony to the possibilities of development through resource substitution, and through the 'appropriate' organisation and management of human labour. (I will come back to the whys and wherefores of these success stories in Chapter 4, but it is perhaps worth emphasising that South Korea's current world leadership in such industries as shipbuilding and steel can hardly be laid at the door of its vast coal and iron ore reserves. These are notable only for their paucity.)

Finally, we might confront Chisholm with the claim that a plentitude of non-renewable resources is a mixed blessing for Third World countries. I do not subscribe to this view myself, but Gunder Frank has argued that 'the greater the wealth available for exploitation, the poorer and more underdeveloped the region today; and the poorer the region was as a colony, the richer and more developed it is today' (Frank, 1972, p. 19). In direct opposition to export base theory Frank accounts for the contrasting facts of North and South American development/underdevelopment in terms of the absence of mines and other raw materials in the former. Meantime, the gold and silver found in Mexico and South America, together with the suitability of these regions for the production of the agricultural raw materials demanded in the metropolis, 'determined that they would be victims of class-systems of ultra-exploitation' (Brenner, 1977, p. 87, paraphrasing Frank).[25]

In a sense though these objections are too easy, and are too easily invited by Chisholm's attempt to knot together a resour-ce–development nexus on the back of a much-criticised export base theory. (Chisholm himself notes that North's work in this field 'is but a variant of the more general stages [of growth] approach' [Chisholm, 1982, p. 120], but he finds nothing excep-tionable in this.)

But suppose we refashion his arguments. Suppose we eschew all thoughts of a deterministic relationship between resources and development, and instead ask ourselves two simple questions: is not the pace and possibility of capitalist development in, say, Mali, made more difficult than that in Brazil by such factors as size, climate, and lack of 'resources', and do not the governments of small socialist countries like Cuba and Tanzania face rather differ-ent, and arguably more difficult, conditions of existence of social-ist *development* than, say, China or the Soviet Union?

Put like this there is surely a case to answer. Mali's terrible plight is not a direct result of its climate or geography of course, nor of its lack of resources. It has far more to do with the commercialisation and taxation of its agricultural sector under colonial rule. Nevertheless these same factors were also at work in Brazil, but the government of that country at least has some latitude in dealing with its historical legacy. It has some coal and iron resources, for example, not to mention offshore oil (and a coastline), and some potential for industrial economies of scale; all of which place Brazil's administration in a rather more favourable position than its Malian counterpart. Moreover the picture is not entirely different when we come to the socialist bloc, as the cases of China and Cuba make clear. Consider China first. After a century or more of imperialistic intervention and exploitation, China's Communist Party swept to power in 1949 and set about a radical programme of economic and social reforms. At first they opted for a Soviet-style programme of rapid industrialisation, based upon a prior socialisation (and collectivisation) of produc-tion in agriculture. Of course there have since been a series of backlashes against this programme, but this is not germane to our discussion.[26] What matters is that these early Chinese efforts were themselves partly made possible by China's large population, and by the country's ability to feed itself and to promote its own basic machine-tools industries. Isolationism was not just another of Mao's bright ideas.

By contrast, Cuba has never had the option of closing its borders to international events and agencies. The revolutionaries who seized power there in 1959 certainly inherited a very similar set of problems to those facing Mao and his followers – in particular an agricultural sector geared almost exclusively to the production of sugar for the US market – and they set about these problems with a clearly socialist prospectus. Within months the First Agrarian Reform Law was promulgated, which dramatically reduced the ceiling on the size of private farms, and this was followed by a series of agrarian laws and other initiatives which emphasised the pooling of land and other means of production in Production Co-operatives.[27] For all this the Cubans' attempt to diversify their economy has faced a set of obstacles largely unknown to the Chinese. For a start there was the simple matter of inertia. Fully 41 per cent of Cuba's total farm income in 1946 came from plantation-style sugar production; a degree of specialisation un-matched in any one of China's main cropping regions. More crucially, the Cuban administration soon came to recognise that to get out of a monocrop spiral a government – any government – has to have money. But where was it to get it? It is all very well to plan to reduce the percentage share of sugar crop production in terms of both GNP and exports, but how is the money to be found to build the necessary replacement industries? Perhaps it will come in the form of a gift from the USSR, but this surely implies a measure of dependence and possible vassalage. (In practice Cuba has obtained most of its development funds from the Soviet Union, mainly because of the Soviets' continuing willingness to buy Cuban sugar at prices well above international market prices).[28] Other-wise the money must come from Cuba's export earnings: but these are dominated by sugar and may be difficult to boost without access to new technologies – which may themselves have to be imported.

Now it might reasonably be objected that what I have presented here is a set of catch-22s which are at best a caricature of Cuba's real problems and its real achievements. It might also be argued that socialism is not about a manic push for industrial growth alone (Cuba has had a lot of success in the fields of health and education) and that significant export earnings from sugar could always be created through the simple renegotiation of the relations of pro-duction that surround the crop. Collectivisation may increase peasant incentives and efficiency. Whilst all this is true, however, or at least arguable, it seems to me that socialists and socialist geographers have nothing to gain from denying that different social governments – just like capitalist governments – will face rather different development possibilities and conditions of existence, in part because of their differing geographical sizes and resource endowments. Far less do they stand to gain from ignoring such issues.

3.3   Perspectives on *homo socialismus*

In practice a stand-off is very much the order of the day, and in this final section I want to offer one or two more general comments on why this should be the case. These comments will also be relevant to later chapters.

One reason has already been suggested: epistemology. We saw in section 3.1 how David Harvey dismisses practically all non-Marxist perspectives on population and environmental issues on the grounds that they are un-Marxist (and are thus deterministic and/or ideological). But there is another reason. Many Marxists add to these epistemological blinkers a vision of a communist future wherein, by definition, economic, environmental and demographic 'problems' could not occur. In this way they reinforce the view that capitalism alone must be responsible for all the world's ills, a view which is itself perpetuated by a failure to think in terms of capitalist relations of production and their specific conditions of existence.

Alec Nove has identified the main elements of this vision for us, paying particular attention to its assumptions of abundance and of a purely relative conception of scarcity (cf. Harvey). Writing of the way in which certain problems are defined out of existence, Nove notes that:

> If one assumes 'abundance', this excludes opportunity cost since there would be no mutually exclusive choices to make. If one assumes that the 'new man', unacquisitive, 'brilliant, highly rational, socialised, humane' will require no incentives, problems of discipline and motivation disappear. If it is assumed that all will identify with the clearly visible general good, then the conflict between general and partial interest, and the complex

issues of centralisation/decentralisation, can be assumed out of existence . . . Everyone will govern, there will not be any governed. Since all competing interests will have disappeared, there will be no need to claim rights of any sort, no need for restrictive rules, laws, judges, or a legislature. Of course there will be no state, no nation-states (and so no foreign trade, or any trade). The wages system will have gone, as well as money (Nove, 1983, p. 10).

Now one can argue over whether or not Marx intended such a vision of the future,[29] or if anyone really holds to all these propositions. What is beyond doubt, however, is that assumptions like these are integral to many modern Marxist discourses, and to modern Marxist politics, just as they are central assumptions in the work of certain radical geographers. On the political front one thinks especially of Chairman Mao,[30] whose thoughts on society and nature were so ably captured by Rhoads Murphey in 1967. According to Mao 'The united will of the people will transform nature' and thus secure for China all the flat land and forestry cover that it requires. So long as the Chinese people accepted that 'Chairman Mao's thoughts are our guide to scoring victories in the struggle against nature' (see Murphey, 1967), they would at long last be able to control the last of China's enemies within: the Yellow River (see Greer, 1979, for a sympathetic account). More generally, it is this image of a perfect society which has allowed so many radicals to distance themselves from 'bourgeois' critiques of the lack of civil liberties in the USSR, or of the developmental 'failures' of Tanzania, or of the renewed need for incentives and population planning and regional policies in communist China. According to Bruce McFarlane (1983) these shortcomings can be explained away as the products not of socialism but of capitalism. He takes the view that by definition, socialism guarantees civil rights and development and an equitable space-economy. At the same time it removes the need for any system of material incentives. Ergo, the introduction of China's new Production Responsibility System (say) is evidence not of the contradictions of socialist development, but of a failure to be socialist enough.

Again, one must be careful not to press this too far. There are worthy exceptions to these remarks,[31] and I have no wish to give the impression that radical development geographers are wrong to join with Marx in opposing a fixed view of human nature wherein man is seen as necessarily territorial, aggressive or selfish. This is the very stuff of determinism, and radical geographers are quite right to steer the discipline away from these ideas of *The Selfish Gene*,[32] or *The Naked Ape*.[33] All the same, there are dangers in opposing such views simply by standing them on their head; by deciding in advance that sociobiology is racist because it argues that men and women are subject to a number of biological determinations, or by decreeing *a priori* that socialist men and women will be everything that capitalist men and women are not – caring, non-sexist, co-operative, non-materialistic polymaths.

The dangers lie in two main areas. First, there is the likelihood of intellectual refutation. Alec Nove writes as a committed socialist, but his devastating critique of 'unfeasible socialism' positively invites a less well-meaning, and possibly less well-directed, attack from the New Right. As things stand it is too easy to point up the romanticism of such Utopian socialism: to point out that no such society exists, or that it depends on a view of the new men and women as 'omniscient angels' (Nove, 1983, p. 17); to point out that it depends on a vision of the world where there is no absolute scarcity (not even of mineral X at time Y in region Z) but only relative scarcity, and thus no opportunity cost; or to point out that assumptions of no money, or of no division of labour, and so of no management, are quite at odds with the degree of specialisation and delegation that is everywhere demanded by all but the simplest of industrial processes. (Nove presents a telling parable on the organisation of Soviet fuel policy.)[34] It is also worth saying that if there is an exception to this rule it is probably 'small-scale socialism'. It may be that material incentives and a regular division of labour can be dispensed with under Kibbutzim-type arrangements, or under the wing of one of Kropotkin's mutual aid teams. But this surely tells us more about the scale of Utopias than about the realities of national, or any other large-scale, socialist development.

The second reason for rejecting the oppositionism that so clearly underlies this vision of a perfect future, is that it makes for a less, not more, relevant radical development geography. This might seem a strange conclusion to draw when one considers that the proponents of such Utopias are generally perceived to be revolutionary socialists or anarchists, but really these people are revolutionary gnostics. They believe in the politics of abstention. Moreover it is a view which is consistent with what is now happening in radical development geography. Throughout this chapter we have seen how some radical geographers have turned their backs on important areas of debate, and on important areas of and for policy and politics. Spurred on by the easy pickings of epistemology some radicals have spurned the chance to engage in dialogue and to win by reasoned argument. Spurred on by a monolithic conception of capitalism and its effects some have spurned the opportunity to investigate the particular demographic and environmental conditions of existence that face specific capitalist societies, and which set in train distinctive and varied problems and possibilities. Finally, spurred on by a 'four legs good, two legs bad' approach to capitalism versus socialism, it seems that some radical geographers are now spurning the chance to comment upon the continuing contradictions and successes of socialist economic development. Sadly, we shall see more evidence of this in the next two chapters.

4
Capitalism, Industrialisation and Development

Introduction

In Chapter 3 we were looking at the way in which environmental and demographic factors can provide variable conditions of existence for capitalist development. As such we were concerned to disaggregate the concept of capitalism itself. In this chapter we shall be changing tack somewhat. From now on we will assume that 'capitalism' is established in the Third World, and will inquire instead into its supposed effects. More precisely we will examine the scope for, and nature of, industrialisation in the Third World. Besides being a topic of intrinsic importance, the debate surrounding this issue strikes at the very heart of radical geography's theories of capitalist underdevelopment.

The chapter falls into three main parts. The first section outlines the arguments of three radical schools of thought on peripheral industrialisation: the stagnationist tendency associated with the early Gunder Frank; the more optimistic 'post-imperialist' school identified with Warren (and Sklar); and the various theorists of the new international division of labour (NIDL) who number neo-Smithians, neo-Ricardians and post-Palloixians amongst their ranks (after Jenkins, 1984). As ever these positions are criticised wherever criticism seems appropriate and I tentatively conclude that the work of Bill Warren has been pivotal both in denying the excesses of the underdevelopment school and in shifting the Left to a critique of peripheral independent industrialisation which turns more on the question of independence than on the facts of industrialisation. (If this sounds cryptic it will be explained in due course.) Whether Warren's critique has itself been answered by the work of the NIDL theorists is a moot point. His arguments are clearly vulnerable in places, but a good deal of the critique of Warren would seem to rest on two unproven assumptions: (i) that transnational-led industrialisation is incompatible with true Third World industrialisation; and (ii) that Third World governments have no useful role to play in promoting a more appropriate industrialisation within their borders.

These assumptions are explored in the second and third sections, where I also take the opportunity to confront the emerging Marxist perspective on the NIDL with a number of non-Marxist writings on Third World industrialisation. Finally, some specific conclusions on the politics of peripheral industrialisation are drawn and these are related back to the more general theme of capitalism and development essayed in Chapter 2.

4.1 Industrialisation in the Third World: competing perspectives

From Frank to Warren

To the extent that Left and Right agree on anything developmental it is that industrialisation is a precondition for successful economic growth.[1] In itself this is hardly surprising. The evidence for such a view is to be found both historically, in the long-standing association between high levels and rates of growth of industrialisation with high levels and rates of growth of national income, and in the positive economic effects supposedly induced by industrialisation. Diversification, the spread effects of backward and forward linkages, attitudinal modernisation, skill upgrading and prestige are just five of the benefits listed in a recent geographical textbook (Dickenson *et al.*, 1983, p. 147).

When it comes to the pace and policies of and for such industrialisation, however, Left, Right (and centre) part company and begin to chase each other's tails. Consider the case of mainstream economics first. Prior to the Second World War most economists of centre and centre-right persuasions adhered to a fairly static version of comparative advantage theory wherein it was assumed that peripheral countries were naturally and eternally predisposed to the production of agricultural crops and other primary commodities; manufacturing was the preserve of the metropolitan powers. To ensure that the thought was truly father to the deed colonial governments acted out this convenient piece of philosophy in a manner most succinctly described by Lord Cromer, Governor of Egypt, 1883–1907:

> The policy of the government may be summed up thus: (1) export of cotton to Europe . . . (2) imports of textile products manufactured abroad . . . nothing else enters the government's intentions, nor will it protect the Egyptian cotton industry, because of the dangers and evils that arise from such measures . . . Since Egypt is by her nature an agricultural country, it follows logically that industrial training can only lead to neglect of agriculture while diverting the Egyptians from the land (quoted in Hayter, 1981, p. 49).

By the end of the Second World War this perspective was no longer in touch with global *realpolitik*. In an era of rising US hegemony and advancing decolonialisation, a new centre-right economics emerged which quickly convinced itself that industrialisation was a veritable panacea for development. The only point of disagreement was the ease of this industrial transition. In the more optimistic Rostovian analysis industrialisation and development are treated in true sausage-machine fashion: development or take-off is all about mobilising savings equivalent to 10–15 per cent of national income, investing it in industry, cranking the handle, and awaiting a happy future (see Rostow, 1960). In the more distinctively *laissez-faire* formulations comparative advantage theory still retains a hold, but it is now cast in terms of the factor proportions model developed by Hecksher and Ohlin (see Todaro, 1981, ch. 12). This holds that comparative advantages are set by the tripartite factors of capital, land and labour, thus allowing for a gradual move towards a comparative advantage in low-level industrialisation as foreign aid flows into a country, and as low-cost labour moves to the cities. (A convenient theory, some would say, given the Lewis two-sector model of the 1950s, and given the current concern with a new international division of labour: see Lewis, 1955 and 1978.)

Meanwhile the Left was also changing its tack, but in the

opposite direction. Prior to the Second World War the Left was almost alone in rejecting the tautologies of static comparative advantage theory, and in warding off the depradations prosecuted in its name.[2] At the same time it foresaw a world where industrialisation would follow naturally enough from the political fact of decolonialisation. By the mid-1960s, however, this would be rejected as untheorised romanticism. For the 'development of underdevelopment' school which grew up around André Gunder Frank the industrialisation of the Third World was deemed to be incompatible with capitalism. In a curious echo of pre-war mainstream economics, Frank argued that capitalism never changed its spots and that the political act of decolonialisation would find no economic counterpart in a world which continued to be dominated by a handful of neo-colonialist capitalist powers.

The proof for this view was supposedly twofold, beginning with the post-war statistics of industrial inactivity in Latin America (and elsewhere). Writing in 1965–6, Frank argued not only that industrialisation was all but absent from Latin America in 1945,[3] but also that the Economic Commission for Latin America's policies of inner-directed industrialisation had signally failed to alter matters. Reasonably enough, Frank took this to be critical. After all the entire ECLA strategy was steeped in the earlier radical tradition which promised that industrialisation would come quickly to any politically independent country brave enough to challenge the 'laws' of comparative advantage. (It will be recalled that Prebisch identified the oligopolistic nature of core commodity and factor markets as the determinants of a secular decline in the terms of trade of Latin America, and that he called upon state-sponsored industrialisation as a way out of this vicious circle. More precisely he looked to policies of 'healthy protectionism, exchange controls, the attraction of foreign investment into Latin American industry, the stimulation and orientation of national investment, and the adoption of wage policies aimed at boosting effective demand' [Palma, 1978, p. 907] to secure the industrialisation which would bring with it the developmental externalities absent from primary-commodity-based growth.) ECLA's apparent failure therefore, which manifested itself in such things as a declining balance of payments position, in mass unemployment and in massive outflows of profits (Bernstein, 1982), led Frank to the conclusion that industrialisation within the capitalist world system was impossible.

This conclusion was strengthened by Frank's parallel 'discovery' that the only periods when Latin America had enjoyed some industrial growth happened to coincide with periods of weakened centre – periphery ties. Thus if a first hypothesis of underdevelopment theory suggested that the 'development of the national and other subordinate metropoles is limited by their satellite status', a second hypothesis held that 'the satellites experience their greatest economic development and especially their most classically capitalist industrial development if and when their ties to the metropolis are weakest' (Frank, 1969, pp. 9–10).

This second hypothesis is almost diametrically opposed to the generally accepted thesis that development in the underdeveloped countries follows from the greatest degree of contact with and diffusion from the metropolitan countries. This hypothesis seemed to be confirmed by two kinds of relative isolation that Latin America has experienced in the course of its history. One is the temporary isolation caused by the crises of wars or depression in the world metropolis. Apart from minor ones, five periods of such crises stand out and are seen to confirm the hypothesis. These are: the European (and especially Spanish) depression of the seventeenth century; the Napoleonic Wars; the First World War, the Depression of the 1930s and the Second World War. It is clearly established and generally recognised that the most important recent industrial development – especially of Argentina, Brazil and Mexico, but also of other countries such as Chile – has taken place precisely during the periods of the two World Wars and the intervening Depression. Thanks to the consequent loosening of trade and investment ties during these periods, the satellites initiated marked autonomous industrial growth . . . The other kind of isolation which tends to confirm the second hypothesis is the geographical and economic isolation of regions which at one time were relatively weakly tied to, and poorly integrated into, the mercantilist system. My preliminary research suggests that in Latin America it was these regions which initiated and experienced the most promising self-generating economic development of the classic industrial capitalist type . . . Internationally, of course, the classic case of industrialisation through non-participation [*sic*] as a satellite in the capitalist world system is [post-Meiji] Japan (Frank, 1969, pp. 10–11).

These comments provided the kernel of a stagnationist account of peripheral non-industrialisation. Frank's work was soon 'extended', however, by the first generation of radical geographers, who talked heatedly about the deindustrialisation of Africa and Asia,[4] and by a group of the more prominent late 1960s' New Leftists. One thinks in particular of Ernest Mandel, whose 'classic' *Marxist Economic Theory* (1968, pp.476–9) deals at some length with 'Imperialism as [an] Obstacle to the Industrialisation of Underdeveloped Countries'. One thinks also of Michael Kidron (1971) who seemed to maintain that no significant progress towards industrialisation is any longer possible in the Third World – even after a socialist revolution in any one peripheral country – because of the growing scale of industrial and technological organisation. As Sutcliffe points out 'On this view all significant progress . . . is now being held up pending socialist revolution in the advanced countries' (Sutcliffe, 1972, p. 180) – a fair anticipation of world systems thinking.

Such stagnationist claims were not destined for a long ascendancy however. Some radical geographers continued to present them,[5] but as the 1970s wore on it became clear that industrialisation was occurring in selected Third World countries, a point brought home to the Left politically by growing Northern fears of deindustrialisation in the wake of a flood of imports from cheap-labour countries. What really brought these trends to the attention of radical development theorists, however, was the work of Bill Warren, an English Communist and self-proclaimed Marxist. In a brace of penetrating articles written for the *New Left Review* in 1971 and 1973, Warren claimed not only to destroy the main tenets of stagnationism (which was galling enough) but to demonstrate that any true Marxist – as opposed to one indoctrinated in the pragmatic ways of Leninist and post-Leninist theories of imperialism – would actually expect, and would certainly welcome, the post-war industrialisation of the Third World. It is this latter claim with which the Left is still coming to terms.

Warren

Warren's articles in *New Left Review* were expanded in 1980 with the posthumous publication of his book *Imperialism: Pioneer of Capitalism*. This text makes it clear that Warren's (in)famous statistical arrays on 'The Facts of Post-War Progress' are meant to be read as the culmination of a fourfold critique of neo-Marxist theories of imperialism and underdevelopment.

The first stage of this critique consists of a re-examination (or for Warren a reaffirmation) of Marx's own thoughts on the historically progressive nature of both capitalism and colonialism. One can detect two strands in Warren's work here. On the one hand he is engaged in an act of critique pure and simple. Warren wants to reclaim Marx from those who would criticise capitalism on 'moral and ahistorical' (and thus anti-socialist) grounds; those who look only to capitalism's darker side and to its behavioural and institutional associates of immiserisation, prostitution, uneven regional development and so on and so forth. Warren has no sympathy for such New Leftism and he wastes no opportunity to remind its adherents that there is another side to the coin: that under capitalism 'the possibility of genuine moral choice . . . increases to the extent that people (and individual persons) can consciously control their own destiny' (Warren, 1980, p. 20); that:

> equality, justice, generosity, independence of spirit and mind, the spirit of inquiry and adventure, opposition to cruelty, not to mention political democracy are not late comers to [but] . . . are either ushered in by capitalism or achieve a relative dominance unequalled by any major earlier or contemporaneous cultures (Warren, 1980, p. 21);

and that 'it is the self-sustaining momentum and rapid pace of technological change under capitalism, and especially industrial capitalism, that distinguish it from *all* earlier societies' (ibid, p. 12, his emphasis). 'Under capitalism to stand still is to perish' (ibid, p. 14).

These reminders issued, Warren seeks to underline them with chapter and verse from Marx himself. The latter parts of the first chapter of *Imperialism – Pioneer of Capitalism* are thus devoted to Marx's own statements on domestic capitalism – 'the bourgeoisie cannot exist without constantly revolutionising the instruments of production, and thereby the relations of production, and with them the whole of society' (Marx, 1967, p. 83) – and on the imperialist mission of capitalism. In this latter context pride of place is given to a series of lengthy quotations from Marx's *New York Herald* articles, the centrepiece of which is his description of England's double mission in India:

The ruling classes of Great Britain have had, till now, but an accidental, transitory and exceptional interest in the progress of India. The aristocracy wanted to conquer it, the moneyocracy to plunder it, the millocracy to undersell it. But now the tables are turned. The millocracy has discovered that the transformation of India into a reproductive country has a vital importance to them, and that, to that end, it is necessary, above all, to gift her with the means of irrigation and of internal communication. They intend now drawing a set of railroads over India. And they will do it' (Marx, 8 August 1853; quoted in Warren, 1980, pp. 42–3).

Marx could not be clearer than this, says Warren, nor more consistent. 'Since Marx and Engels considered the role of capitalism in pre-capitalist societies progressive, it was entirely logical that they should have welcomed the extension of capitalism to non-European societies' (Warren, 1980, p. 39) – warts and all.

The question that then arises is this: if stagnationism has no roots in Marx's own writings, where does it come from and what sort of radical heritage can it claim? Warren is in no doubt as to the answer. In the second section of his critique he argues that:

The traditional Marxist view of imperialism as progressive was reversed primarily by Lenin . . . in his *Imperialism: The Highest Stage of Capitalism*. In effectively overturning Marx and Engels's view of the character of imperialist expansion, Lenin set in motion an ideological process that erased from Marxism any trace of the view that capitalism could be an instrument of social progress even in pre-capitalist societies (Warren, 1980, p. 48).

We have already met the gist of Lenin's work (section 2.3) so we can pass quickly enough over his equation of imperialism with an age of monopoly capitalism (and thus with a lack of competitive dynamic, and with the need for inter-imperialist rivalries and capital export). Instead, we can turn to Warren's critique of Lenin, which is basically threefold. First, the details of Lenin's theory of imperialism are examined. Warren joins a long line of critics in pointing out that it cannot be shown either that capital export was characteristic of a specific stage of capitalism, or that it was decisively connected with the scramble for territories. More specifically, he demonstrates that:

capital export, far from being a symptom of a particular (degenerate) stage of capitalism, has been a significant feature of industrial capitalism since its inception . . . The two leading capital exporting countries, Britain and France, were already quite active in this field as early as the 1820s and 1850s respectively (Warren, 1980, pp. 61–2).

Warren then challenges Lenin's thesis that monopoly capitalism is necessarily parasitic and decadent. In an important and much neglected passage, he argues that:

The rise of oligopolistic market structures – or monopoly firms as they are popularly called – has not reduced competition but on the contrary has intensified it. The development of oligopoly and various forms of association and combination (in individual economies) has been associated with the disappearance of monopoly on a world scale and its replacement by competition – the disappearance, that is, of the British world monopoly of manufacturing with the rise of vigorous competition towards the end of the nineteenth century. These two phenomena – growth of monopolistic, cartelized firms and industries, and intensification of competition internationally – were closely connected; indeed it was the latter that generated the former (along with technical factors, themselves connected to increased competition, which tended to increase the size of the individual unit). The development of large monopolistic firms also permitted major advances in efficiency, primarily through economies of scale and the systematic application of science and new organizational methods to production (Warren, 1980, p. 79).

Readers will note how far removed this is from Baran's discussion of monopoly capitalism, which I have already urged is the link between Lenin and Frank and thence to a whole series of stagnationist arguments that still continue with today's cruder denigrations of the transnational corporations (TNCs). It might also be noted that Warren rebukes the 'myth of consumerism' which so agitates Baran, and in particular the notion that the advertising industry is creating artificial wants to make up for the lack of dynamism in monopoly capitalism. Not so, says Warren: 'monopoly capitalism [has proved] far more responsive to the needs of the masses than nineteenth century capitalism ever [did]' (Warren, 1980, p. 80) and has actually provided them with a range of consumer durables at which only intellectuals are prone to sneer.

Finally, Warren attends to Lenin's reasons for writing his pamphlet on *Imperialism*. With some vigour he argues that Lenin was well aware of capitalism's progressive mission abroad – witness Lenin's *Development of Capitalism in Russia* (1974) – but that he chose to turn his back on Marx's theory for propagandist reasons. In essence, Lenin arrived at his theory of imperialism (and so of monopoly capitalism) as a way of explaining the inexplicable: the fact that at the height of the First World War (and *Imperialism* was written in 1916) the working classes of Europe were slaughtering each other in the name of patriotism. As Warren has it:

> Although his results were logically and analytically lamentable, Lenin did score Marxism's glittering propaganda success of the twentieth century, for the pamphlet was able really to explain *both* the cause of the war *and* the reasons for the opportunist, nationalist proletarian support for it by one and the same phenomenon: imperialism (Warren, 1980, p. 49, emphasis in the original).

This concern with propaganda is taken further in the third section of Warren's critique, where it is suggested that the inadequacies in Lenin's theory of imperialism continued to be papered over as it came to prove useful first for the Comintern (and Soviet security) and later for the nationalistic bourgeoises of the Third World. Again it is difficult for me to give more than the drift of these charges. Taking them in turn, though, we find Warren dealing first with the Comintern and in particular with the Sixth Congress of the Communist International in 1928. It was at this Congress, says Warren, that 'The Marxist analysis of imperialism was . . . formally . . . sacrificed to the requirements of bourgeois anti-imperialist propaganda and, indirectly, to what were thought to be the security requirements of the encircled Soviet state' (Warren, 1980, p. 8).

This sacrifice involved the endorsement of two theses that were at best only implicit in Lenin's original pamphlet: (i) that imperialism actually retarded the industrialisation of the colonies, and (ii) that consequently the Soviet Union and the industrial bourgeoises of the colonial countries were natural allies in the fight against imperialism. For Warren this is pure cant, but he recognises it as a brilliant piece of propaganda. Here we have an ideology – imperialism – which not only served the immediate defensive interests of the Soviet Union (which could now retreat from internationalism), but which also went some way to meeting the demands of Asiatic Marxists like M. N. Roy of India, who was seeking to prioritise the anti-imperialist struggle over the socialist aspirations of the Western proletariats.[6] In the longer run, however, these theses proved most critical in sustaining the 'nationalist mythologies' of post-war dependency and underdevelopment theories. The immediate roots of such theories may well lie in a critique of the alleged failures of import-substitution industrialisation, notes Warren, but their real genealogy, and certainly their real appeal to the political elites of the Third World, can be traced back at least as far as 1928. For Warren there is a direct line of descent from Lenin and the Comintern to all that is most distinctive and most misleading in modern dependency theories: that the Third World is being exploited and underdeveloped by a set of monopolistic metropolitan powers, and that the Third World's bourgeoisies (and workers and peasants) can be absolved of all blame for not promoting a faster industrialisation of their countries than has already occurred.

In the fourth and final section of his book, Warren attempts to show just how misleading these propositions are. In this section he presents a wealth of empirical material to support his contentions that imperialism has given way to interdependence in the post-colonial era, and that, as it has done so, so an already 'powerful engine of progressive social change' [imperialism] has found full fruition in the 'substantial industrialisation and capitalist transformation' of the Third World (Warren, 1980, p. 9).

Once more, the full extent of Warren's documentation defies summary here, for he deals not only with the recent industrialisation of the Third World, but with the corollary 'facts':

1. that 'economic progress as measured in conventional terms by GNP per capita was rapid and fairly generalised throughout the Third World (although very uneven between countries) during the post-war period' (Warren, 1980, p. 250);
2. that 'the wide belief that rapid economic progress in the Third

World since the Second World War has generally been associated with worsening aggregate inequality is not borne out by the . . . time-series data, or by the more plentiful cross-section data' (Warren, 1980, p. 200);

3. that marginalisation is not characteristic of recent Third World development: 'the relevant non-tautological indicators, such as open unemployment and underemployment as measured by short hours show very little evidence of marginalisation . . . and possibly declining unemployment rates in the majority of countries' (Warren, 1980, p. 251);

4. that 'the patchy available evidence of physical indicators measuring fulfilment of the basic needs of the population in health, education, nutrition and housing . . . strongly suggests that major advances in the material welfare of the population has been registered in the Third World post-war' (Warren, 1980, p. 250).

Nevertheless, it is the statistics on industrialisation which are supposed to underlie these various claims, and which have provoked the most righteous indignation. It follows that it is reasonable to deal with them at greater length. In effect Warren is seeking to do two things here: to argue that 'the underdeveloped world as a whole has made considerable progress in industrialisation during the post-war period' (Warren, 1980, p. 241), and to ward off the more obvious assertions, predictions and countercharges that might be made to the contrary. (By 1978, remember, when Warren wrote the book, he had some experience of damning reviews.)

Given these guiding lights Warren advances in three stages. He deals first with the aggregate levels and trends of post-war industrialisation in the Third World, pointing out (or claiming) that in the 1950s, 1960s and 1970s Third World manufacturing output grew much faster than its First World counterpart, despite record growth in the latter. In this first section too, Warren dismisses the notion that these high statistical growth rates (7 per cent annually from 1960 to 1968) are illusory either because they start from low base levels, or because they ignore population growth rates in the less-developed world. Inspection of the figures, says Warren (and see Table 4.1), shows that 'many underdeveloped countries are able to maintain faster rates of growth of manufacturing output

TABLE 4.1   *Annual average rates of growth of manufacturing, 1951–69 and 1965–74, for selected countries*

	1951–69	1965–74		1951–69	1965–74
Brazil	7.8	11.2	Panama	14.2	8.5
Costa Rica	9.7	–	Peru	7.5	7.8
Iran	11.2	13.3	Philippines	8.5	5.8
Iraq	6.8	7.6	Puerto Rico	6.5	–
Jamaica	5.0	–	Singapore	14.8	15.3
Jordan	15.2	–	Taiwan	16.1	–
Korea (Rep of)	16.9	24.4	Thailand	8.7	–
Malaysia	6.4	9.6	Trinidad/Tobago	10.0	–
Mexico	7.4	7.6	Turkey	11.5	–
Nicaragua	7.6	–	Venezuela	10.5	5.0
Pakistan	15.0	–	Zambia	13.8	7.4

SOURCE   Warren (1980).

than the industrialised countries . . . over a long period' (Warren, 1980, p. 242). Furthermore, 'to take the growth of per capita manufacturing output as a basis of comparison is to apply an extremely demanding criterion . . . from the standpoint of the distribution of world industrial power . . . growth rates are the central issue' (ibid, p. 243).

The second stage of Warren's presentation deals with the share of manufacturing in GDP, both within selected less-developed countries over time, and between developed and less-developed countries. His basic argument is clear enough: 'For the LDCs as a whole, manufacturing accounted for 14.5 per cent of GDP in 1950–4; the figure rose to 17.9 per cent in 1960 and 20.4 per cent in 1973. In the developed capitalist countries manufacturing contributed 28.4 per cent to GDP in 1972. *The difference is therefore becoming rather small*' (ibid, p. 244; emphasis in the original). To ward off sceptics again this argument is further developed with the table reproduced here as Table 4.2.[7]

Finally, Warren turns his attention to the supposedly elitist pattern of manufacturing output that is said to characterise Third World industrialisation. Arguing that this 'is plainly incorrect for

TABLE 4.2   *Selected countries' manufacturing as a percentage of Gross Domestic Product at current factor cost (1973) and percentage of active labour force employed in manufacturing (latest estimates)*

Country	Manufacturing as % GDP[a]	% of active labour force employed in manufacturing[b]
Egypt	21.6	12.9
Taiwan	29.8	n.a
South Korea	24.3	20.5
Argentina	38.3	19.7
Brazil	24.6	11.0
Chile	25.9	15.9
Costa Rica	21.9	11.9
Mexico	25.4	17.8
Peru	21.4	12.5
Uruguay	23.0	18.8
average =	25.6	average = 15.7
Australia	26.6	24.8
Canada	20.1	18.0
Denmark	26.6	23.1
Norway	25.4	24.4
Sweden	24.8	26.5
USA	24.7	22.4
average =	24.7	average = 23.2
Greece	20.4	17.1
Spain	26.7	25.7
Malta	26.5	27.8
Hong Kong	32.1	44.4
Singapore	26.1	25.6
average =	26.3	average = 32.1

SOURCE   [a] World Bank, *World Tables*, 1976
        [b] ILO, International Yearbook of Labour Statistics, 1977, Geneva (1977), Table 2.
        (after Warren, 1980)

the Third World countries that include the vast majority of the population of Africa and Asia, where the market for 'luxury goods' is too small to sustain profitable production' (Warren, 1980, p. 247), Warren concludes that such an argument is once more expressive of Western intellectual snobbery. The fact is that the Third World actually wants consumer durables and in Latin America at least, which tends to be more advanced than Africa and Asia, a wide market for such goods reaches 'well into the lower income urban groups' (Warren, 1980, p. 248. This obviously bears upon Warren's remarks on the myth of marginality).

Together, these arguments and statistics attain a powerful effect, and Warren draws on them to make three more general remarks: (i) that stagnationism is a chimera (the more so for these developments happening in years that could not conceivably be called years of crisis, war or depression); (ii) that 'there is nothing to gain from a refusal to recognise the existence of developing capitalist societies' in the Third World; and (iii) that to the extent that 'there are obstacles to development they originate not in current relationships between imperialism and the Third World, but in the internal contradictions of the Third World itself' (Warren, 1980, p. 10) – with its policy blunders and with its neglect of agriculture.

Reactions to Warren

It was inevitable that such views would be roundly, even abusively, criticised by the Left, but what is of interest is the way in which the attack on Warren shifted its ground over the later 1970s and early 1980s.

To begin with (that is, after the publication of the articles in the *New Left Review*) Warren was attacked largely from within the underdevelopment paradigm. Thus various critics took issue with his statistics on the post-war industrialisation of the Third World and pointed out:

1. that Warren's evidence for 'substantial and sustained progress' is based on absolute figures of manufacturing output over time. A volumetric study would give a less heartening but more realistic comparison, given the low base levels of industrialisation (see Table 4.3);

TABLE 4.3 *World production of manufactures by continent (by volume)**

	1937	1959
Imperial countries	103	244
Third World countries	12	35
	91	209

* No indication of scales is given in the original; nor is the time period justified.

SOURCE Reproduced from Petras *et al.* (1978), p116.

2. that Warren's portrait of rapid Third World industrialisation is sustained only by an unrepresentative choice of sample countries (compare Table 4.1 with Table 4.4);
3. that Warren's notion of industrialisation is so poorly specified that it is not clear whether he is dealing with '(a) [the] simple elaboration of raw materials; (b) [the] transformation of processed raw materials into parts; (c) [the] assembly of parts; (d) [the] creation of machinery (capital goods) to sustain the process of industrialisation; (e) [the] consumption of a substantial proportion of industrial output; or (f) [the] research and design of products and machinery' (Petras *et al.*, 1978, pp. 110–11; see

TABLE 4.4 *Annual average rates of growth of manufacturing, 1960–70 and 1970–81, for selected countries*

	1960–70	1970–81
Burma	3.4	4.6
Senegal	6.2	2.0
Zambia	n.a.	0.3
Argentina	5.6	0.7
Uruguay	1.5	4.3
Central African Republic	5.4	−4.3
Togo	n.a.	−10.4
Zaire	n.a.	−2.3

SOURCE World Bank, *World Development Reports*, 1983, Table 2.

also Emmanuel, 1974, who berates Warren for failing to distinguish between handicrafts industries employing, say, ten people, and vast integrated iron and steel plants employing thousands with different skills).

By the later 1970s, however, this sort of critique was losing its bite. Warren's statistics continued to be decried as selective and misleading – and rightly so – but the overall thrust of his argument could not be gainsaid. No matter how one massaged the figures one could not disguise the fact that a number of Third World countries were industrialising apace throughout the 1970s.

As a consequence the critique of Warren changes tack and we begin to find him attacked less for his statistics *per se* than for the political and theoretical interpretations he put upon them. We will come to the theoretical objections soon enough. For the moment let us consider Warren's politics. For critics like Petras *et al.*, and Lipietz, these are best described as 'neo-liberal' (Petras *et al.*, 1978, p. 104) or even 'positivistic' (Lipietz, 1982, p. 58). Warren is said to have embraced a vulgar empiricism – that is the 'arrangement of various discrete "facts" ' (Petras *et al.*, 1978, p. 107) which renders him incapable of seeing the capitalist development of the Third World for what it really is: limited, dependent, brutal and exploitative. Indeed he actually seems to welcome the darker side of capitalism (the cheap labour, the prostitution, the shanty towns),[8] dismissing its dehumanising effects as the necessary conditions of a future capitalist development which will in time bring the world to socialism. In a powerful attack on the 'stages theory' of politics to which Warren, like Rostow, so clearly adheres, Lipietz reminds us that for Marx capitalism always involves exploitation, and that it is not enough to talk about low wages being functional for capitalist accumulation. More woundingly, he accuses Warren of using the charge of 'moralism' to deflect the attack which should rightly be made upon his own immoral defence of the 'necessary' development of capitalism. In a brilliant concluding passage, Lipietz argues that:

In essence [Warren] is saying: Don't fight imperialism, since it helps to spread capitalism, and capitalism itself is all right, 'functional', 'appropriate to economic growth'. Such is the thesis worn thin by so many writers from Adam Smith to Walt Rostow yet still hegemonic today, which Warren's final chapter trumpets forth in every way. So much the better if inequality is on the rise: it will promote the 'necessary diversification of skills and operations'; it will kindle 'energies previously dormant'; and it will mobilise 'scarce or underutilized entrepreneurial talents'. This side of things is 'likely to be most severe in the earliest stages', but eventually, with the generalization of the modern sector, the gates will open on the post-industrial paradise promised by Colin Clark and Walt Rostow. So much the better if the teeming humanity of the shanty-towns has to survive through the informal economy: this permits very cheap production of basic consumer goods, and it is therefore entirely functional to the development of the modern sector – which leads us (see above) to paradise. Indeed, should not the activity of prostitutes 'be regarded as socially beneficial in cities with large male immigrant populations'? Can such a deplorable observation be redeemed by any intended irony? (Lipietz, 1982, p. 56).

Although I will later want to challenge some aspects of this critique of Warren I do want to endorse the thrust of Lipietz's remarks here.[9] Warren really is so obsessed with capitalism serving as the 'bridge to socialism' (Warren, 1980, p. 25) that he quite abandons any moral critique of capitalism as it now exists. He also fails to consider the alternative social systems that could be constructed in its place, and which might act as catalysts to the future socialist golden age to which he claims to be looking forward. Having said that, it seems to me that certain of Warren's prognoses on industrialisation in the Third World do stand or fall independently of these shortcomings. One does not have to be as impressed as Warren with recent developments to recognise that they are taking place. It follows that a conclusive critique of Warren must also challenge the more narrowly industrial and developmental segments of his thesis; a point which seems to be well understood by all those Leftists (including Lipietz and Petras *et al.*) who have sought to oppose Warrenite interpretations of post-imperialist industrialisation with an explanation cast firmly in the dependency framework. Central to this critique is the concept of the New International Division of Labour.

Theories of the New International Division of Labour

Discussions of the NIDL have been circulating for some time now, and the more precise formulations of the concept to which I will be coming cannot always be traced back to an engagement with Warren: the recent restructuring of the world economy has been at least as forceful in its impact. Nevertheless, if one re-reads the original Petras review of Warren one finds that the bulk of his criticism is already predicated on an alternative interpretation of Third World industrialisation. Already the talk is of the need to theorise the 'global system . . . rather than . . . distinct national economies' (Petras *et al.*, 1978, p. 133), and of the need to focus on the way in which selected value-added activities are being transferred to repressive Third World countries as assembly operations under the control of metropolitan TNCs. For Petras and his colleagues the real failing of Warren is the way in which he fragments the totality. 'To equate the fragmented, externally integrated, and technologically dependent industrialisation of the Third World with that of the Western imperialist countries is to ignore the vast qualitative differences in the levels of development of the productive forces, as well as the tentative and vulnerable nature of the industrial efforts in the Third World' (Petras *et al.*, 1978, p. 111).

Since the mid-1970s, however, this early concern for the possible non-independence of Third World industrialisation (itself an accomodation to Warren)[10] has been superseded by a number of more formal models of a NIDL. These seek not only to describe recent changes in the world economy, but to account for them in terms of Marxist economic theory. Apart from Warren's own efforts in this field, and the associated theory of post-imperialism propounded by Sklar (1976) – and since taken up by Becker (1984) and Schiffer (1981) – there seem to be three main versions of this new orthodoxy: the neo-Smithian approach, the neo-Ricardian approach and the post-Palloixian approach. (The first two terms are taken from Jenkins, 1984; the last is mine). All of them extend the critique of Warren either explicitly or implicitly, and I will review them in turn before examining possible counters to each.

The neo-Smithian and neo-Ricardian approaches   It is convenient to deal with the neo-Smithian and neo-Ricardian approaches in tandem for they are both theories of the world economy, and of changes therein, which have their roots in an 'exchange-oriented' or neo-Marxist perspective (Jenkins, 1984, p. 29: that is, their emphasis is upon circulation rather than production). The major difference between them is that the neo-Smithians look to an explanation of the NIDL in terms of the changing world market for labour-power and production sites. Thus Fröbel, Heinrichs and Kreye (1980) structure their account of the NIDL in terms of: the development of a world-wide reservoir of potential labour-power; the development of the labour process in manufacturing (which has led to the decomposition of the production process into elementary units and the deskilling of the labour force); and the development of the forces of production in the fields of transport and communications which has made industry less tied to specific locations. By contrast, the neo-Ricardians[11] trace the origins of the NIDL to a profits squeeze specific to the Western industrial powers. They argue that the processes of centralisation and concentration which are characteristic of the post-war accumulation of capital, plus the fact of full employment, strengthened the hand of organised labour to such an extent that profit rates in the metropolitan countries began to dip in the late 1960s. To escape this crisis the capitalists in the core had either to *automate* (that is, fight the working classes at home by unemployment, rationalisation and the extraction of higher rates of relative surplus value), *evaporate* (that is, give up), or *emigrate* (that is, exploit the cheap labour of the unorganised, peripheral working classes).[12] Given that the first option was thought to be politically inexpedient, and the second unthinkable, it followed that a 'decentralisation of accumulation to the periphery [made] an extremely attractive strategy for capital . . . [Moreover] although industrial location is determined on the basis of all relevant cost factors, wages [in this model] are the crucial determinant' (Jenkins, 1984, p. 30).

Aside from these different explanations of the origins of the NIDL – different both from each other and from Bill Warren – the implications and pitfalls of these two perpectives are remarkably similar and tell tales of a common logic.

Consider the implications first. Both theories are united on two basic points: (i) that the NIDL was not established in response to either the changing development needs or strategies of the Third World countries themselves (for Fröbel *et al.* the NIDL is an

'institutional innovation of capital itself' – Fröbel, 1982, p. 46),
and (ii) that the NIDL (*contra* Warren) does not alter the fundamental structures of inequality between core and periphery established in mercantilist and colonial times. Rather the reverse. For
Gyorgy Adam, all that is happening now is that 'banana republics
are becoming pyjama republics' (Adam, 1975, p. 102).[13] This
observation has since been endorsed by those critics who have
sought to characterise and criticise it in terms of four more specific
attributes:

1. It is said that the NIDL is predicated on the fact of (necessarily)
   cheap labour. This factor is crucial to both neo-Smithian and
   neo-Ricardian accounts in their different ways (the former
   emphasising the role of cheap labour in extending the world
   market for labour power,[14] the latter emphasising its role in
   restoring profits) and no effort is spared to itemise the long
   hours, the short holidays, the intensity of labour, the high
   turnover, and the high female participation rates that are the
   supposed counterparts of low wages.
2. This super-exploitation upon which the NIDL is said to be
   based, is itself held to be guaranteed by the actions of com-
   pliant, if not client, Third World governments. The regimes in
   the Newly Industrialising Countries (NICs) are not only
   thought to be attracting export-production capital through such
   means as tax incentives, subsidies and free-trade assembly
   zones, they are also deemed to be opposed to the democracy
   which Warren so blandly assumes to be the natural complement
   of capitalism. Instead they prefer and encourage the repressive
   anti-union and anti-labour policies which Lipietz calls 'Bloody
   Taylorism' (Lipietz, 1982, p. 41) and of which Frank, archetypally, has claimed 'that this repressive political policy has the
   very clear economic purpose and function of making these
   economies more competitive on the world market by lowering
   wages and by supporting those elements of the local bourgeoisie
   who are tied to the internal market' (Frank, 1981, p. 324).
3. Despite the successes of selected NICs in attracting capital to
   the periphery, the industrialisation that is occurring can in no
   sense be welcomed as 'real', 'developmental' or independent
   industrialisation. There are a number of reasons for this. On the
   one hand it is argued that such industrialisation as is occurring is

creating very few jobs when compared with the size of the massive industrial reserve army now encamped in the Third World. At the same time it is argued that industrial control remains firmly in the hands of the TNCs. As a result the industrialisation is of an enclave nature: few linkages are forged because the manufacturing is usually of an assembly nature; production is still dependent on the vagaries of the world market; and dependency is being forged anew by the TNCs' emerging monopolies over technology and marketing.

4. Finally, the NIDL is said to be detrimental to the interests of the working classes in the core countries too. In an interesting 'annexe' to their main analysis, Fröbel *et al.* argue that the relocation of industry to the periphery has been a prime cause of the crisis now afflicting the major metropolitan powers, and which threatens the social harmony that has prevailed in the core. In particular it has provoked: a decline in domestic investment, which has been increasingly directed towards rationalisation as opposed to the expansion of productive capacity: a rapid growth in OECD unemployment; and a fiscal crisis of the state (after Jenkins, 1984).

A critique of exchange-oriented theories There can be little doubt that charges such as these have had a powerful impact on the Left, where they have met with widespread approval both as a rejoinder to Warren and as a reaffirmation of dependency (if not underdevelopment) theory (see Bienefeld, 1981).[15] This is especially true of radical development geography. Already there is a sizeable literature which concurs that 'the international economic relationships which dominated the immediate post-war period have been overturned' (Cohen, 1981, p. 287), and which traces through this movement from world trade to world factory in terms of the classic concerns of neo-Marxism. Today's emphasis is upon the global corporation (Susman and Schultz, 1983) and footloose capital;[16] upon the way in which the 'potency of an industrial reserve army is [being] resuscitated (Gibson and Horvarth, 1983, p. 180) as a 'global sub-mode' of capitalism replaces monopoly capitalism; upon the way in which this new global capital uses its mobility over space to 'subvert . . . each local advance or reform' (Ross, 1983, p. 145), and upon the role 'of wages, the discipline of the labour force, and public policy perceived to be favourable to capital' as

TABLE 4.5   *Hourly wage rates and fringe benefits in the apparel industry (in $US)*

Sweden	7.22
Netherlands	5.68
Belgium	5.49
New York (Legal)*	4.58
USA	4.35
Puerto Rico	2.57
New York (Sweatshops)*	1.75
Singapore*	1.10
Hong Kong	0.96
Brazil	0.86
Taiwan	0.56
South Korea	0.41

* = no fringe benefits
SOURCE   Reproduced from Ross (1983) Table 3.

determinants of the decision 'to stay, leave or enter a locality' (ibid, p. 144: see also the table from Ross reproduced here as Table 4.5, and designed to show the critical role of low wages in directing a NIDL).

Whether or not such concerns are warranted, however, is another matter. Along with Jenkins and Brenner, I have my doubts as to whether these neo-Marxist perspectives can ever transcend the more general failings which bedevil them, and with which I dealt in Chapter 2. It may be attractive to think of the growth of the world market (and thus of the role of transport and communications, capital mobility and the conquest of space: in a word, geography) as a basis of the NIDL, but it is evident that such thinking owes more to Smith and Babbage than it does to Marx. As Jenkins puts it:

The emphasis placed by these writers on the Babbage principle as a fundamental factor underlying the fragmentation/relocation of production processes is illustrative . . . of its failure to ana-lyse the tendency of capitalism to expand through increasing relative surplus value by raising the productivity of labour . . . Babbage's emphasis on reducing labour costs through the fragmentation of tasks in order to take advantage of workers with the minimum level of skill required for each task is characteristic of what Marx referred to as the arena of manufacture as opposed to machinofacture. It therefore highlights the tendency to neglect the role of technological change in increasing labour productivity in this approach (Jenkins, 1984, p. 33).

More to the point, these theoretical failings can be shown to have their empirical counterparts. In effect, the neo-Marxists are ignoring four things:

1. that whilst wages are considerably lower in the Third World than in the core capitalist countries this does not mean that unit labour costs are necessarily lower too. Tables like Table 4.5 (from Ross) can thus be quite misleading, if not entirely meaningless, because they fail to take into account the higher productivity of labour in the core countries. (Bettelheim, 1972, showed some years ago how this undercut Emmanuel's neo-Ricardian theory of unequal exchange. The gist of what he said then is true today. If Ford workers in the UK are paid four times as much as their Brazilian counterparts but are five times as productive, then it is the British workers who are the most exploited in terms of Marxist economic theory.)[17]

2. a concern for production costs alone, as opposed to those associated with the technical development of a product, can lead to an analysis devoid of any consideration of demand conditions and factors. In practice these may be critical. Jenkins gives the example of the semi-conductor industry, whose post-1960s relocation to the periphery can be traced back to a shift in demand away from military and government uses towards industrial and consumer applications (Jenkins, 1984, p. 34).

3. a neglect of points (1) and (2) must give a highly one-dimensional picture of the NIDL whereby it is associated only with the centre-periphery relocation of branch plants to cheap labour, free trade zones. This may be true of selected industries, such as textiles and semiconductors. However, it neither acknowledges the role of Third World governments in promoting their own local industries, nor does it admit the existence of more highly skilled and more highly paid industries such as shipbuilding, the manufacture of vehicles, metalworking and so on.

4. just as the neo-Marxist account downplays the role of the Third World state by tracing the NIDL back to the 'needs of metropolitan capital',[18] so too does it overestimate the full extent of Third World industrialisation. Setting too much store both by Warren and by their own theories of metropolitan crisis, the neo-Marxists fail to see that industrial relocation is only one possible response open to Western capital, and that relocation to the periphery is only one possible relocation response. In fact the export of capital is still predominantly between the countries of the core, rather than from the high-wage countries to the low-wage countries (Grahl, 1983).

Put together, these theoretical and empirical shortcomings leave our exchange-oriented theories in something of a mess. Moreover they suggest that if the Left is to fashion a coherent, as opposed to merely speculative, critique of Warren, it must challenge Warren's optimism on independent industrialisation and democracy from a position which is more firmly rooted in Marx's analysis of the production, distribution and exchange of commodities.

Palloix, Jenkins and the internationalisation of capital This is certainly Jenkins's conclusion and in response to Warren's original argument Jenkins advances a third Marxist perspective on the industrialisation of the Third World.

In effect Jenkins's work has emerged out of his critique of what he calls exchange-oriented and productionist (that is, Warrenite) theories. He argues that these are necessarily one-dimensional theories and that a 'more promising starting-point is found in Marx's analysis of the circuits of capital which emphasises the unity of production, distribution and exchange' (Jenkins, 1984, p. 40). This point is further elaborated via Palloix. Using the latter's distinction between the circuits of commodity capital (world trade), money capital (international capital movements) and productive capital (the operation of the TNCs) Jenkins argues that the crisis which is now upon us is in fact an attempt not just to restore profits but to restore 'harmonious relations between production, distribution and exchange' (Jenkins, 1984, p. 41). Less opaquely, it is Jenkins's contention that the industrialisation of the Third World – or the internationalisation of capital as he prefers to call the NIDL – must be understood as but one moment forced upon capital by its inability to stave off a declining rate of profit either by increasing productivity, by exploiting cheaper raw materials, or by drawing on female or immigrant labour. Of equal import in this restructuring, he argues, has been the introduction of new production techniques (often via bankruptcies and/or centralisation) and thus the typical (domestic) drive for increasing relative surplus value.

Three further sets of observations follow. First, in keeping with this idea of 'choice in crisis', Jenkins points out that the relocation of production to cheap labour countries has only been of limited significance. In the late 1970s 'imports of manufactures from the Third World accounted for less than 2 per cent of total consumption of manufactured goods in North America, the EEC and Japan' (Jenkins, 1984, p. 43). It has also been concentrated in particular branches of industry (for instance clothing) where further accumulation via relative surplus value was not a practical possibility. (Jenkins suggests that Warren is wrong to assume that late 1960s and early 1970s industrial growth rates in the Third World will continue. This period was 'relatively short-lived' he says, and may be discontinued if new production technologies arise which can be reimported to the core countries.)

Jenkins's second point is that the conditions for the industrialisation which has occurred must often be traced back to developments in the circuits of commodity and money capital which are ignored in the other three theories. In particular he draws our attention to the way in which the financial sphere made available vast numbers of export credits and other loans for the industrialisation of the Third World in the 1970s. Similarly, he notes that investment is made in some Third World countries not so much because of their cheap labour as because of the markets they offer (*pace* Warren) and because the expansion of relative surplus value through technological innovation often presupposes a degree of mass production and economy of scale that must be provided globally. He also suggests that such factors as legalised shift-working and state incentive policies may have been critical in inducing a limited NIDL.

Finally, Jenkins contrasts the political implications of his approach with those of Warren and the neo-Marxists. Naturally he benefits from the comparison. Whilst the exchange-oriented theorists are said to make contradictory demands for the international solidarity of the working class and for core protectionism, Warren is accused of being too insensitive to the evils of industrial capitalism in the Third World. He is also too convinced that an industrial labour force divided by nation, race and sex will one day unite to overthrow capitalism at the global level. By contrast the implications of Jenkins's work are less bombastic. Since his perspective points up the limited scale of the NIDL and the fact that it necessitates neither authoritarianism nor super-exploitation (though this characterises some countries and some industrial branches and accumulation processes), he can suggest that:

> the implications of the NIDL for the working class in the advanced capitalist countries is not nearly as catastrophic as exchange-oriented theories imply since it is not a major factor in rising unemployment and the decline of manufacturing . . . This approach emphasises the different forms taken by the internationalisation of capital and the need for different forms of struggle in order to counter the strategies of capital. Thus a strategy for workers in the car industry might be quite different from one which would be appropriate in the clothing industry (Jenkins, 1984, pp. 52–3).

Warren reconsidered: Conclusions and pointers

How right Jenkins is. The entire thrust of Jenkins's remarks here backs up our argument in Chapter 2: that accounts of development and underdevelopment must be sensitive not only to the dynamic of the world system, but also to the relations of production and their conditions of existence that are characteristics of particular countries and development sectors. Moreover this disaggregating approach suggests both a middle line on the debates surrounding capitalism and the industrialisation of the Third World, and a number of pointers to the investigation of two more empirical debates which follow on from these: on the developmental role of the TNCs, and on the role, capacity and constitution of the state in the Third World.

Consider the more 'abstract' debate first. Having reviewed the work of Warren and his critics at some length it would seem that the pendulum is now swinging back towards Warren. Of course there are still provisos that need to be entered. Warren does tend to eulogise the darker side of capitalism, just as he tends to overestimate the temporal and spatial significance of the Third World industrialisation which has occurred. Nevertheless, it is clear that stagnationism has had its day, and that it is no longer acceptable to dismiss Warren on the grounds that 'his' industrialisation is of a dependent, authoritarian and super-exploitative type. This may be true of some Third World countries and industries but it is not true of all. In any case the whole thrust of this neo-Marxist critique is based on two clear fallacies. On the one hand it denies the possibility that Third World states might stand up for themselves against the all-powerful world system (which for some reason is assumed to be forever and always dead-set against them alone). On the other hand it measures what is going on in the Third World against a stylised and idealised model of balanced, independent industrial growth which is (wrongly) imagined to have occurred in the West. To paraphrase Henry Bernstein (1982), the world system theorists continue to oppose capitalism and Third World industrialisation at a philological level. By definition, and *a priori*, they know that nothing good is happening, or could happen, in the Third World.

Aside from pure theory Jenkins's work implies that we also need to look with fresh eyes at two of the more empirical issues that are embedded in these wider ideological perspectives on the NIDL. One thinks first of the debate on the TNCs where neo-Marxists and radical geographers have been particularly keen to paint global capital as a bully-boy or Leviathan figure (Ross, 1983), the new enforcer of unequal exchange and Third World underdevelopment. Alongside this one thinks of the debate, or lack of it, on the significance of the newly industrialising countries and on the role of the state in the Third World.

4.2 Transnational companies and the industrial development of the Third World

Attacking the TNCs has become something of a *rite de passage* for radical development geographers and others on the Left, and is clearly central to the radicals' case against Warren. In effect the Left has set itself against the comfortable earlier orthodoxies which held that TNCs would fill certain gaps in the developing world – foreign exchange gaps, technology gaps, skill gaps and so on.[19] (In geography there is also opposition to the sort of growth-centre TNC-led industrialisation once advocated by Mabogunje, 1973.) Against these views the Left urges that the TNCs are the new enforcers of an old imperialism. The TNCs monopoly powers are supposed to enable them to enslave the developing countries in new forms of unequal exchange, and thus to maintain the continuity of an asymmetrical world system which first came into being in 1492.

In this section I want to review the emerging debate about the TNCs and their developmental role. I will look first at the arguments against the TNCs, and then at the counter-arguments produced by comparative empirical research. Finally, I will attempt some sort of resolution of this debate, stressing (again) the need for disaggregation by country and by industrial sector, and on a product-cycle basis.

The case against the TNCs

I have already hinted that the radical case against the TNC hinges upon a wider critique of monopoly and of the capitalist world system. Nevertheless, the strengths and weaknesses of this critique do emerge in a number of more restricted sub-debates: on the size and power of the TNCs; on their fiscal impact on LDCs; on their technological and cultural implications; and on their capacity to generate linkages and true economic development.

TNCs: size and power   Most critiques of the TNCS begin with a discussion of the economic and political clout which these institutions wield as a result of their sheer size, scale and organisation. In this vein it is emphasised that the TNCs are not the 'current end point of a continuum of development that begins with the small, privately owned, single-plant firm' (Taylor and Thrift, 1982, p. 14). Rather they must be understood as qualitatively new phenomena on the post-war economic scene. Following Hymer we might say that the 'early' (US) multinationals were a response to the peculiar conditions of the 1950s: conditions of market saturation and oligopoly in the USA; of an increasingly sophisticated transport and communications system; of an evolving hierarchical corporate division of labour; and of an emerging corporate challenge to the USA from Europe and Japan. It was against this background that the leading US corporations decided upon an 'outward thrust to establish sales production and bases in foreign territories' (Hymer, 1975, p. 47), and it was the success of this strategy which encouraged the major European and Japanese corporations to follow a similar course. What has happened since is that this same logic has worked itself out. From an initial export of capital from the economies of one advanced country to another, we have now reached the era of the global corporation. Today's world economy is structured by a clutch of truly transnational companies, still mainly based in the USA, the UK, Japan, France and Germany, whose increasing penetration of the Third World (Table 4.6) is matched only by their own increasing magnitude.

Some figures will bear this out. Consider, first, the multinational nature of the TNC. Table 4.7 shows that there has been a remarkable expansion in the number of countries in which a typical TNC maintains subsidiaries. In 1950, of 315 US- and European-based TNCs only three had subsidiaries in more than twenty countries, and only fifty-nine in between six and twenty countries. The vast majority (154) had branch plants in six or less foreign countries, most of them elsewhere in the developed world. By 1970 this picture had changed substantially: all but forty of these 315 TNCs were operating in six or more countries, itself an indication of a drift towards the Third World. Then there is the question of size proper, where the statistics are truly staggering. A quick glance at Table 4.8 reveals that the largest TNCs (and the statistics on the Japanese conglomerates include their multinational banking allies) have turnovers that are in excess of the GNPs of several advanced countries. For example, the Mitsubishi group ranks seventeenth in a list of today's major economic powers, putting it ahead of such countries as Austria, Switzerland and South Africa, and fully nine transnational groups can claim a place in a league table of the world's thirty leading economic entities. If we add to these figures the facts that today's TNCs are involved in a wide range of manufacturing activities in the Third World (as opposed to just mining); that these same TNCs are 'increasingly financially oriented [and sourced by] . . the Eurocurrency and other international money market and institutions' (Taylor and Thrift, 1982, p. 2), where they can create and exploit currency differentials; and that intra-firm trade is now equivalent to something like 35–40 per

158

TABLE 4.6 Flows of foreign direct investment from developed economies to developing countries by major home country, 1970–81 (in million of $US)

Country	1970	1971	1972	1973	1974	1975	1976	1977	1978	1979	1980	1981
Australia	106	48	102	104	117	48	75	84	68	113	136	n.a.
Austria	5	0	4	5	8	7	33	18	20	13	20	31
Belgium	46	28	58	48	49	69	236	69	138	254	198	123
Canada	64	76	176	125	193	300	430	390	558	–100	400	700
Denmark	8	25	9	16	26	30	30	n.a.	76	66	79	66
Finland	1	1	1	0	0	2	1	2	6	15	26	17
France	235	170	231	287	239	274	245	265	413	681	899	1137
Germany FR	317	358	601	787	701	816	765	846	1025	818	1579	1352
Italy	123	214	280	246	100	150	213	162	71	455	316	132
Japan	261	222	204	1301	705	223	1084	724	1318	691	906	2426
Netherlands	183	130	321	88	242	228	245	486	443	167	135	354
New Zealand	n.a.	n.a.	–2	1	3	1	1	9	10	7	24	15
Norway	19	11	7	14	15	17	43	16	30	8	9	8
Sweden	36	40	42	22	49	82	125	126	115	127	90	86
Switzerland	55	66	73	81	128	208	226	211	174	416	353	340
UK	341	233	391	699	719	797	986	1178	820	1029	1231	1217
USA	1888	2010	1976	2887	3788	7241	3119	4866	5619	7986	3367	6475
Total	3688	3632	4474	6711	7082	10493	7851	9452	10904	12746	9768	14479

SOURCE UN Centre on Transnational Corporations, *Transnational Corporations in World Development – Third Survey* (1983) New York; after Lall (1984).

TABLE 4.7 *The foreign manufacturing subsidiary networks of 315 large multinational corporations in 1950 and 1970*

Number of enterprises with subsidiary networks including:	180 US-based MNCs		135 MNCs based in the UK and Europe	
	1950	*1970*	*1950*	*1970*
6 countries	138	9	116	31
6–20 countries	43	128	16	75
20 countries	0	44	3	29

SOURCE Taylor and Thrift (1982), ch. 1.

cent of total world trade (Lall, 1980, p. 121), then it is apparent that we are indeed dealing with institutions of unparalleled economic importance.

But this is not all. According to their critics, the TNCs' economic power has brought them an unrivalled degree of corporate power, which has been used for counter-developmental purposes in a number of different ways on a number of different occasions. In the most extreme case the TNCs are said to have indulged in sabotage pure and simple. Thus Anthony Sampson has written persuasively of the secret history of ITT, *The Sovereign State* which, not 'being concerned with anything except the company's profits' (Sampson, 1974, p. 254) joined forces with the CIA to destabilise and ultimately overthrow the democratically elected government of Salvador Allende in Chile. Similar stories could no doubt be told of the operations of the United Fruit Company throughout Latin America, and they continue to surface from the vulnerable states of Black Africa. One of the more revealing is related in Lanning and Mueller's account of *Africa Undermined* (1979). In a chapter dealing with the mining companies and the state in Zaire they pay particular attention to the way in which the Belgian corporation *Union Minière* catalysed the Katangan secession movement in that country. This bid for a copper monopoly was thwarted by the actions of the USA, which was equally keen to intervene to see the integrity of Zaire maintained for its own future operations.

TABLE 4.8 *Some of the world's largest multinational corporations, ranked by turnover*

	Country of origin	1976 ($m)	1978 ($m)
Mitsubishi Group	Japan	75 000	106 400
DKB Group	Japan	54 500	79 300
Sumitomo Group	Japan	51 200	78 100
Mitsui Group	Japan	48 800	76 500
Fuyo Group	Japan	57 000	71 000
Sanwa Group	Japan	46 100	64 500
General Motors	USA	47 200	63 200
Exxon	USA	48 600	60 300
Royal Dutch-Shell	Netherlands/UK	36 100	44 000
Ford	USA	28 800	42 800
IBM	USA	16 300	21 100
General Electric	USA	15 700	19 700
Unilever	Netherlands/UK	15 800	18 900
ITT	USA	11 800	15 300
Philips	Netherlands	11 500	15 100
Hoechst	West Germany	9 300	12 100
US Steel	USA	8 600	11 100
Nestlé	Switzerland	7 600	11 000
El du Pont	USA	8 400	10 600
Thyssen	West Germany	7 900	9 200
ICI	UK	7 500	8 700
British Steel	UK	5 000	5 700

SOURCE Taylor and Thrift (1982), ch. 1.

Nevertheless, the political actions of the TNCs are not confined to these acts of virtual warfare. A more subtle case continues to be argued against them by critics like Sunkel (1973) and Godfrey and Langdon (1976) who look upon 'transnational capitalism' as the new agent of national cultural disintegration in the Third World (see also Peet, 1982), and by Holland (1976) and Ross (1983) who see in the hypermobility of capital a serious threat both to the international working-class movement, and to any given host country's room for manoeuvre. Finally, there is the more general point which sociologists are fond of prosecuting in terms of multiple regression models: namely that TNCs favour, help (and even need) authoritarian host governments. This may appear to contradict an earlier claim that the TNCs erode national sovereignty, but for critics it is evidence of the contradictory, as well as the malevolent, nature of transnational capitalism. As Martinelli puts it: 'The TNCs need strong states and stable societies, but cannot help undermining them to some extent' (Martinelli, 1982, p. 86).

Fiscal effects   A second line of criticism of the TNCs has focused more exclusively on the pricing and tax-minimising policies of these global capitals, seeing in these activities the transmission mechanisms linking increasing corporate size and power with the erosion of national sovereignty in the Third World.

Again this critique has assumed a number of forms. In its most simplistic guise we are faced with the charges of the young Gunder Frank. He totalled up the book value of private foreign investment in countries such as Brazil, compared this with the value of the profits and interest payments that were later remitted to the host countries of the TNCs concerned, saw that the latter exceeded the former, and concluded that the TNCs were agents 'not of aid, but of exploitation'. In his own words:

> It is widely believed that the US and other developed capitalist countries contribute more capital to the underdeveloped countries than they receive from them. Nonetheless . . . [the] facts of economic life completely vitiate this American logic. If the disparity between the capital inflow and outflow to Brazil is as normal and legitimate as its defenders claim, then why is it that according to the late President John F. Kennedy the capital inflow into the US from the underdeveloped countries in 1960 was $1300 million and the capital outflow from the US to the same countries $200 million? (Frank, 1969, pp. 162–3).

The problems with this sort of argument, however, is that it is very dependent on flow as opposed to stock and flow figures (see Jackman, 1980) and it makes a number of heroic assumptions about the unearned nature of profits and interest charges. This is less the case with two more contemporary accounts of TNC fiscal subtractions: on tax incentives and on transfer pricing.

The matter of tax incentives can be dealt with briefly. The two points that need to be made are (i) that tax incentives are now widespread in the Third World,[20] whilst (ii) for critics, there is 'no support for the belief of most less developed countries that the provision of fiscal incentives is necessary to attract direct foreign investment, and that the greater the generosity of these incentive programmes the greater would be the level of such investment' (Lim, D., 1983, p. 207).

By contrast, the practice of transfer pricing demands a fairly extensive treatment, the issue being absolutely crucial to the wider debates concerning the TNCs and Third World development. The practice may reasonably be defined as an attempt to exploit international tax differentials to maximise joint profits on intra-firm trade, and the case against it embraces three main points.

First it is argued that the capacity of the TNCs to transfer price is growing almost yearly. The fact that something like 40 per cent of total world trade is now between the subsidiaries and parent companies of TNCs means that 40 per cent of world trade is no longer subject to open market prices where 'buyers and sellers are trying to maximise their profits at each others' expense' but to intra-firm transactions where 'the price is merely an accounting device and the two parties are trying to maximise joint profits' (Lall, 1980, p. 111).

Next, it is pointed out that the TNC's incentive to transfer price is as strong as ever; an observation which has the gravest implications for any host country which suffers as a result. This incentive exists wherever effective tax rates on remissable profits are not equal between the countries host to various parent and subsidiary firms of a TNC; wherever there are restrictions on remissions and/or price controls on the output in either country; wherever import duties exceed effective tax rates; wherever the exchange rate of the two concerned countries is not stable; and wherever there are political or other pressures on the level of declared, present or future profits (after Lall, 1980, p. 112). To turn it around this means that a TNC will have an incentive to transfer price in a number of different situations; where it can exploit international differences in tax and tariff rates; where it can take advantage of multiple exchange rates; or where it can move profits back to the core in anticipation of political instability in the Third World. In fact the list is endless. It is harder to imagine the equilibrium conditions in which transfer pricing would not pay off.

Finally, the critics of transfer pricing are convinced that there is evidence to show that this practice is having a detrimental impact on the fiscal capacities of LDCs. In a sense this is surprising, for proof of transfer pricing is by its very nature difficult to come by. (One must compare parent and subsidiary traded prices with arms-length prices which it is assumed would have operated otherwise.) Nevertheless there have been some important and disturbing case studies, the most notable of which were concerned with transnational pricing of pharmaceuticals in Colombia in the late 1960s. Researchers from Colombia's Planning Office and its Import Control Board conducted extensive surveys of local and open-market prices in this sector and discovered, respectively, 'a weighted average of overpricing for a wide range of pharmaceutical imports of 155% (for 1968) and. . .of 87% (for 1967–70), the difference in findings being accounted for by differences in coverage over time and products, with the latter [study] being more comprehensive' (Lall, 1980, p. 125). Lall later refined these figures himself by looking in detail at fourteen of the pharmaceutical firms concerned. He discovered that whereas some firms were overpricing by a 'mere' 33.5 per cent (as a weighted average), others were obtaining a mark-up as high as 338 per cent by transfer pricing (see also Patel, 1983). More importantly, the collective impact of these activities was found to be costing the Colombian government something like $3.3 million annually (out of a total pharmaceutical import bill of $15 million). If this pattern held throughout Colombia's import sectors it is apparent that the country would suffer considerable fiscal damage. So too would other Third World countries placed in a similarly vulnerable position. Wherever it is practiced 'the use of transfer pricing means that the net gains from foreign investment are less, or losses more, than they otherwise would have been' (Lall, 1980, p. 130).

Inappropriate technologies and products A third set of arguments against the TNCs has concerned itself with the manner and appropriateness of the technologies and products which these corporations are transferring to the Third World.

Looking first at the technology issue, there seem to be two main points of attack. In its least strident form the argument against the TNCs is that they are costly and highly imperfect organs for the transfer of technology to the developing world. For critics like Vaitsos a more acceptable form of transfer may lie with unbundled licensing and patenting agreements which, for all their shortcomings, relieve the purchasing government of the necessity to buy an entire technology package (which in any case will remain under TNC control).[21] Drawing on the recent experience of Japan and the leading South-east Asian NICs, these critics detect in unbundled transfers a greater capacity both for local technology adaptations and developments, and for labour-intensive activity. The Third World is said to be better off copying its way to development through labour-intensive adaptations of licensed technologies than it is relying on large-scale direct foreign investment.

Not all critics would agree, however. A more radical line on the question of technology transfer argues that the TNCs are extremely unlikely to agree to these licensing and patenting agreements. It is more likely that they will either use their research and development capacities, to reinforce pre-existing relationships of dependence, or that they will license only inappropriate and second-hand technologies – which has the same effect. Either way these critics see in the transnational's control of technology a capacity to mould the NIDL in the image of the corporation's own vertical division of labour. Thus in Hymer's classic study, 'The MNC and the Law of Uneven Development' (first published in 1972) we find him arguing not only that TNCs are introducing inappropriate technologies to the Third World, but also that the Third World is becoming the site of their lowest level (Level III) activities. Anticipating the views of Fröbel *et al.*, he foresaw a situation wherein the pull of cheap labour and raw materials brings blue-collar assembly type technologies and jobs to the periphery. At best a small group of workers is taught a degree of technological 'know-how' – how to attend the track in Vokswagen's Brazilian plants, for example, or how to combine semi-conductor components in northern Mexico. Meantime Level II activities, 'because of their need for white collar workers, communications systems and information, tend to concentrate in large cities' (Hymer, 1975, p. 50) in the core and semi-periphery, and real 'know-why' activities of research and development, and strategic planning management, become still more concentrated in a handful of Level I cities like London, New York and Tokyo (a concentration since graphed out by Cohen, 1981). The result is a degree of Third World industrialisation, says Hymer, but of an increasingly capital-intensive, isolated and inappropriate type. The TNCs brings renewed dependence rather than development.

Aside from these arguments about inappropriate technology, the TNCs have also been accused of introducing the 'wrong' products into the Third World. (Richard Peet talks about 'cultural imperialism', Peet, 1982, p. 297). A liberal economist, Frances Stewart, was among the first to develop this charge. In a series of articles (1972, 1973, 1978) she examined the main assumptions of free-trade theories of technology transfer and found that they were contradicted by the monopolistic activities of the TNCs. In effect the TNCs take their product decisions with respect to their own international factor environments. These are often quite at odds with the factor proportions which are appropriate to Third World countries, and which are central to the Hecksher–Ohlin model. As a result Stewart believes that the TNCs have little incentive to modify the products they introduce into the developing countries. Instead they have every reason for pushing inappropriate products to the periphery — cigarettes, coca-cola, videos or whatever. 'So long as developing countries are following a free trade strategy with the developed countries, their technology and consumption patterns, will be largely dictated by product and taste developments in the developed countries' (Stewart, 1973, p. 255).

These predictions have since been borne out by events say critics. In one particularly infamous example Mike Muller (1974) found considerable evidence to show that certain multinational food companies were pushing powdered milk compounds upon Third World mothers, even though their preparation was known to involve access to clean (and/or boiled) water and feeding bottles, and even though such 'milk' was known to be inferior to breast milk insofar as it lacked certain infant immune systems (see Chetley, 1979), and a considerable contraceptive effect (Page *et al*, 1981). More recently Muller has extended his researches on the unethical marketing practices of the health-related TNCs. In studies described in *The Health of Nations* (1982) he found further evidence of company workers dressed up as nurses; of unsafe drugs being dumped in LDCs; of free samples being showered upon Third World doctors; and of transnationals undermining generic drug codes by covert political action (see also Melrose,

1982) and by their own marketing of the more expensive brand-name medicines. Not for nothing does Muller conclude that developmental 'damage will continue to be done by the ultranationals through the wasteful, harmful and ultimately irrational medicine which they promote' (Muller, 1982, p. 226).

Linkages, growth and development   Finally, we come to a fourth set of objections to the role of global capital in the developing world. The gist of the case this time is that the TNCs are failing to promote the necessary linkages which will lead to development, as opposed to mere growth. They are instead accused of promoting a premature concentration of industrial structures in LDCs, and thus of closing opportunties for local innovation and competition.

Any protestations of 'not guilty' from the TNCs are brushed aside on two counts. Consider first the claim that the TNCs have generated a series of backward and forward linkages of the type that Hirschman (1958) envisaged when he proposed his strategy of 'imbalanced growth for entrepreneurship and competition'. Sanjaya Lall answers this by pointing out that a crude demonstration of such and such a linkage between a TNC and a local firm:

> does not show (a) if the local enterprises would have been set up in the absence of TNC investments; (b) whether they gained or lost by having TNCs as major customers (where this is the case); (c) if the host country could have created the same linkages at lesser cost, say by replacing the TNC by a local firm; (d) if the linked local enterprises are desirable from the social point of view (where the linkages are fostered behind heavy protective barriers); and (e) whether negative linkages were created by stifling potential local investment (Lall, 1980, p. 30).

Whilst admitting that the evidence on all of these topics is flimsy, Lall's own review of the literature leads him to believe that:

> TNCs establish relatively few linkages in small or industrially backward economies; that in larger economies they may create linkages, mostly because of government pressure; and that a substantial part of these linkages in import-substituting industries may be excessively costly and uneconomical (Lall, 1980, p. 33).

This impression has since been confirmed by two pieces of work published under the rubric of radical development geography.[22] Thus Newfarmer and Topik (1982) have examined Moran's (1978) hypothesis that a monopolistic domination of an international industry by TNCs can in time be expected to evolve into a state of workable competition. Looking at the structure of Brazil's electrical industry between 1880 and 1945 they found no evidence of this. Instead, the data point to a deepening oligopolisation of market structures and to a premature concentration of Brazil's industrial structure. This can in turn be traced back to the weaknesses of the Brazilian State and to the transnationals' control of 'the supply of products, production technology, international finance and domestic Brazilian demand for heavy equipment' (Newfarmer and Topik, 1982, p. 55). Not unrelated conclusions have been reached by Susman and Schutz. Looking at the relationship between IBM and its client suppliers they 'found' that the former's monopoly pricing and buying strategies were pricing its competitors out of the market, and was thus distorting (if not always concentrating) the industrial sector which it dominates. Their analysis also leads them to the conclusion that any linkage between 'The Big Blue One' and its suppliers cannot be seen in the dynamic and developmental terms of modernisation theory. In reality 'many competitive sector firms may be considered . . .to be mere appendages of the dominant firms' (Susman and Schutz, 1983, p. 175).

Findings such as these have in turn been used to head off a second defence of the TNCs: that they promote growth. Believing that this is debatable in itself, critics argue that growth is one thing and development another, and that TNCs are not aiding the latter. At best they are credited with fostering a process of growth without development, whereby spatially isolated, enclave economies[23] are set up which employ a labour aristocracy of workers on condition that this labour-power is reproduced within the unchanging and underdeveloped relations of production that are characteristic of the countryside (see Arrighi, 1970, for a classic discussion). This distortion is said to be further borne out by the available aggregate statistics. With the help of yet more multiple regression models, Bornscheir *et al.* (1978) discovered that whilst 'flows of direct foreign investment . . .have had a short-run effect of increasing the relative rate of economic growth of countries. . .stocks of direct foreign investment. . .have had the cumulative long-term effect of decreasing the relative rate of economic growth of countries'. Moreover, this same cross-sectional evidence suggests that 'the effect of direct foreign investment has been to increase economic inequality within countries' (Bornscheir *et al.*, 1978, p. 651).

TNCs reconsidered

The sheer weight of the case against the TNC has made a majority of development geographers rightly sceptical of their role in the developing world. Nevertheless, there is another side to the story. One need not hold any brief for the transnationals to realise that their critics are trying to have it every which way and the other. On the one hand they want to argue that the TNCs are the new agents of Western imperialism and the false industrialisation of the Third World. On the other hand the TNCs are blamed for the deindustrialisation of the old world, and for being the standard bearers of a global capital which knows no home and which owns no allegiance.

It strikes me that these are contradictory perspectives. It is right and proper to accept that the TNCs are imperfect organs of Third World development, and that their potential for the exploitation of a weak state is greater than their potential *vis-á-vis* a strong state. What we must have done with, however, is the notion that all transnationals are Western TNCs committed to the bogus industrialisation of the Third World (unlike the Third World's own bourgeoises). Recent studies have shown that that this is far from being the case (see Evans, 1981). If we briefly reinvestigate the four main segments of the case against the TNC we find that a less clear-cut picture is emerging; one which is the logical counterpart of the more recent and less didactic vision of a NIDL.

Consider first the question of size and power. In section 4.1 I drew on Taylor and Thrift, and Sampson, to paint a fairly grisly picture of the TNC as Leviathan unbound. To my knowledge this picture is accurate as far as it goes, but as always it can be qualified and reshaped. We might challenge, for example, the representativeness of the Chilean tragedy. A number of scholars have argued that a propensity to intrigue and authoritarianism is not a characteristic of the transnationals. According to Becker 'the transnationals are indifferent, not antagonistic, to democratic governance' and in Latin America at least he finds a positive 'correlation between direct foreign investment and the potential for capitalist democracy – exactly the opposite of the *dependencia* prediction' (Becker, 1984, pp. 422–3).

Then there is the question of the size of the TNCs. No one denies that the TNCs are getting larger and larger, or that their sheet size holds the gravest of implications for conceptualising today's world economic order. Nevertheless the assumption tends to be that giantism alone is indicative of monopoly and thus of inefficiency, a double leap of logic which is surely open to question. (IBM is an interesting case in point. Undoubtedly it is a large 'monopoly', but are we really to believe that it is inefficient or that it has prevented developments within the general field of computing and office systems?)[24] Finally, there is the matter of location. Again it is true that a majority of TNCs are based in a handful of metropolitan powers. Even so one needs to be wary of presenting the transnationals in a First World versus Third World context. Already a number of largish multinationals are emerging from the Third World itself (Lall, 1983), and it remains the case that a majority of transnational investment in the Third World is located in the NICs of Wallerstein's 'semi-periphery', where cheap labour considerations take second place to such attractions as the availability of an industrial infrastructure and an educated workforce (see Table 4.9).

Now consider the fiscal impact of the TNCs in the developing world. The critics of the TNCs are on safer ground here for there can be no doubt that the TNCs do have an incentive to transfer price, and that they have done so to the detriment of many Third World countries. What may give rise to objections, however, is the way in which the magnitude of this practice is calculated and presented. In a striking *volte-face*, Lall now argues that:

> part of the early anxiety [was] based upon misconceptions about what the phenomenon was all about. Most of the evidence came from one industry, pharmaceuticals, and involved the comparison of prices charged on intra-firm transactions with what would be charged by a non-patent observing imitator. The price differences were enormous, leading analysts to believe that the impact of the practice was huge; furthermore it was felt that the pharmaceutical industry was representative of all sectors inhabited by TNCs. More reasoned analysis showed that the initial basis for assessing transfer prices was wrong – an innovating firm

TABLE 4.9 *Distribution of foreign direct investment and other resource flows from OECD countries among groups of developing countries, 1978–80 (percentage)*

	Gross National Product 1979	Stock of foreign direct investment end-1978	Flows from OECD countries: Annual average 1978–80		
			Foreign direct investment	Bank loans	All resources
Total developing market Economies	100.0	100.0	100.0	100.0	100.0
By income group					
Less than $380 per capita GNP	16.9	13.5	3.1	1.4	16.8
$380–1000 per capita GNP	14.7	13.5	8.7	11.4	19.4
Above $1000 per capita GNP	68.0	58.2	49.5	86.8	50.2
Of which: tax havens	0.3	14.2	14.8	0.2	3.6

By region					
Europe	3.0	0.4	1.7	6.4	3.7
West Asia	14.6	3.2	−2.6	3.4	11.5
South Asia	9.9	5.0	4.7	13.0	8.5
South and East Asia	13.9	22.1	18.7	12.3	12.5
Socialist Asia	13.7	0.0	0.1	0.2	0.8
Latin America	30.7	56.7	64.4	62.7	33.7
Africa	14.1	12.4	13.1	13.7	29.4
Other country groups					
Least developed countries	2.9	1.5	0.4	0.6	9.0
Oil-exporting countries	21.8	16.6	10.7	12.2	13.4
NICs	27.1	33.7	40.1	56.9	20.1

SOURCE As for Table 4.6.

had to charge more than an imitating one. By choosing an imitator's price as the reference point, the host country was in effect asserting that it wanted to opt out of the innovation process (Lall, 1984, p. 13. Emphasis in the original).[25]

To this I would add one further observation or query: why should it be thought that Third World countries, pre-eminently, suffer from transfer pricing? It is true that their governments may often be weak, and their customs and excise departments unsophisticated. Nevertheless these same countries are often low-tax countries or even tax havens, in which case one might expect the transnationals to transfer price against the core. Finally, whilst we are on this question of taxes and regional revenue retention rates, let me commend the recent work of a British geographer, R. M. Auty (1983). In a fascinating dissection of the hitherto classic work of Girvan's *Corporate Imperialism: Conflict and Expropriation*, Auty demonstrates that the cruder 'fiscal drain' views of the Frankian school are based on a poor understanding of (reasonable) corporate strategic and accounting procedures. His 'findings indicate that aluminium's capital-intensive production function and cost-minimising geographical fragmentation of the production chain are prime factors accounting for low regional revenue retention, rather than multinational ownership [or] transfer pricing' (Auty, 1983, p. 4).

A third area of debate concerns the question of technology transfer and possible product dependence. Again I have no wish to detract from the thrust of this case, but it may be in need of one or two qualifications. In particular it has to be said (i) that a preference for licensing as opposed to direct foreign investment may not be practicable for many leading-edge technologies where it is a case of the TNCs or nothing; (ii) that to base the case for unbundled technology buying on Japan may be misleading given that country's early and rather extensive educational and infrastructural capacities; and (iii) that to blame the TNCs, alone, for introducing inappropriate products to the Third World begs the question of what is appropriate [the baby-milk issue is unusually clear-cut] and quite ignores the distorting influence of local, pre-TNC income inequalities and consumption patterns.

More substantively, one might criticise the assumption that the TNCs do not adapt their technologies and products to particular local environments. Empirical work by Baer (1976) gives us some grounds for believing that they do, and Lall is now of the opinion that:

> Every application of a technology entails considerabler adaptive effort. The core process may not be significantly altered, but changes in scale, inputs, outputs, automation, etc., may constitute between 10 and 60% of total project costs. [Moreover] . . . Product ranges of TNCs in developing countries are very different from those in advanced countries, and new products are developed specifically for developing country conditions. There is no evidence that TNCs lag behind local firms in generating 'appropriate technology' in this limited sense' (Lall, 1984, p. 10).

In itself this proves very little of course. It might still be objected that the very presence of monopolistic TNCs is an obstacle to the production of local know-why technologies, and to the forging of domestic linkages which, properly protected against competition in their early days, will call forth real development; but we do need to object carefully. We need to be wary to assuming that policies of protectionism and of excluding TNCs will necessarily catalyse locally appropriate industries, technologies and products. If the experience of India is any criterion this is not the case. India has certainly chalked up some notable achievements in the field of technology generation, and it retains a relatively independent economic base. At the same time it is suffering from massive over-capacity in spheres like iron and steel and from chronic inefficiency in such vital sectors as power and heavy engineering. In India the local bourgeoisie has not used the benefits of protectionism for a dynamic development effort. Instead it has sheltered behind tariff walls to such an extent that its now overpriced and uncompetitive products are a drag on the rest of the economy: a clear illustration of the foibles of a 'foreign capital bad, local or state capital good', philosophy.[26]

There are also a number of more prosaic reasons for treading carefully. For example, it is now emerging that TNCs can be persuaded to site a certain amount of their research and development activities in selected Third World countries (Lall, 1984, p. 11). It has also been shown that domestic enterprises can sometimes mount a challenge to the domination of the transnational corporations. In a case study of the Argentine pharmacuetical industry Chudnovsky (1979) found that levels of foreign participation and business concentration were being kept down by judicious policies of technology transfer, of joint ventures (as opposed to Newfarmer-type take-overs: Newfarmer, 1979), and by using the techniques of product differentiation. Chudnovsky concludes that: 'Domestic firms are reversing the denationalisation process of the industry' (Chudnovsky, 1979, p. 55).

Finally we come to the question of growth and development, and the sociologists' multiple regression models. The point to make this time is the simple one that no matter how well specified these models are they find it extremely difficult to compensate for the equifinality implicit in their equations. It will come as no surprise to most geographers that for every study reaching the conclusions of Bornscheier *et al.*, another discovers a positive relationship between direct foreign investment and growth (see Papanek, 1973; Kaufman *et al.*, 1975; Jackman, 1980). In the end we are left with the conclusions of the most sophisticated and up to date of these studies: Jackman's (1982) review of the relationship between direct foreign investment and country growth over the period 1960–78. Tests on his data revealed that 'the level of foreign capital has *no* effect on economic growth for the Third World as a whole, one way or the other. At the same time they suggest that growth in foreign capital (like both the level and growth of domestic capital) contributes to economic growth' (Jackman, 1982, p. 191. Emphasis in the original).

The TNCs and the Third World: *towards a new orthodoxy?*

Conclusions such as these will be greeted with shock in some quarters and disbelief in others. It will be reiterated that the TNCs are definitely not the best agents of development and that they are incapable of providing for an integrated, possibly rural-based, basic-needs approach to development: to all of which I will gladly assent. But ripostes such as these are clearly shifting their ground. In this chapter I have deliberately not concerned myself with the proper role of industrialisation in the development process, though it is clear that this is a crucial debate and that many admirable articles have contributed to it.[27] Instead I have assumed that a degree of industrialisation is vital to any development strategy, and have asked to what extent it is progressing in the Third World, and to what extent it is being fostered , distorted or prevented by the TNCs.

The conclusions which I have reached may seem ambiguous but that is how it should be. In the first part of this chapter I was concerned to argue for a disaggregative approach to the new international division of labour and to this end I endorsed Jenkins's conclusion that a measure of industrialisation is taking place in selected Third World countries. Having now reviewed the more detailed literature on a major agent in this industrialisation – the TNC – I see no need to retract this judgement. The evidence shows that TNCs in certain countries and in certain industrial sectors (say mining in Zaire) are indeed the new face of imperialism, and need to be opposed for sponsoring growth without development in what are little more than dual-economy puppet states, but this is not the full story. If we look east, to the NICs of South-east Asia, we find considerable evidence of TNCs exporting up-to-date technology and skills, of governments demanding joint ventures and licensing agreements, and of significant positive correlations between TNC involvement and high levels of growth of GNP, exports and wages.

Disaggregation is the key. I entirely agree with Becker when he says that we must 'abandon the teleology and stasis of system maintenance ideas' (Becker, 1984, p. 418) of the kind typified by Fröbel *et al.*, and by others who resort to the most blanket 'world systems' denunciations of the TNCs. However, disaggregation need not mean empiricism. Although I am advocating an approach to the NIDL which is sensitive to both national and sectoral differences, this objective can be pursued with the help of two existing, if rather less grandiose, theories of the TNC in the developing world: those of Vernon (1978, 1979) and Girvan (1976).

Again I do not wish this to sound too contrived, nor do I want to review these lower-level theories at any length. But consider the gist of each. Vernon's product-cycle theory is well known to industrial geographers,[28] and it is not without its critics (Newfarmer and Topik, 1982). Nevertheless Vernon's claim that there is a cycle of industrial location associated with oligopolistic competition (whereby industrial competition within the Third World follows earlier stages of core innovation and an oligopolistic transfer to the low-cost periphery) is suggestive to say the least. Were it to be recast with a stronger sectoral (and thus secular) component one could envisage a theory well able to distinguish between the likely development effect of TNCs both on product cycle and industrial concentration grounds. In effect one would associate a greater developmental stimulus with those TNCs at the mature stage of their product cycles (for instance textiles) and with those in sectors of lower-than-average industrial concentration (semiconductors, microelectronics, foodstuffs and the like). This framework could then be allied to the rather different insights that emerge from Girvan's model. He deals at length with the issue of corporate and [versus] national political power, and the conclusion which I draw from him is this: that all other things being equal, the political power – and thus the capacity for exploitation – of a TNC is greater wherever it is in a situation of global monopoly, duopoly, or limited oligopoly, and wherever it draws upon a number of different raw material sources (see also Kaplinsky, 1979). *A priori* one would expect to find a greater developmental effect associated with a Case 1 situation (see Figure 4.1) where some body like OPEC collectively faces up to the might of the oil multinationals, or a Case 3 situation where a number of large firms are bargaining with a limited number of suitable host countries. By

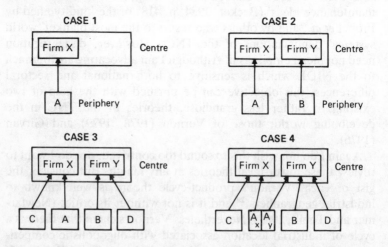

FIGURE 4.1   *The framework of output determination (after Girvan)*

contrast, an enclave economy and political interference may be all that the government of a Case 4 country can expect. Case 4 is supposed to manifest itself in the Caribbean bauxite industry, where Girvan believes that a TNC duopoly is consistently playing off and exploiting competing raw material sources.

As ever, these conclusions are subject to a number of *ceteris paribus* conditions, but it is not difficult to see how the two models might be co-joined to give a less bombastic picture of the link between transnational capitalism and the industrialisation of the developing world. In the remainder of this chapter I want to explore one or two of these conditions in more detail, looking in particular at the role of state policy in the Third World, and at the capacity of individual Third World nations to bargain with TNCs and/or to sponsor a more locally-based pattern of industrial development. Inevitably this has its own difficulties, for the potential for state action against the TNCs is to some extent conditioned by that country's prior insertion into the world system. (Thus the weak States of Black Africa must partially reflect a history of corporate imperialism). Equally, a comprehensive review of the NICs is out of the question. What I propose to do therefore is to look at the Taiwan experience – the so-called deviant case (Barrett and Whyte, 1982) – and to probe both the logic and pattern of Taiwan's development and the lessons that it may or may not hold for other Third World countries and for academic discussions of the NIDL.

4.3 Taiwan, the NICs and the new international division of labour

The world systems perspective on the NICs is most concisely expressed in Frank's article on 'Asia's Exclusive Models' (1982). Focusing there on Hong Kong, Singapore, Taiwan and South Korea (his 'Gang of Four') and with occasional sideswipes at Brazil and Mexico,[29] Frank advances a thesis that at once highlights and condemns an exchange-oriented outlook on the NICs and the NIDL.

Frank's argument falls into eight main parts and I propose to let him introduce these snippets himself before dissecting them piece by piece. Frank's first claim is probably his most cogent: that it is a mistake to hold up the 'Gang of Four' (or six) as a miraculous model of export-led growth and development to be copied by the rest of the Third World. Frank rejects this suggestion on two grounds. To begin with he notes that the idea of a 'miraculous model' is incongruous:

> If the experiences of South Korea, Taiwan, Hong Kong and Singapore (and sometimes of Mexico's border region with the United States and of Sao Paulo in Brazil) are really miraculous, that is extraordinary and almost inexplicable in normal terms, then they can hardly serve as a model for the remainder of the Third World (Frank, 1982, p. 22).

More pertinently, he explains that:

> export-led growth by a few small countries and the absorption of their exports by the rest of the world is one thing; the generalisation of the same export-led growth to that same rest of the world (which would export to whom?) is another matter . . . Consider the prospects and problems of Hong Kong and Taiwan-style exports on a Chinese or Indian, let alone Third World, scale! . . . The sheer impossibility of such a model is intuitively clear (Frank, 1982, p. 22).

Frank follows this with a second methodological point. Re-emphasising that only a few export-based 'miracles' are permissible within the world system, Frank argues that the real reason for 'the inability of much of the world to follow [the NICs] . . . is that this development or ascent has been misperceived as taking place in particular countries when it has really been one of the processes of the world system itself' (Frank, 1982, p. 22). Frank is sticking to his systemic principles here: any growth which has occurred has happened at the bidding of the metropolis. Nevertheless he still feels obliged to explain why this growth was allowed in South-east Asia's 'Four Little Tigers' specifically,[30] and why this growth cannot be considered significant or developmental. This brings him to point three and points four to eight.

Consider point three first, where Frank explains the location of the NICs. Capital, he tells us, has chosen to relocate in South-east Asia not just: 'To reduce costs of production and to make room for more technologically advanced development elsewhere' but because:

> All four [countries] are fundamentally characterised by very particular political reasons for their establishment and survival, and two of them, additionally, are city states for the same reason . . . South Korea and Taiwan clearly came about as a result of the Cold War against China and the Soviet Union and have been politically and economically supported for their strategic value. Hong Kong emerged from history to a similarly peculiar position, and Singapore became a state because of the ethnic situation on the Malayan Peninsula (Frank, 1982, p. 22).

Once again, growth has nothing to do with local initiatives or structures. Nor has it anything to do with development: Frank's fourth point is that 'beyond the impossibility of following the NICs as a model, the desirability of their miracles as models of development is also questionable to say the least' (Frank, 1982, p. 23).

The reason for this is that export-led growth 'scores very badly in the test of experience' (ibid), when it comes to the crucial considerations of balance-of-payments performance, unemployment, skill improvement and so forth. Thus a fifth point is that:

> Far from improving the balance of payments, export-led growth makes it deteriorate to the point of generating serious balance of payments crises, as the three largest NIC exporters, South Korea, Brazil and Mexico [note the switch in emphasis – SC] have found to their, and the banking community's alarm. To export the NICs have to import raw materials, components, technology and high-priced businessmen, that are frequently overpriced through transfer pricing within the multinationals which in turn underprice the resulting exports, thus reducing or eliminating the foreign exchange earnings and tax-paying value added in the NIC (Frank, 1982, p. 23).

Moreover, this national value added is low anyway because 'the principal attraction of the NICs is their low wages' (ibid). As a result the 'NICs have to borrow increasingly to pay for their import requirements which grow additionally – especially for agricultural products – as export production interferes with domestic production' (ibid). All of which brings Frank to points six and seven: that export-led growth is spatially unbalancing and 'draws more labour into the cities than the jobs it creates' (ibid), and that whilst wages stay low 'technological development is also uncertain' (Frank, 1982, p. 22). Finally it leads him to his grand conclusion: point eight. Here Frank argues that the NICs are being 'allocated the least remunerative and technologically obsolete contributions to a worldwide division of labour . . . and [thus] correspondingly meagre benefits' (ibid). Overall, 'The new dependent export-led growth of manufacturing and agribusiness production for the world market are in no way significantly different from the old raw materials export-led growth that underdeveloped the Third World in the first place' (ibid).

Frank could not be more forthright than this, and I trust readers will now understand why I have quoted him so extensively. All the same, he is not alone in these judgements. A number of writers have looked at Latin America, with its terrible debt problems, its shanty towns, its repression, its low wages and so on,[31] and concluded that there must be some general characteristics which are definitive of the NICs and the NIDL. The work of Fröbel *et al.* is an obvious example, and I have also cited the views of Bienefeld, who maintains that 'extremely high levels of political repression and violence have accompanied NIC strategies from their inception . . . [especially] in Brazil [where] income distribution has not improved, and even the absolute level of wages of unskilled workers has changed little over the whole period of the miracle' (Bienefeld, 1981, p. 93; a point confirmed by Bacha and Taylor, 1978). Another authority who can be added to this list is Geoff Lamb. Although critical of some aspects of the dependency literature, Lamb suggests that there are six main characterictics of the emerging NICs (as typified by Sri Lanka and Trinidad in this case): (i) a sustained attempt to demobilise the power of organised labour; (ii) the development of a strong, and by its nature growing, political constituency committed to sustaining 'openness' and dependent capitalist development; (iii) the rapid assumption of external economic interests in the political calculations of the regime concerned; (iv) a growing (political) role for state employment; (v) a politics of primary exploitation; and (vi) a tendency to hive off high-growth activities to enclaves where they can be politically protected (after Lamb, 1981, pp. 102–4).

Whatever the merits of this case (and I would want to enter a number of caveats)[32] Frank is supposedly concerned with Asia's exclusive models, not with Latin America. Judged against this background it does seem that there are a number of methodological and empirical errors in his perspective; errors which in the case of Taiwan, at least, are suggestive not so much of 'deviancy' as of an exception which disproves the rule.[33]

Let me elaborate on this. Frank dismisses the Taiwan experience on the grounds that it is externally controlled, that it is not new, and that it is quite opposed to real, democratic development. What he fails to tell us, however, is why Taiwan, exceptionally, should have grown at the unprecedented rate of 9 per cent annually throughout the period 1953–72, and why its export growth should have averaged 17.8 per cent each year over this same period (Barrett and Whyte, 1982, p. 1066).[34] Clearly external conditions cannot be everything and Frank would be hard pushed to argue that Taiwan has been the USA's only, or even its most favoured, client over these years (although it did receive vast aid inflows up to 1968).[35] What of Taiwan's internal conditions? As one might expect Frank quite ignores the internal economic and political histories of his 'Gang of Four'. As a result he seems quite oblivious to a good deal of informed research on Taiwan and Korea – especially Taiwan – which points to three factors as being of crucial importance in Taiwan's post-war economic miracle.

The first of these may be termed the Japanese legacy. This may seem a strange candidate for praise, and it would clearly be absurd to suggest that colonialism and a sizeable outflow of resources to Japan over a fifty-year period is a precondition of growth. Nevertheless the Japanese did bring certain unintended benefits to Taiwan. In their efforts to turn Taiwan into a sugar- and rice-producing colony, and industrial importer, the Japanese endowed the island with remarkably well integrated transportation and financial systems. The Japanese also transferred to Taiwan their own belief in the importance of education, and of an educational system geared (censoriously) to mass literacy and practical skill formation. When the Japanese were ejected in 1945 Taiwan enjoyed a literacy rate well above the regional average (Ho, S. P. S., 1978) and something like '3000km of railroads, 2600km of highways, and over 13 000km of feeder roads' (Ho, S. P. S., 1979) transected this island of 35 989 square kilometres.

A more important factor in the Taiwanese 'miracle' was the land reform of the early 1950s. By lumping together all the NICs of South-east Asia and Latin America Frank quite fails to see that Taiwan is unburdened by a large landless peasantry (with all that this implies for the urbanisation process and for trends in real wage rates).[36] Yet this is the case. The rent reduction and land-to-the-tiller programmes of 1949 and 1953 respectively, ensured (i) that farm rental rates fell from an average of 50 per cent to a maximum of 37.5 per cent of the annual main crop yield; (ii) that 96 000 hectares of public land was sold by the government to 200 000 previously tenant families; and (iii) that a further 60 per cent of Taiwan's total privately tenanted land would be purchased by the government and resold to 200 000 previously tenant families (Lee, 1974, pp. 188–9). Collectively this left post-war Taiwan with what Johnston and Kilby would call a unimodal distribution of operational land holdings. In Taiwan something like 80 per cent of all farming households are operating farms which fall within one acre of the average farm size. Needless to say this is not the case in Latin America.

This is important. When set alongside the prior integration of the island's space-economy, the Taiwanese land reforms and the associated co-operative movements had the effect of institutionalising a pattern of rural demand which was at once supportive of low-level agrotechnologies (as distinct from combine harvesters and Mercedes)[37] and which could be met largely by local production in a decentralised industrial strategy. It has been argued that Taiwan escaped the worst effects of enclavism and over-urbanisation because its essentially egalitarian, literate, skilled and accessible rural labour force was progressively able to transfer to more remunerative forms of rural non-farm employment. This is clearly evident in the fact that whilst Taiwan's rural population declined by less than 8 per cent (relatively) in the period 1956–75, 'the share of income from non-farm sources in total farm household income increased from 25 per cent to 43 per cent [over the same period]' (Ho, S. P. S., 1979, p. 77. See also Chinn, 1979, and Galenson, 1979). It is also apparent in the diversified nature of Taiwan's rural industrial base. If I might draw on Ho again:

In 1970 over 1.2 million farm household members worked at least 30 days off their farms. Of these, 996,000 or 81 per cent, were employed by others, 13 per cent were self-employed, and 6 per cent were involved in home handicrafts. The distribution by industry was as follows: public administration and education, 5.6 per cent; commerce, 11.7 per cent; industry and mining, 26.5 per cent; agriculture, forestry and fishing, 33.0 per cent; home handicrafts, 5.8 per cent; and other activities, 7.3 per cent. Of the 534 000 who worked, but not on their farms, nearly all were engaged in non-agricultural activities, particularly in industry and mining which employed over 40 per cent of the total (Ho, S. P. S., 1979, p. 89).

In short, Taiwan is not Brazil or Mexico. Its physical infrastructure and its rural skills, together with its equitable distribution of land, has ensured that a growing population has not been forced to the cities or turned into permanently cheap labour reservoirs for the new corporate imperialists. Instead, it has laid the groundwork for a spatially balanced pattern of growth and development which continues to set great store on the local industrial production of goods to satisfy an 'appropriate' pattern of local (mainly rural) demand. Export-led growth is only one side of the story.

Nevertheless, exporting is an important part of Taiwan's tale and it would be idle to pretend that labour is not relatively cheap there or that it is not put to work in the assembly plants of a number of western TNCs. However, even when we turn to this better known face of the NIDL it is apparent that Frank is ignoring a third factor of local significance: the fact that successive Taiwan governments have sought actively to foster and shape that country's industrial and export structures. This is evident not only in the sheer weight of the rural industrial sector which has grown up (and which Frank quite ignores); it is apparent, too, in the government's more acknowledged two-stage model of industrial development. In effect this committed Taiwan to a fairly archetypal pattern of import substitution in the 1950s and early 1960s, when large inflows of US aid made it possible for the Taiwanese to sink capital into industries such as textiles, electronics and shipbuilding. These industries were in turn protected by an array of tariffs and quotas. In the mid-1960s, however, Taiwan shifted course. Claiming to have recognised that protectionism only makes sense in terms of an infant industry argument, the Taiwan government opted out of the second stage of import-substitution on which countries like Brazil and India were then about to embark – what Balassa (1981, Essay 1) would call permanent protection for inefficiency and uncompetitiveness. Instead, Taiwan's authorities opted for an export orientation based upon a modicum of continued subsidisation and a larger dose of 'realism' in the setting of relative factor prices and exchange rates. For advocates of such a strategy and such a government choice the results are self-evident: sustained and rapid development.

No doubt Frank would dispute this. Even if he could be convinced that Taiwan's growth owes something to its own people, and to economic and political decisions in part dictated by its own history and class structure, Frank would still challenge the desirability of such 'growth without development'. Once more he would be on shaky ground. The plain fact is that export-led growth has not led to serious balance-of-payments crises in Taiwan, and there is no clear evidence that Taiwan has suffered disproportionately from the transfer-pricing activities of the TNCs to which it plays host. Similarly, it is not apparent that an enclave economy is being set up in Taiwan which 'draws more labour into the cities than the jobs it creates', or that Taiwan is suffering new forms of technological dependence which will inexorably push down the low wages which are supposedly its principal attraction. If anything the opposite is true. Over the past twenty years real wage rates have risen markedly in Taiwan as urban labour demand began to outstrip its supply,[38] and it is now clear that Taiwan's 'exports are no longer limited to textiles, shoes and plastic toys, but include supertankers, steel and vehicles' (Lim *et al.*, 1982, p. 25). Add to this the fact that Frank is both overestimating the dependence of Taiwan and other NICs on the TNCs, and underestimating their ability to deal with the multinationals,[39] and it is clear that his conclusions about the 'oldness' of the new dependence are quite inaccurate. In trying to force Taiwan (and South Korea) into the teleological and deterministic framework of a world systems or NIDL framework, Frank is overlooking all that is most significant in recent South-east Asian history. He merely re-emphasises the circular and undiscriminating nature of a theory which by definition equates real development with US wage levels and with a purely indigenous manufacturing and technological presence. By this logic the developing countries are always destined to fail.

Lessons from South-east Asia

Frank's errors should not lead us to an unthinking and uncritical acceptance of the Taiwanese (or the more repressive Korean) experience. It seems to me that we need to tread carefully when it comes to the lessons that are to be learnt from these NICs. On the one hand Taiwan's level of growth and development surely knocks on the head the sort of exchange-oriented theorising of a NIDL, against which Warren fought, and which threatens to become dominant in radical development geography. To group together the likes of Taiwan and Brazil, and then to point to both as examples of purely systemic change, is completely meaningless. In so far as this approach does not distinguish between the various NICs it is effectively saying to Taiwan's farmers and workers that they may as well be living in Latin America, where the system is 'essentially' the same: a conclusion which would be very properly resisted in Taiwan.

At the same time it would be grotesque to hold up 'Korea, Taiwan, Brazil, etc., as triumphs for the free play of market forces [and free choice: SC] when in fact they are among the more corporate, planned and *dirigiste* economies in the world' (Lamb, 1981, p. 107). One does not have to agree with Lamb's remarks in their entirety to see that Taiwan's growth has owed a great deal to economic planning, fiscal interventionism and even protectionism. More crucially, whilst it is fair to point to Taiwan and South Korea *today* as 'open market' economies which like to respond to undistorted price signals, it must be emphasised that the appropriateness of such a policy in a development sense depends on a series of prior structural reforms in these economies. In other words it is the comparatively egalitarian economic base of Taiwan and South Korea which has ensured that their reliance on open market prices is not hopelessly at odds with the relative factor endowments of these countries. To extend the same logic to countries like Bangladesh would be disastrous. In an economy almost totally lacking in physical and educational infrastructure, and where patterns of commodity demand and labour supply are 'distorted' by a grossly unequal distribution of resources and massive rural to urban migration,[40] a reliance on open market prices can only reinforce a comparative advantage in agricultural exports and a commodity import profile heavily geared to 'elite' goods.

In other words, the lesson from Taiwan is not a free market lesson. It is that *dirigisme* for development will be inescapable wherever open market prices are not reasonable representations of a country's relative factor endowments. Where there is such a correspondence, however, – in other words where there has been significant prior political activity in favour of equality – open market prices should not be ruled out of hand. I noted in Chapter 3 that there is a tendency for some radicals to reject such things as the market mechanism on ideological grounds, in the process forgetting that its effects will be specific to the particular relations of production governing the operation of any given economic system.

Of course the question that then arises is whether it is possible and/or likely that other developing countries will be able to reproduce Taiwan's recent political and economic past. At one level this seems unlikely. If we are concerned with precise questions of growth rates, of investment levels and patterns, of aid inflows and so on, it is clear that Taiwan's preconditions for growth were fairly unusual. In a telling, if still broadly sympathetic, review of Fei *et al.*'s Taiwan-based *Growth With Equity* model (1979), Chinn points out that Taiwanese development has been highly dependent on (i) high levels of US aid; and (ii) a land reform inspired and carried out by an incoming nationalist government which itself had very little to lose from land expropriation.[41] By contrast:

> The major problem in most other developing societies is that assets, particularly land, are extremely unequally distributed, and since economic and political power are highly correlated, governments lack the political will to carry out any form of land reform (Chinn, 1982, p. 882).

This much is clearly true and it would be churlish to deny the importance of Chinn's remarks here. Nevertheless, if we conceive of the Taiwanese model in slightly wider terms it is apparent that there are lessons to be learnt, and that these lessons do undermine both neo-classical and world systems perspectives on international development.

I say this for two reasons, the first of which concerns the role of local class structures and histories in the determination of development patterns. Whether or not Taiwan's changing balance of power can be copied is irrelevant in this context. What matters is that Taiwan has responded very differently from Brazil, say, when faced with the changing 'demands' of a supposedly all-determining world system. Its class structure and its past history have ensured a far more benign integration into an evolving international division of labour than could ever be the case in its Latin American counterpart.

Internal factors do matter, then, and they do set significantly different policy agendas and opportunities in developing countries, but even then these agendas do not have to be heeded. Thus whilst it is right to affirm that Taiwan's leaders did not just hit upon a successful development strategy by accident, that they did not simply look it up in an economic textbook, or pick a winner as Balassa seems to imply,[42] nevertheless the element of scope and of active choice within limits does need to be drawn out. If Taiwan has a second lesson for us, it is that there can be room for manoeuvre. The world economy sets many imposing constraints, but it is wrong to imply that all options are closed to all Third World countries, or that they are always predetermined by the metropolitan powers. In a number of areas which are of significance to the local population governments can intervene for better or worse. The differing experiences of Frank's six NICs is testimony to that.

4.4 Conclusions

This chapter has suspended all but the most implicit judgements on the desirability, and correct role, of industrialisation in a unified development strategy. Instead it has assumed that industrialisation is a necessary component of growth and development, and has attended to three of the key debates which surround this issue: on the possibility and characteristics of capitalist industrialisation in the Third World; on the role of the TNCs; and on the significance of the NICs (especially Taiwan). The conclusions I wish to emphasise here are also threefold.

First, it is clear that industrialisation is proceeding apace in a growing number of Third World countries. Second, it is not enough to write off this industrialisation as dependent come what may, and thus non-developmental. Such a critique is not borne out by the facts, and in any case is predicated on a wholly unreason-able conception of a perfectly balanced, perfectly autarkic, and in some respects already developed, mode of industrial develop-ment. It is also at odds with our review of the TNCs and the NICs. This emphasised the differential experience of countries and com-panies, and pointed up the need for a more disaggregated ap-proach to the relationship between capitalism, industrialisation and development. Capitalism *per se* has no one industrial 'effect'. This is also the substance of my third point. Once capitalism is defined in terms which do not demand its teleological reincarna-tion as core versus periphery, it is apparent that many of the issues now worrying the Left must disappear. At the moment it is only an obsession with the evils of foreign as opposed to domestic capital; of independent as opposed to interdependent development; and of system continuity as opposed to system change, that prevents some critics from seeing that the conditions for Third World industrialisation are now more established than ever before, and should be built upon. As Jenkins has it: 'There is only one thing worse than being exploited by capital and that is not being ex-ploited at all. Given the alternatives which at present exist in most Third World countries it is by no means clear that workers em-ployed in export production would be better off if these factories did not exist' (Jenkins, 1984, p. 51).

5
Capitalism, Interdependency and Development

Introduction

The notion that we are living in an interdependent world has become an insistent catch-phrase in recent years. It is a phrase which has been adopted with particular vigour by geographers, who have tended to see it either in the liberal–interventionist terms set out by Brookfield (1975), or in the more pessimistic tones of world systems theory. In this latter vein there has been a tendency to follow Wallerstein in arguing that because 'the modern world system more than ever comprises a single world capitalist economy . . . it follows that nation-states are not societies that have separate parallel histories, but are part of a whole reflecting a whole' (Wallerstein, 1979, p. 53).[1] According to this new orthodoxy there is no longer any room for conventional national economic planning or policies. As Radice puts it: 'the capitalist world economy is now so thoroughly integrated across national boundaries that an autonomous national economic strategy is no longer possible' (Radice, 1984, p. 113).

In literal terms this is clearly the case, but in this chapter I want to step back from the wider thrust of this judgement.[2] I want to make the case for a conceptualisation of world development which accepts that the world system is greater than the sum of its component parts (of course), and thus sets limits to localised political action, but which accepts also that these component parts, and nation-states especially, can still mould and change the system itself. More generally I want to continue the theme of disaggregation which was so central to Chapter 4. I will argue that an

189

adequate conception of interdependent development must find room for the still-dominant role of the US economy, and for that country's problematical and largely asymmetrical power relations not just with a dissolving 'South' but with its increasingly fractious Northern 'allies'. The world system I map out is thus a good deal more complex than that which usually informs talk of a North-South dialogue or a New International Economic Order (NIEO). It is my belief that such macro-labels are of little help in theorising contemporary global geopolitics. Political action in support of a more equitable world order is indeed possible, but it is most likely to emerge from those less grandiose forums where groups of Southern countries are able to exploit selected points of cleavage in Northern bloc thinking – notably on trade and the international monetary system.

These arguments are unfurled in three sections. Section 5.1 reviews three 'traditional' accounts of the interdependent world system: the Keynesian–interventionist account, the 'new' neo-classical account, and the radical–world systems account. Each perspective has something to offer, and collectively they remind us that a model of the world's geopolitical economy can no longer be cast in terms of nation-states alone. As I have said before, it is not my intention to disregard the evidence of competing perspectives: in this case on the increasing scale of North–South trade, on the increasing synchronisation of global interest rates and monetary indicators, or on the continuation of imperialist political action against sections of the Third World. My purpose is merely to offer a counterpoint. To that end I suggest that the very different insights of these three perspectives on the world economy may each be marred to the extent that they share one common assumption: that the capitalist world system could and should be theorised in terms of the interlocking workings of North and South alone. This seems to me to render the concept of interdependent development meaningless, for it adopts a level of aggregation which conceals as much as it reveals. Above all, it fails to examine the way in which changes in this interdependent world system are opening up new opportunities for (as well as constraints on) national economic and political action.

This theme is further developed in section 5.2 which is a short linking section. At this point I return to an important debate on the role and significance of the nation-state in an evolving capitalist world system. This debate exercised some sections of the Left in the early 1970s when two of the main protagonists were Robin Murray and Bill Warren. Murray maintained that the contradictions between national capitalisms were becoming increasingly insignificant in an age of ultra-imperialism.[3] Warren, unsurprisingingly, argued the converse: that imperialism was giving way to independent national capitalisms in North and South. Standing in the middle was Bob Rowthorn. In an article which has clearly influenced the thinking of this chapter, Rowthorn argued that 'the prospect is one of imperialist rivalry, in which a number of relatively autonomous states, which we have called "imperialist metropolises", are in conflict with each other as they try to support their respective capitals' (Rowthorn, 1980, p. 73). In other words, Rowthorn foresaw a world of increasing national rivalry and strife precisely as a result of the internationalisation of capital which Murray took to signal the end of the nation-state.

This crucial insight is explored at greater length in section 5.3 in which I draw on the work of Riccardo Parboni to argue that a major determinant of recent geopolitics (of the debt crisis, of the hostile responses to calls for a NIEO, of trade wars, even of Middle Eastern tensions) has been the response of the USA to its changing, and ultimately deteriorating, position in the world economy. Paradoxically, it has been the very ability of the USA to ward off its long-term decline *vis-à-vis* its trilateral allies[4] that has made it so willing to 'unhesitatingly pursue its own national interest and [so] become the principal source of perturbation of the international economy' (Parboni, 1981, p. 50). The reasons for such action, and the manner of its execution, will have to be explained in some detail. For presentation purposes, however, it is convenient to expand upon the Rowthorn–Parboni thesis in the context of an empirical review of recent Northern bloc responses to the crucial international (North–South?) issues of trade and finance. Since these are also the principal concerns of the two Brandt Commission reports, it is doubly convenient to tie our more general discussion to an analysis of the logic and proposals of these reports, and to the different intellectual and political responses made to them. Such a structure has the added advantage of allowing us a ready comparison between our three traditional accounts of the world order and the more complex geopolitical-economy outlined by Parboni. It also directs us to a number of concluding remarks on the sort of geographical theorising which radical development geography must produce if it is properly to understand the complicated and evolving world system in which we all live. As certain political geographers have already discovered, this is not a world system which lends itself to the more simplistic visions of centre and periphery.

5.1   Three views of interdependency

Although I will later want to challenge the interdependency perspective, there are good reasons for the growth of this paradigm in development studies. Whether one looks at the build-up of North-South trade flows since 1945, at the multiplication of global institutions and agreements, or at the transnationalisation of capital, it is apparent that a world system exists which cannot be reduced to the sum of its component parts. Nevertheless the workings of this system continue to be theorised in three quite different ways and it is as well to familiarise ourselves with these views before attempting a deconstruction of their dominant spatial metaphors.

Interventionism

The interventionist perspective defies a quick and easy summary for it embraces three competing strands. Nevertheless there have been certain common themes to its progress, the most important of which are: (i) a mistrust of the equilibrating nature of free market forces (this establishes the economic case for interventionism); (ii) a fear of the political movements which are likely to occur in the periphery in response to an unregulated, and thus polarising, world system (this makes the political case for interventionism); and (iii) a belief that in an age of greater trading and investment interdependence certain decisions must be taken in the global interest by global political communities (it is in this way that the nation-state is downgraded in the interventionist account).

The early Keynesians   The early Keynesians presented the most optimistic, and in some respects the most altruistic, model of interdependency. Drawing on the principles of demand management that Keynes had established in his General Theory, these men and women looked forward to a post-war international order governed by two basic objectives.

The first of these was stability. Shocked by the waste of men and resources that had accompanied pre-war policies of deflation and competitive devaluation, the international Keynesians wanted to ensure that the pursuit of national interests would never again subvert the entire international economic and monetary order. To this end Keynes himself was instrumental, in 1944, in setting up the Bretton Woods institutions of the International Monetary Fund (IMF) and the International Bank for Reconstruction and Development (IBRD),[5] charging the IMF with the particular duty of guaranteeing fixed exchange rates. Later on this idea of stability for growth through trade was extended with the introduction of the General Agreement on Trade and Tariffs (GATT). Proponents would claim that the benefits of such interventionism are there for all to see. Between 1945 and 1980 the world system really did become interdependent as world trade multiplied by a factor of ten, and as North–South exchanges, specifically, grew twelvefold.[6]

The second Keynesian principle was growth. Believing that growth and full employment would not necessarily be created by a free market system, Keynes suggested that governments should act to secure levels of aggregate demand sufficient for growth. In time this idea was transferred to the international stage. In the work of Harrod and Domar we find an emerging intellectual justification for concessional international money and capital transfers, and for international deficit financing. The basic idea was that the South suffered from a series of 'gaps' (savings, foreign exchange and technological gaps especially) which could be plugged either by government fiscal activities within the Third World or by foreign aid transfers from the North. There was also a philosophical reworking of Keynes's ideas. In the 1950s we see the emergence of a fully-fledged paternalism whereby the North would discharge its duty to the South without thought for its own future. In the heady years that led up to the First Development Decade (1960–9) economic philosophy was relatively untroubled with the zero-sum problems that would soon afflict it, and which would lead it to a more tardy appreciation of the South's needs and demands.[7] Finally there was the institutional question. Again this had been partially solved by Keynes. Back in 1944 he had pressed for the IMF and the IBRD to have certain credit creation facilities, notably the power to issue 'global money' (which became the Special Drawing Right). Not surprisingly the Americans cavilled at this.[8] Nevertheless they did agree to the reconstructionist and developmental brief of the World Bank and they did agree to the creation of various credit tranches at the IMF which could be used by member countries in exceptional circumstances (and under particularly stringent rules). When set alongside the later multiplication of multilateral aid agencies these concessions allowed for a flowering of the views of the early international Keynesians. For close on twenty years their vision of a world growing to interdependence through aid and managed free trade held sway.

The physicalists   In some quarters that vision still does hold sway, but by the mid-1960s there were some cracks appearing in this edifice. Specifically, as the Keynesian boom years came to an end, so too the South (through UNCTAD)[9] began to question the equity of this increasingly interdependent world. I shall come back to this later. For the moment let me leave it as a coincidence that it was at about this time that a new interventionist vision of interdependency began to appear: that of the global 'doom-and-gloom' school.

We have already met the main proponents of this view. What I have in mind here is the sort of physical systems theorising to be found in Barbara Ward's *Spaceship Earth* (1966), in the Meadows' *Limits to Growth* (1972), in Schumacher's *Small is Beautiful* (1973), and in the more recent publication of the *Global 2000* team (Barney, 1982). Texts such as these turned the interventionist account upside-down. Instead of urging the North to pour money and technologies into a growing South, the 'physicalists' set up a no-growth model wherein the fabric of the entire world system was said to be threatened by any further and future industrialisation. Amid dire warnings of over-population and photo-chemical smog they presented a vision of interdependency which was dominated by fragility and positive feedback, and which, politically, cautioned the South to forego its (entirely understandable) pursuit of growth for the more critical demands of a global system teetering on the brink of resource depletion. In the interests of an interdependent world the South was once more asked to play the white man (*sic*).

Ankie Hoogvelt has suggested that this sudden awareness of the global interaction of physical variables can be traced back to a lack of confidence in the economic performance of the North. As the South began to appear as a competitor for scarce resources, she suggests:

> Liberal thinkers . . . became conscious of the fact that it is not just the Third World that is dependent on the First World but that the relationship works the other way as well, and that there is a real threat to the future survival of the world capitalist system if, for instance, lack of international redistribution of resources leads to political violence on the part of Third World countries, or if, indeed, quite the opposite occurs and successful industrialisation on the part of all Third World countries leads to complete resource depletion of materials used by the advanced world (Hoogvelt, 1982, pp. 122–3).

Whilst her views are suggestive however, and though she goes on to discuss the origins of the basic needs perspective and NIDL theorising in the same terms, her thesis takes us rather too quickly to the radical critique of interventionism. For the moment it is important to stress that these physicalist views did not last long. No matter how hard their proponents tried to soften the blow of Southern no-growth with similar demands of the North, the fact remained that the South was unconvinced by the evidence of these global 'gloom-and-doom' scenarios, and its leaders were rightly sceptical of the claim that redistribution must substitute for growth. As their challenge mounted so the interventionist perspective began to change its spots once more.

International Keynesianism, mark II Today we are living in the third era of interventionism, or the age of international Keynesianism, mark II. In some respects this new philosophy of interdependency is best described as a philosophy of redistribution for growth, though this may conjure up a rather narrow equation with the work of Chenery *et al.* (1974) and with the basic-needs approach of McNamara's World Bank. What I have in mind is a good deal wider: a paradigm that would include also the works of the Pearson Commission (Pearson, 1971), and more especially the reports produced by the Tinbergen and Brandt teams (Tinbergen & Dolman, 1976, Brandt, 1980).

These latter texts have a particular importance, for the progression from Tinbergen to Brandt tells us much about the re-emergence of a modified international Keynesianism within the interventionist ranks. Consider the work of Tinbergen first (or more properly the work edited by Tinbergen and Dolman, 1976). Caught between the no-growth school and its emerging critique, Tinbergen's call for a reshaped international order (RIO) makes confusing reading. On the one hand it endorses the physicalists' claim that the Third World should give up its quest for material richness. The idea that the South can catch up with the North on its own terms is dismissed as simply impracticable.[10] At the same time the Tinbergen collective sugars this pill in a rather novel fashion. First, it paints a picture of a new international order wherein every individual has an unalienable right to a life of well-being and equity. Next, it defines these rights in terms of a right to survive, a right to work, a right to education, and a right to socio-cultural activities. Finally, it suggests that these rights must be secured by an international redistribution of growth, of jobs and of income. The paradox is that this redistribution must be secured economically, through a new international division of labour, rather than politically, through the Charter for a New International Economic Order (though this is discussed). Third World countries are thus at one and the same time expected to make strides towards local self-reliance and independence (for ecological stability) whilst opening their doors to more international trade and investment (for growth).

Inevitably this sets up certain tensions in the Tinbergen model and it is not clear that these are overcome with a recommendation for a more functional conception of national sovereignty. (In effect the RIO collective suggest that the global population and the individual, and not the nation-state, are to be seen as the primary units of any development strategy. It follows that whenever decisions taken by one nation-state are likely to affect the individuals of another – almost always? – these decisions should be referred to an international forum which can represent the global population. In this way the territorial conception of national sovereignty is progressively undermined). What is clear is that texts such as Tinbergen and Dolman's *Reshaping the International Order* found an echo in the better contemporary geographies, where Brookfield was already warning that the 'voices from the periphery' would grow more strident unless a set of global managers acted to protect them from the free market forces which were deepening the 'uneven distribution of scarce resources [which] underlies the whole development problem' (Brookfield, 1975, p. 206). It also paved the way for the more sophisticated, and in some respects more practicable, global Keynesianism of the two Brandt Reports (Brandt, 1980, 1983).

This is especially true of the first Brandt report, *North–South* (1980). This text firmly rejects the resource pessimism scenario which so besets Tinbergen. Instead it turns the interventionist clock back to the late 1940s, though with a subtle twist. Once more the focus is on the developmental role of aid and managed free trade, but the sting in the tail of this new international Keynesianism is the concept of mutual interests (as opposed to true altruism). I will expand upon this later on, but the gist of the concept is well understood: the Commissioners urge Northern politicians to develop Southern economies if only to reflate their own economies as they head into recession for want of sufficient demand.

By a careful mixture of analysis and presentation the Commissioners manage to bring to a head most of the surviving themes of the interventionist perspective. On the one hand they restate the central tenet of interdependency. By stressing a mutuality of interests the Commissioners speak to the fact of growing post-war North–South trade, whilst holding out the promise of its future growth as the salvation of both economic blocs. At the same time the Commissioners make plain their distrust of an unregulated world system. Their vision of interdependency is truly Keynesian in its suggestion that a lack of global demand is the principal cause of recession, and in its recommendation of greater global liquidity as a cure. It also looks to global institutions and agreements to stand above purely national and regional economic calculations. Indeed, one of the report's most distinctive features is its call for an extension of the existing Bretton Woods machinery. Having acclaimed the present international institutions as part of an 'indispensable system . . . central to the task of world development' (Brandt, 1980, p. 257) the Commissioners have since come out in favour of a more frequent resort to international summit meetings, and the merging of GATT and UNCTAD under the auspices of an International Trade Organisation. As if to crown this global polity, and as if to make sure that free market forces are indeed harnessed for the managed and harmonic growth of North and South, the Commissioners have also proposed that a World Development Fund be set up. This would sit alongside the IMF and the World Bank, and would create a triumvirate of international guardian angels to watch over our interdependent world.

The new neo-classicism and interdependency[11]

At least that is the theory. In practice international Keynesianism no longer exercises significant political power, and academically its vision of interventionism for interdependency is under attack. As ever this offensive has been slow to make its mark in geography where interdependency theory is still largely Keynesian in tone. Nevertheless its impact has been significant in the wider field of development studies, where the onslaught has been joined by two scholars whom we shall have cause to meet again: Deepak Lal, Reader in Economics at the London School of Economics, and Michael Beenstock, Professor Finance of Investment at the City University, London.

Lal's chief concern is with *The Poverty of 'Development Economics'* (1983a), and his work is more in the way of a polemic or a critique than an exercise in alternative theory construction. Nevertheless his thinking is instructive. He argues that 'development economics' has its roots in the belief that neo-classical economics is of little validity in the Third World. Its principal hallmark is a 'paternalistic denial that the poor and ill-educated masses of the Third World could respond rationally, as either consumers or producers, to changes in relative prices' (Lal, 1983a, p. 55). Lal believes this to be quite untrue and he proceeds to 'show' how such an assumption has promoted a *dirigiste* perspective on welfare which is actually making the situation worse: 'Most serious distortions in the current workings of the price mechanism of Third World countries are due not to the inherent imperfections of the market mechanism, but to irrational government interventions' (ibid). Lal thus concludes that open market prices are the best route to development, and that 'despite the current problems of the world economy, the best service that the North can give to the Third World is to ensure that the post-war liberal international economic order is maintained by refusing to surrender to the blandishments of either the Southern *dirigistes* of the NIEO or the

Northern advocates of the 'new protectionism" (Lal, 1983a, p. 55). Should this advice be heeded there will be no need for yet more global institutions, and there will be no place for the sort of 'pseudo-economics' that has for so long passed as international Keynesianism.

No doubt these same general thoughts have been at the back of Michael Beenstock's mind. The virtue of his work, however, is that he has sought to provide an alternative model of world interdependence, which he calls his new neo-classical 'Transition Theory'. In a stimulating recent text Beenstock argues that the world economy is now in a post-Keynesian stage of transition in which the principal dynamic comes not from the North but from the South. To be precise, the recession and de-industrialisation that is now racking the economies of the trilateral powers is said to be a temporary phase brought on by the sudden and prior industrialisation of the South in the late 1960s and 1970s.

According to Beenstock, this industrialisation was probably induced by 'the more open economic policies that were implemented in the so-called "newly industrialising countries"' (Beenstock, 1983, p. 14), though he admits that the Transition Theory does not examine this proposition: it simply takes it 'as a matter of fact, as an autonomous development' (ibid, pp. 14–15). What matters is that this industrialisation has altered the balance of power between North and South. As far as the North is concerned, it has suffered from the lower relative prices of manufactures on world markets consequent upon their greater supply. As Beenstock puts it 'The rise in the relative price of raw materials that began towards the end of the 1960s was brought about by supply shocks in the market for manufactures rather than or as much as supply shocks in the market for raw materials' (Beenstock, 1983, p. 15). (At this point I should add that one of Beenstock's more important claims is that worker militancy in the North and/or the OPEC price shocks are but secondary features to the changes induced by the long-run trend to North–South equalisation.) This fall in the relative prices of manufactures has in turn provoked a set of market signals which causes resources to shift from the manufacturing sector to other sectors of the economy in the bloc of developed countries. This is called the de-industrialisation effect because industry suffers while the rest of the economy expands.

Meanwhile the South is gaining. On the one hand it gains from the rise in worker militancy that is induced, paradoxically, by the first round of de-industrialisation in the North. As Beenstock explains: 'Militancy is circumscribed by market power' (ibid, p. 15), and in the late 1960s and early 1970s de-industrialisation actually favoured wages against profits. 'This is because the manufacturing/industrial sectors of the economy are assumed to be relatively capital-intensive, so that a relative contraction of the manufacturing sector results in a fall in the marginal product of capital and an increase in the marginal product of labour' (Beenstock, 1983, p. 15). At the same time the South has reaped the rewards of greater foreign investment. As the rate of return on capital improved in the South relative to the North so investment began to flow to the Third World.

All this is simple enough. Beenstock's model may be firmly in line with the equilibrating and equalising traditions of neo-classical economics, but its analysis of recent changes in the world economy would be accepted by many Keynesians and even by some radical theorists of the new international division of labour. Where these latter theorists would depart from Beenstock, I suspect, is over his political conclusions. Although his politics are never made explicit, it is apparent that Beenstock's work carries a quite different message to Northern governments and labour leaders (and the British government and unions especially) from that of the Brandt report, or the texts of Fröbel *et al* or the Cambridge Political Economy Group.[12] Where the Brandt Commissioners favour the global politics of aid and managed free trade, and many radicals a new protectionism, Beenstock urges a more open and positive push for 'adjustment'. He believes that whilst current high levels of unemployment in the North have their roots in the transition now gripping the world economy, they are also being dragged out by 'restrictive practices and natural causes of friction' which threaten the North's necessary movement away from a manufacturing base. Within the general transition theory he calls this the 'mismatch thesis'. 'Mismatch unemployment is inherently temporary' he suggests (Beenstock, 1983, p. 17) but it will be prolonged wherever governments enact policies which amount either to protectionism (as in the 1981 Multi-Fibre Agreement) or labourism. Beenstock concludes that:

> The Transition Theory implies that LDC industrialisation inflicts a terms-of-trade loss on the developed countries, and in the

shorter term it generates mismatch costs. In a narrow sense the theory thus implies that policies designed to thwart LDC economic development are desirable as far as the rich countries are concerned. Despite the economic arguments, politicians seldom base commercial policy on terms-of-trade considerations and instead regard protectionism as the basis for policy. In so far as the Transition Theory implies that unemployment will be temporary this would serve as an argument against protectionism. This would leave as the main political challenge the reduction in man-made frictions which contribute to mismatch effects (Beenstock, 1983, p. 20).

This is not the place to discuss what these frictions might be, or what Beenstock would advise governments to do about them. Nor do I yet want to develop a critique of the Transition Theory, though it must be clear that Northern governments are once more being asked to act in the long-run global interest. Instead, let me re-emphasise the central feature of this neo-classical resurgence: its emphasis on the world economy. Beenstock's model may be more 'optimistic' (his word) than its Keynesian and radical counterparts, but its focus is still on *the* developed world and *the* developing world. Specific national economies and political policies appear as mere residuals in an account which concludes that: 'After a century, the balance of world economic power in the 1960s began to shift in favour of the developing countries' (Beenstock, 1983, p. 226). For Beenstock 'The greatest challenge to the world economic order is coming to terms with the inexorable spread of economic development over the next hundred years. It will be as much a test of the integrity of man as it is a challenge to policy-makers' (Beenstock, 1983, p. 226).

Radical theories of dependent interdependency

A similar emphasis upon the world system is apparent in most radical development theories, though their conclusions tend to be a good deal less sanguine than Beenstock's. As we have seen before, the dominant Marxist and neo-Marxist accounts of development and underdevelopment present a model of the global system in which the North is perpetually exploiting the South through a series of unequal and asymmetrical relations of production and exchange. Of crucial importance here are the terms of trade and the international division of labour, but we have already discussed these at some length. In this section I want to explore three further aspects of the radical critique of interdependency, looking at the transnationalisation of finance capital, at the aid issue, and at the question of global economic and political management.

Transnational finance capital   An emphasis upon finance capital is a recent but important addition to the radical thesis. Many radicals (see Coakley and Harris, 1983) believe that the internationalisation of Northern industrial capital is now being surpassed by the transnationalisation of finance capital. They further believe that this dual reproduction of capital on an extended scale has the effect of eroding intra-Northern bloc differences and of enforcing a collective core identity and will.

In more detail, this thesis depends upon a consideration of the booming Eurocurrency markets. There seem to be three points at stake here. First, there is the question of a break from the past. Coakley and Harris's account draws a clear distinction between the relatively rooted financial capitals of the 1950s and the footlose finance capitals of the post-1950s era. This distinction takes us to the heart of the Euromarket phenomenon. Prior to the late 1950s, these authors suggest, dollars were comparatively scarce in the world economy, and those governments and companies lucky enough to hold them were happy enough to deposit them in the USA (where they were usually returned to pay for US imports). In New York and elsewhere these deposits were subject to a similar range of laws and constraints as domestic deposits: notably a maximum rate of interest and a requirement that a certain proportion of the deposit be held as non-interest-bearing 'reserves' at the central bank. By the early 1960s, however, things were changing. From this point on the USA began to run a balance-of-payments deficit against the rest of the world (of which more later) and increasing numbers of dollars began to flow into Europe, Japan and elsewhere. More crucially, these deposits began to be deposited in Europe (hence 'Eurodollar'), as investors sought to escape the prying eyes of the US authorities. At the centre of this market was the staunchly unregulated banking sector of London, and London's position was further consolidated in the 1970s as exchange rates became freely floating and as vast numbers of OPEC petrodollars were recycled through its exchanges.

The essence of the Euromarket phenomenon, then, is the trans-nationalisation and deregulation of financial capital. Nevertheless, it is not the geographical relocation of 'offshore' banking facilities that really worries the radical scholar. What is far more important to him or her is the loss of national sovereignty that this transnationalisation induces. As Coakley and Harris put it, 'the Eurodollar credit system greatly reduces the power of democratically elected governments' (Coakley and Harris, 1983, p. 49). The reason for this should be obvious. Since the Euromarkets allow and even encourage the liberation of financial capital to chase the highest international interest rates, so finance capital progressively detaches itself from the national industrial capitals which it might once have been expected to serve. This decoupling would appear to have gone furthest in Britain, where financial capital has long been politically dominant, and where exchange controls have recently been scrapped. Nevertheless it is thought to have affected most of the trilateral powers. Throughout the developed world governments are thought to be losing control of their strategic planning capabilities as the fear of capital flight prevents them from adopting the low-interest-rate policies necessary for industrial regeneration and economic growth.[13]

Side by side with this national degeneration, however, is a solidification of the interests of Northern capital as a whole. According to this element of Leftist thinking, financial capital is regrouping at a hemispheric scale and is there seeking to use its powers to enforce global policies which are best suited to its interests. In effect this means acting to secure international aid policies which are supportive of transnational capital. It also means acting upon the IMF, especially, to ensure that its Charter requirements are progressively brought around to the twin claims of deflation and sound money.

Aid and imperialism This new emphasis upon the IMF parallels a critique of foreign aid programmes which has long been central to the radical vision of dependent interdependency. Ever since the interventionists set up their gap-models, and ever since foreign aid was heralded as evidence of supra-national altruism, the radical school has sought to depict aid as, at best, propaganda, and, at worst, imperialism. Resisting the glowing homilies of the Keynesians these radicals have joined with certain critics of the Right (notably Bauer, 1974) in pointing to four flaws in the pro-aid case.

A first flaw concerns the amount of aid that is actually transferred. It must be well known by now that radicals have delighted in attacking the rhetoric that lies behind the pronouncements of the First and Second Development Decades. Noting that these Declarations committed OECD countries to transferring 1.0 and 0.7 per cent of their GNPs, successively, as foreign aid, radicals like Byres (1972) and Hayter (1971) have had no trouble in showing that these targets have only rarely been met. Indeed only the Netherland and Sweden seem to have taken their responsibilities seriously.[14] Most of the economically more powerful Northern bloc countries preferred the promise to performance. In the 1970s the USA managed to transfer just 0.265 per cent of its GNP as official development assistance, and countries like Japan, the UK and West Germany did little better with figures of 0.25, 0.46 and 0.385 per cent respectively.[15] But that is not all. Once it is recalled that aid programmes usually consist of concessional loan agreements it becomes important to work out the degree of concessionality implicit in these figures. This involves computing the grant element, a figure dependent upon the interest rate of the loan, the grace period involved and the total repayment period.[16] The story uncovered is not a happy one. Although the British government has recently taken steps to improve the concessionality of its aid, throughout the 1950s, 1960s and 1970s it was not uncommon to find Britain and others offering aid with grant elements as low as 20 or 30 per cent. Even the soft-loan arm of the World Bank rarely managed to provide loans with a grant element of more than 75 per cent.[17]

Of course the financial status of a loan is not the be-all and end-all of radical concern. Of much greater import is the question of the terms on which aid is offered: the fact that its transfer is often tied to economic and political preconditions. This practice has again provided the radical critique with an armoury of telling quotations which can be turned against their supposedly pro-aid instigators.

One thinks of Richard Nixon's remarks, for example, when he reminded prospective voters in the 1968 Presidential campaign 'that the main purpose of American aid is not to help other nations but to help ourselves' (quoted in Hayter, 1981, p. 84). A similar observation had previously been uttered by Eugene Black, President of the World Bank in the 1950s:

Our foreign aid programmes constitute a distinct benefit to American business. The three major benefits are (1) foreign aid provides a substantial and immediate market for US goods and services; (2) foreign aid stimulates the development of new overseas markets for US companies; (3) foreign aid orients national economies to a free enterprise system in which US firms can prosper (from Hayter, 1981, p. 83).

It is not just the USA, however, which favours a system where recipient countries have to spend a fixed percentage of their incoming aid on the goods and services of the donor country, despite the fact that such purchases may be, on average, 20 per cent above the prevailing free market price.[18] UK governments long ago recognised the value of this aid–trade connection, and they have recently set out to formalise these arrangements in the post-1978 Aid–Trade Provision (ATP). This allows and encourages British firms to tender for large 'development' contracts (usually in Middle-Income Countries) in the knowledge that a grant may be made to their clients in the event that they are undercut by a competitor. The classic example to date concerns the Sicartsa Steel Plate Mill in Mexico. Towards the end of 1981 a £35 million ATP grant was made to the Mexican government on the understanding that the Sicartsa contract would be given to the British firm of Davy McKee rather than to a cheaper German competitor. This occurred despite the fact that Mexico is not a country which either traditionally, or under the new poverty-related criteria, would qualify for such British aid (see Independent Group on British Aid, 1982, p. 15).

But aid-tying goes beyond even this. So far we have been looking at the way that aid can be used to reinforce the interests of private Northern capital in a project assistance context. In the earlier submission of Eugene Black it was further suggested that aid might create a suitable political climate for the TNCs. It is thus an important part of the radical critique that programme aid is offered by Northern governments because they can then more directly control the development strategy of a client country. By insisting that its aid is tied to Green-Revolution-type programmes, or to transport improvement schemes, the North can foster that spirit of openness and private enterprise which in the long run is as crucial to the interests of private capital as an ATP scheme. What the North will not support is radical egalitarian policies. According to Hayter 'It is clear that the policies to be promoted by aid are not to involve any direct and radical attack on the causes of poverty' (Hayter, 1981, p. 95).[19]

The truth of this is further inscribed in the form in which aid is given. Quite apart from the question of commercial tying, radicals are concerned about the amount of 'aid' that is transferred for military purposes or as food aid. The case against military aid appears to them self-evident. Such aid is not aid at all but is clear proof of the North's massive financial stake in maintaining governments willing to go along with its imperialist designs. One has only to consult a table of the major recipients of Northern military aid to see this (see Table 5.1). As for food aid, this is used both to dump unwanted Northern food surpluses in a manner that will not affect domestic food prices, and to encourage a new dependence of taste. South Asians are given a taste for wheat, the critics say, in the hope that they will later provide a commercial market for such a product. More sinisterly, food aid may be used for political blackmail. This sentiment was once openly expressed in the USA, where Senator Hubert Humphrey said, in 1957:

I have heard . . . that people may become dependent on us for food. I know that was not supposed to be good news. To me that was good news, because before people can do anything they have got to eat. And if you are looking for a way to get people to lean on you and be dependent on you, in terms of their co-operation with you, it seems to me that food dependence would be terrific (quoted in Hayter, 1981, p. 86)

Today few politicians are likely to be as forthright, but that does not mean that Humphrey's sentiments are not still being put into practice. In a terrifying account of the politics of food and famine in Bangladesh, Rehman Sobhan has described how the USA sought to depose the vaguely left-of-centre Mujib government in 1973–4 by withholding two crucial food grain shipments even as tens of thousands of people were starving in that country (Sobhan, 1979 and 1983). Less dramatically, John Tarrant[20] discovered that in these same years of high need, EEC food aid to South Asia dipped to its lowest 1970s level precisely because these were years when EEC food prices were on a par with world market prices. In

TABLE 5.1 *The ten top recipients of US military assistance ($ millions proposed, financial year 1981)*

Israel	1 000.0
Egypt	551.0
Turkey	252.0
Greece	182.7
South Korea	176.5
Spain	125.6
Philippines	75.7
Portugal	75.7
Jordan	52.7
Thailand	51.4
Ten top recipients	2 543.3
All other recipients	286.7
Total military assistance	2 830.0

SOURCE Lappé, Collins and Kinley (1980)

other words when the EEC could sell its excess wheat and dairy products, it did. 'Needs' appeared to be a minor consideration in its food aid policy (Tarrant, 1982).

Finally, there is the question of where the North's aid is sent. For radicals the evidence is once more instructive. The major beneficiaries of US aid (which amounts to about half the world's total aid budget) have been a consistently motley bunch. As Table 5.2 makes clear, what unites them is not so much a common level of poverty – only three of the top ten would qualify as Low Income Countries[21] – as a common political outlook. Most of these countries are sympathetic to the goals of US foreign policy, and in return the US supports them notwithstanding their often gruesome human rights records.[22]

Even so, that USA is not alone in giving aid to countries which meet its political and economic 'needs' rather than to the thirty-four countries which now comprise the poorest in the world.[23] One has only to look to the aid policies of the UK, or to the food aid policies of the EEC, to find a similar lack of discrimination. John Tarrant suggests that the level of correlation between national needs and EEC food aid receipts is a paltry +0.08, whilst my own

TABLE 5.2 *The ten top recipients of US bilateral economic assist-*
ance ($ millions proposed, financial year 1980)

Egypt	969.6
Israel	786.0
India	245.5
Indonesia	205.0
Bangladesh	184.1
Turkey	98.8
Portugal	90.0
Pakistan	86.9
Philippines	83.3
Syria	65.5

SOURCE As for Table 5.1

calculations concerning UK aid between 1976 and 1981 yield a
correlation coefficient of +0.22 (which is also insignificant).[24]
Moreover, even if one takes the optimistic view (as Tarrant does)
that reforms are now being made, the fact remains that channelling
aid to poor countries is not in itself a guarantee that it will be used
to help the poor people of those countries. In their book *Aid as
Obstacle*, Lappé *et al.* remind us that some 100 000 Ethiopians
died in the last two years of the Haile Selassie regime (1973–5),
even though the Emperor's own National Grain Corporation held
17 000 tons of Australian wheat in storage at the time, and even
though 150 000 tons of free food was pouring in from the aid
donors. At one point, indeed, the Selassie government even tried
to sell back some of its stored grain to the USA 'with the idea that
the US could then donate it back for relief inside the country'
(Lappé *et al.*, 1980, p. 116).

Collectively, then, the radical case against foreign aid, or of the
motives and purposes behind it, is a strong one, and it has led
some critics to the conclusion that the aid industry is beyond
reform. As far as Lappé, Collins and Kinley are concerned, the
rationale for aid-giving is so clearly imperialist, and is so clearly
designed to reinforce the North's power over the South, that for
them 'Ending foreign aid to most Third World governments may
be our most important contribution to overcoming hunger and
poverty abroad' (Lappé *et al.*, 1980, endpiece). Moreover, they

TABLE 5.3 *The ten top recipients of World Bank assistance ($ millions, 1 July 1978 to 30 June 1979)*

India	1 429.0
Indonesia	830.0
Brazil	674.0
Mexico	552.0
Korea, Republic of	397.0
Philippines	395.5
Morocco	349.0
Egypt	322.5
Turkey	312.5
Colombia	311.5

SOURCE As for Table 5.1

hold to this conclusion notwithstanding the fact that an increasing percentage of aid transfers is now being made good under the auspices of the multilateral agencies: the World Bank Group, the Inter-American Development Bank and so on. Rather, it is because of this fact. From the point of view of Lappé *et al.* these institutions are simply more efficient organs for the implementation of Northern (and especially US) foreign policy. Under their cover of neutrality and supra-nationality these institutions actually enforce a set of practices and biases that individual Northern governments would find it difficult to apply without challenge. This claim is apparently borne out both by the strong overlap in the aid beneficiaries lists of the US and the World Bank (compare Tables 5.2 and 5.3), and by the sevenfold increase in World Bank lending to Chile *after* the advent of the Pinochet regime, and in a period (1973–9) when World Bank lending rose by an average of only threefold.[25]

The global institutions These latter observations are strongly in keeping with the wider radical line on the purpose and functions of the global institutions and on the nature and relevance of the so-called North–South dialogue.

Again Theresa Hayter has taken a lead in this critique. Along with Cheryl Payer (1974, 1982) and certain radical geographers,[26] she has decried the global institutions on three main counts. First there is the question of accountability. Hayter notes that the Bretton Woods institutions were set up in such a way that voting rights would be determined by the levels of financial support for the relevant institution. Thus in the case of the IMF today the Third World may well be represented by 114 of its 141 member countries but its collective voting weight comes to no more than 36 per cent of the total. As if that is not handicap enough, the South is further restricted in seeking to change the rules and the practices of the IMF by the requirement that major changes must command the support of 60 per cent of the members and 85 per cent of the voting power. In effect this means that the South must have the support of some OECD countries and, more realistically, of the USA. Since the USA has more than 15 per cent of the vote it alone can block any changes which it deems undesirable – such as a further issue of SDRs, or a change in the IMFs voting structure.

Of course this lack of accountability might not matter so much if the rules of the Bretton Woods institutions were really as neutral as their proponents like to claim, or if it could be shown that the Third World exercises a similar degree of power from its institutional power bases within the United Nations, but this is clearly not the case.

Regarding the former, Hayter claims that the 'World Bank and the IMF were set up after the Second World War to solve the problems of the rich countries' (Hayter, 1981, p. 88), a duty which they still discharge. Most radicals concur. Pointing to the Charter of the IMF they note that the principal function of this institution has always been to make the world safe and predictable for private capital and free trade. It is to this end that the IMF advocates 'sound money' policies and it is to this end that both the IMF and the World Bank make development financing conditional upon agreement to certain pre-specified objectives. More often than not these commit Third World governments to lower levels of public spending, to balancing their books and to open-door trade regimes. Whether or not this is to their liking, or for the long-term good of their people, seems to be a secondary consideration.

Radicals are equally sceptical of the role of the United Nations and the United Nations Conference on Trade and Development. They will happily acknowledge that these forums have been important sounding-boards for the South. It was at UNCTADs III and IV that the Group of 77 put the detail on its programme for a

New International Economic Order.[27] Similarly it was at the 29th
Annual Session of the United Nations General Assembly that the
global community accepted, on a majority vote, the Group's
accompanying Charter on the Economic Rights and Duties of
States. Nevertheless there are clear limits to the power of these
institutions. Circumscribed by a lack of money,[28] and by the
North's triple veto in the UN, radicals judge that it has been all too
easy for the North either to bypass these assemblies – preferring to
co-opt the likes of Brazil, Saudi Arabia and pre-revolutionary Iran
into extended Group of Ten meetings[29] – or to string them along
with an institutionalised North–South dialogue. In this latter context Hoogvelt has paid a grudging tribute to the so-called Kissinger
strategy. Defining this as a strategy based upon four main tactics –
the watering-down of resolutions, the suggestion that hard details
should be worked out in technical committees, the fragmentation
of the NIEO programme, and the endless buying of time – Hoogvelt notes how the mid- to late-1970s saw an endless and usually
fruitless multiplication of North–South committees and meetings,
task forces and commissions, the whole lot culminating in the
Brandt Commission. More interestingly she argues that this 'dialogue' can be seen as the finale to a long running North–South
farce in which the North has consistently appeared to take up
certain themes important to the South before turning them to its
own advantage. Thus we have a progression from international
Keynesianism, mark I, through a no-growth era, on to basic needs,
and now on to redistribution, reciprocity and dialogue. At all
times, says Hoogvelt, it is the North which holds the reins.
Beneath the 'myth of mutual interests' (Hill and Scannell, 1983,
p. 13) it is the North which calls the shots, setting the stage in its
capitals and forums, and directing the actors to its well-scripted
conclusions (see Hoogvelt, 1982, ch. 4).

Finally, if any country should get out of hand and start to mouth
the wrong lines, or act out the wrong actions, the North has
recourse to one last prop: force. If all else fails the North will
intervene bodily in the affairs of a Southern country, as El Salvador, Nicaragua and Grenada have all recently discovered. For
most radicals it is this willingness to wield the club which reveals
the true and unchanging nature of the 'interdependent' world
system: a system where appearances continue to cloak the truth of
repression and asymmetry.

5.2   Ultra-imperialism or inter-imperialism?

It is likely that all three of these accounts of the modern world system contain significant elements of truth (even if my own preference is for a version of the radical account). If nothing else the interventionists remind us of the growing volume of trading interdependence, whilst Beenstock reminds us that for all the remaining inequalities in North–South relationships the arrow of causality does occasionally run from South to North.

But there are also problems with these accounts, and not just the everyday problems that rack any academic perspective. For what all these accounts have in common is a willingness to contest each others' interpretations according to an agreed point of reference: the North–South divide. Very rarely is there any acknowledgement that this is only one of many lines of cleavage in current world affairs, or that global geopolitics might be responsive to such 'recent' complications as the rise of the socialist bloc, the partial industrialisation of the Third World, and the relative decline in US hegemony. As a consequence the political understanding on offer is shaky to say the least.

In Beenstock's model the Third World is presented with an inevitable route to future glory in which collective action against the North is dismissed as unhelpful. In this account there is no conception that Northern nations may seek to put off their 'adjustment problems' for entirely rational reasons, resorting to trading restrictions to minimise mismatch unemployment. Nor is there any recognition of the depths of recession which individual Southern nations might themselves plumb, as they wait for the North to come to terms with the changes which are undoubtedly occurring. (In this context I will later want to challenge Beenstock's rather blasé interpretation of the debt crisis.)

Meanwhile, the interventionist account is equally bland. Obsessed with its kindly vision of international co-operation, the modern global Keynesian quite fails to see that the macroeconomics of mutual interests may appear quite differently to the individual countries concerned. Try convincing the British Prime Minister that more aid for the South is good for Britain if he or she believes that the majority of these funds will be spent on the goods of our German, Japanese or American competitors. Finally, what of the radical perspective? Having demonstrated to its satisfaction that the collective weight of the South can never match the collective weight of the North, the radical perspective too often counsels the politics of despair. Even the developing socialist countries are assumed to be so downtrodden by the collective rule of the North that Frank can refer to Mozambique and Vietnam, for example, as fakes, berating them for not de-linking from the international system which guarantees their continued subjugation (Frank, 1983, p. 342).

Must the radical perspective be so pessimistic? I think not. There are already signs that Northern governments suffering a loss of sovereignty in one direction will seek to make up for this in other arenas, stoking up intra-Northern bloc rivalries in the process. (The transnationalisation thesis further forgets that even financial capitals run to their home governments and central banks in times of crisis.) More generally we might suggest that current changes in the world economy are both opening and closing doors on national economic and political actions – a possibility debated at some length by the Left back in the early 1970s.

If we return to these discussions we find that the sort of ultra-imperialist line now dominant (and propounded then by Robin Murray) was already being contested by Warren and Rowthorn, especially the latter. Whilst Warren looked upon the decline of traditional imperialism as the liberator of independent Southern capitalisms, Rowthorn outlined a rather more subtle critique of ultra-imperialism and its US super-imperialism variant.

Rowthorn noted that the debate turned on three crucial issues:

(1) The relative strength of US capital and the related question of the degree to which it can dominate Europe and Japan by capturing most key industrial sectors; (2) the severity and nature of the antagonisms between different national capitals; and (3) the extent to which the common fear of socialism can overcome those antagonisms which do exist (Rowthorn, 1980, p. 48).

Regarding the strength of US capital Rowthorn argued a position upon which I shall later want to expand. Briefly, he noted that whilst American firms are still on average larger than their rivals in the EEC and Japan (and were so in the early 1970s), the gap is closing, and in many industries is not significant. Mergers, takeovers and high rates of accumulation have made their mark. Second, although it is true that American firms are the leading innovators, and often monopolise the most advanced product markets, Rowthorn says that an emphasis upon this alone can be misleading. For one thing the Japanese and Europeans are again catching up. Their rate of technological progress is greater than that of the USA. More importantly: 'As leaders, American firms must spend enormous amounts making mistakes which others can avoid and discovering things which others can imitate or adopt cheaply' (Rowthorn, 1980, p. 52). In short they pay a price for being leaders, and it is this fact, coupled with the faster industrial growth in Europe and Japan, which has led to the Americans' transnational invasion of Europe (to reap high profits) and to the consequent erosion of America's domestic economic and political supremacy.

Rowthorn next examines whether this shift in the spatial balance of power is likely to induce a greater degree of antagonism between the trilateral capitalist powers. On the whole he suggests that it will. Although he admits that tensions of some sort (and usually over trade) have always been present, he sees three new developments which are likely to promote more, and not less, rivalry: the fact that 'European and Japanese capital is [now] strong enough not only to fight back against [incoming] American capital but also to counter-attack by expanding overseas; the fact that 'the overseas expansion of big European and Japanese firms will increasingly take the form of direct investment in other countries including the US itself'; and the fact that 'continent-wide mergers in Europe and further consolidation in Japan [will] accelerate the process considerably and enable the firms of these countries to invest overseas on an enormous scale' (Rowthorn, 1980, p. 65).

Rowthorn foresaw all this in the early 1970s, and in a later postscript he is happy to claim that events have borne him out, but will not these tensions still be forestalled by a wider Northern fear of socialism? Rowthorn believes that this will indeed be the case in some arenas – defence is one – but not in all. Rowthorn suggests that if the Common Market becomes more of a political force, or if actual European unity is brought about, then the USA, the EEC and Japan might confront each others as apparent equals, though with very different growth potentials: an explosive mixture.

To date a united Europe has yet to emerge, and Japan is only just beginning to match its foreign policy to its domestic strength. Nevertheless Rowthorn's conclusions are still interesting. Having reviewed the changing state of Northern economic power, and core political interests, Rowthorn concludes that the 'prospect is one of imperial rivalry, in which a number of relatively autonomous states, which we have called "imperialist metropolises", are in conflict with each other as they try to support their respective capitals' (Rowthorn, 1980, p. 73).

5.3   North–South and the geopolitics of the modern world system

Since the early 1970s the relative decline in US competitiveness has continued apace, and this fact, plus the fact that we are now living in the lean years of recession, has strengthened inter-imperialist rivalries to a dangerous extent. David Harvey captures this very well in *The Limits To Capital*. He writes there that:

> At times of savage devaluation interregional rivalries typically degenerate into struggles over who is to bear the burden of devaluation. The export of unemployment, of inflation, of idle productive capacity become the stakes in the game. Trade wars, dumping, international interest rate wars, restrictions on capital flows and foreign exchange, immigration policies, colonial conquest, the subjugation and domination of tributary economies, the forced reorganisation of the division of labour within economic empires, and, finally, the physical destruction and forced devaluation of a rival's capital through war are some of the methods at hand (Harvey, 1982, p. 438).

But why should this be the case and what precisely are the driving forces behind the regional rivalries which we now see around us: in the US–EEC steel and food policy wars,[30] in the US–Japan computer wars, in the EEC–Japan trade access wars, in the disputes over a proper stance towards the Soviet Union, in the criticisms that have built up over US policies in Latin America and the Middle East (and of Europe in Nato) and so on? And what are the political implications of all this as far as the South is concerned? In the final section of this chapter I want to address these questions, following an intellectual trajectory which takes us on from Rowthorn towards the more recent work of Riccardo Parboni. In a difficult but rewarding book, Parboni argues that the present crisis is 'fundamentally the fruit of a grand inter-imperialist conflict the stakes of which are the global redivision of economic and political power between the US on the one hand and the major powers of the second world–Germany and Japan–on the other' (Parboni, 1981, p. 118). Less conspiratorially, he sees this battle being fought out in the arena of international monetary policy. The key geopolitical fact behind the present crisis is said to be the unwillingness of the USA to contemplate international liquidity reforms which challenge the hegemonic position of the dollar.

Do note, though, that I want to move towards Parboni's work. Rather than arrive there directly I think it may be more helpful to build up our more complex model of the world's geopolitical economy in a step by step fashion. In this way we can lend a bit of context to a discussion which tends to be rather abstract and technical. Specifically, I propose the following plan of action. In the first sub-section I will simply challenge the relevance of a politics determined by a resolutely North–South world-view. Taking the first report of the Brandt Commission as my set text (for obvious reasons) I will show how this vision falls foul of a more disaggregated reading of the relevant trade statistics. (Trade is the principal concern of the first Brandt report.) I will also offer some thoughts on why it is that British and American officials have felt able to dismiss all appeals to their 'mutual interests' when their Japanese counterparts have felt constrained to respond to Brandt in more conciliatory tones.

In the next sub-section this theme of Northern disaggregation is taken a stage further and we begin to stress the geopolitical significance of the US economy. Once again this is done gently. The sub-section opens with a discussion of the second Brandt report's analysis of the international debt crisis (its principal concern). This is favourably contrasted with the monetarist perspective advanced by Lal and Beenstock, and a broad nod of approval is given to its major recommendations; notably the call for a significant new issue of Special Drawing Rights. Where I take issue with the Commissioners is over their political calls for greater global cooperation and common sense. Such calls may be fine in theory, but I follow Parboni in arguing that the USA has good, if selfish, reasons for resisting any such movement to a more neutral unit of account. These reasons are bound up with the concept of financial seignorage and they are explored at some length. To the extent that America's trilateral allies do not share these reasons, however, and more especially to the extent that they feel threatened by current US policies, the South may yet find an ally in its search for a less asymmetrical world order. Equally, sections of the South might yet find themselves the renewed victims of a three-way division of the world into spheres of interest. This is the ambiguous political conclusion of the chapter.

Brandt I: North–South and the mutuality of trade and aid

The first report of the Brandt Commission, *North–South*, is the epitome of a certain type of interdependency thinking. More interestingly, the responses to it have highlighted certain blind-spots in the radical critique of this interventionist perspective.

To my mind the radical critique has focused rather too exclusively on just one aspect of the Commission's case: its suggestion that Southern people will gain from massive transfers in aid and a measure of international trading reform. This is clearly the point of attack which Seers seizes on when he notes (correctly) that 'aid to governments of "poor countries" is one thing, aid to poor people of these countries another' (Seers, 1980, p. 684)[31] and it is apparent, too, in Frank's charge that 'From the point of view of the Commission it [appears] to be a relatively minor point that the proposed "massive transfer" would be to Southern governments and through them to the high income receivers in the South and not to the massively poor masses' (Frank, 1980, p. 673). What these critics have tended to overlook are the two remaining elements of the Commission's case: the assumption that the North has a mutual interest in developing the South, and the assumption that there is one common interest in the North to which this appeal can be addressed. In my judgement neither assumption is warranted, and both are illustrative of the political vacuum which descends upon any such broadly North–South (be it North and South or North versus South) perspective.[32]

Consider, first, the question of mutuality. As with so many of the Brandt Commission's concepts this is never clearly specified.

In broad terms, though, it proposes that Northern economies are heading into permanent recession for want of Southern consumers and mass markets for their goods. Greater trading interdependence and a relaxation of protectionism are then the preconditions for growth in both North and South because 'the South cannot grow adequately without the North. The North cannot prosper or improve its situation unless there is greater progress in the South' (Brandt, 1980, p. 33), and because 'a quickened pace of development in the South also serves people in the North' (ibid, p. 20).

But is this true? I have argued elsewhere (Corbridge, 1982b) that whether or not such an increased trading interdependence will materialise depends upon the validity of the Commission's three unwritten assumptions. These are (i) that the crisis of the North is indeed a realisation crisis, manifested in a lack of demand for goods and services; (ii) that this underconsumption can only be made good (and indeed is slowly being made good) by an expansion of Southern markets, this being the North's incentive to develop the South; and (iii) that such an expansion of Southern demand is dependent on the prior raising of the incomes of the mass populations of the South.

None of these assumptions is as innocent as the Commission suggests. Already the idea that the coming crisis of the North is a straightforwardly under-consumptionist crisis has been strongly and effectively challenged by Frank (1980). The evidence which exists on such things as the long-run decline in the rates of profit made by many Northern industries suggests that the crisis may be more usefully conceptualised as a crisis of accumulation.[33] Indeed some commentators would argue that the crisis is so deeply rooted that piecemeal economic and political interventions–whether along the lines of Brandt's strategy or the British Left's Alternative Economic Strategy–can never exert a sufficient force to counteract the underlying trend in the declining rate of profit (Glyn and Harrison, 1980).[34] In fact even the Commissioners seem to be at odds with their under-consumptionism when they go on to state that the crisis of the North comes at the end of a decade or more of *growing* trading interdependence: 'the dependence of the industrial countries on the markets of the South is substantial and is becoming larger still' (Brandt, 1980, p. 70). In which case why the move to recession now?

Moreover, even if it were to be accepted that certain Northern countries are suffering a realisation crisis, it by no means follows

TABLE 5.4 *The regional destination of developed countries'*
exports, 1948–82 (percentages)

From To: Developed North: market economies	Developing market economies		Centrally planned economies
	Non-OPEC	OPEC	
1948 64.2		30.9	3.0
1955 67.6		26.7	2.0
1960 69.2		24.9	3.0
1965 74.4	16.6	3.9	3.8
1970 76.9	15.3	3.5	3.7
1978 70.9	14.6	9.2	4.9
1982 72.6	12.5	9.8	4.8

SOURCE United Nations, *International Trade Yearbooks* (1960,
1978, 1982).

that this state of affairs can only be rectified by increasing the
demand of the South. The Commissioners may assert that the
North's dependence on Southern markets is substantial and becoming larger still, but like most interdependency theorists they
seem loth to support this conclusion empirically. In part this may
reflect the Commissioners' disdain for any detailed quantification
of their assumptions, but it might just as probably reflect a suspi-
cion that the thesis of increasing trading interdependence would
not be unequivocally confirmed. Certainly the tables which follow
would seem to offer the Commissioners little comfort.

Looking first at the regional distribution of Northern countries'
exports (Table 5.4) it is clear that the Commissioners' identifica-
tion of a growing Northern export dependence on Southern markets has been spotted more with the eye of faith than with an eye to
the evidence. Although an increase in the volume of North–South
trade is a feature of the 1970s, this should not obscure the fact that
over the post-war period as a whole, the North has maintained its
highly incestuous trading patterns–and without noticeable economic stagnation. Second, such dependence, or diversification, as
has occurred has been directed towards OPEC and certain newly

industrialising countries. The North's trade with the rest of the developing world has suffered a relative decline. Third, this fracturing of the notion of one 'Third World' finds its echo in the North where the degree of export dependence varies widely between the EEC, the USA and Japan (Table 5.5). Taken together all this must qualify the relevance of a strictly North–South divide (even if one allows for the recent transnationalisation of capital and the growth of intra-firm trade). It is not a question of the North as a whole making good its demand shortfall by pump-priming the economies of the South *en bloc*. It is more accurate to predict that most Northern nations will continue to rely on domestic intra-Northern reflation to maintain their demand profiles, with some becoming slowly more reliant on the demand generated in certain of the richer countries of the South.

Of course it may be objected that even if Northern economic reflation is a likely response to the current crisis, it by no means follows that it is the most rational response. The Brandt Commissioners may argue that in the longer run the North still has it in its interest to develop the South, thus releasing the demand of the Southern masses. But does it? This is an argument which completely overlooks the nature of the products which are likely to be exported from North to South. If it could be demonstrated that these products are of a type which depend on a mass market demand, the Commissioners' equation of Northern reflation--Southern development might indeed hold up. No such optimistic conclusion could be drawn, however, if the North's exports were instead shown to be of a type dependent upon the demand generated by a rich elite-cum-government stratum.

Once again this is not an issue discussed by the Commissioners, and they do not present any of the requisite disaggregated trade statistics. Table 5.6, however, does offer some tentative and rather discouraging evidence. It shows that Northern exports to the South are overwhelmingly (and unsurprisingly) in the form of manufactures, chemicals and arms. None of these is likely to be dependent upon the existence or growth of mass markets in the South. Indeed, were Southern countries to develop along more egalitarian, consumption-goods oriented lines, it is possible that their demand for many of these products would initially decline. In the longer run it is possible that a structural transformation of Third World agricultural systems would unlock a more wide-

TABLE 5.5 *The regional destination of the exports of the USA, Japan and the EEC, 1948–1982 (percentages)*

From North:	To:	Developed market economies	Developing market economies		Centrally planned economies
			Non-OPEC	OPEC	
USA	1948	56.4		40.4	0.5
	1955	61.9		37.3	0.05
	1960	63.9		35.8	0.8
	1965	64.5	25.0	4.9	0.5
	1970	69.5	24.8	4.8	0.8
	1978	60.7	24.1	11.6	2.3
	1982	63.5	23.0	12.1	2.2
Japan	1948	38.5		57.7	1.5
	1955	39.6		58.2	0.5
	1960	47.7		50.9	1.5
	1965	51.4	36.4	6.4	5.6
	1970	54.6	34.9	5.1	5.4
	1978	47.2	31.5	14.5	5.8
	1982	49.4	31.9	13.1	5.6
EEC	1948	63.9		32.2	2.9
	1955	62.3		31.8	5.3
	1960	72.5		22.7	3.3
	1965	78.9	13.1	4.1	3.4
	1970	80.1	10.7	3.4	3.7
	1978	76.8	10.2	8.6	4.2
	1982	77.4	9.3	8.5	4.4

SOURCE United Nations *International Trade Yearbooks* (1960, 1978, 1982).

ranging consumer demand, but this transformation would first presuppose a level of political activity within Third World countries well beyond that envisaged in the first Brandt report.

All in all, then, a future dismantling of Northern protectionism based on a recognition of trading 'mutualities' is unlikely to be in

TABLE 5.6 *Exports of developed countries to developing countries: by product, 1960–82 (percentages)*

	Food, raw materials and fuels	Chemicals, machinery and other manufactures	Chemicals and machines only
1960	20.20	75.14	44.1
1965	20.72	77.42	48.2
1970	16.94	78.98	52.0
1977	14.21	82.97	57.7
1982	13.07	84.39	56.8

SOURCE United Nations *International Trade Yearbook* (1978, 1982), Special Table C.

the immediate offing. Any demand slack which does exist in the North is most likely to be taken up within that trading bloc, or from within the privileged classes of certain richer Southern countries.

This is not to say that the world economy is not moving towards a greater degree of interdependence. It is only to suggest that the exact nature of that interdependence (increased multinational penetration of the periphery, booming arms sales and a selective industrialisation of the South) is in no way the same as the Brandtian scenario of interdependence-cum-mutuality. This is an important point. If concepts of mutuality, and specifications of Northern interests, are to form the basis of a worthwhile and practicable politics, they need to be constructed from detailed and disaggregated surveys of world trading and investment trends. They should not be deduced, *a priori*, from a generalised theory of economic development.

The truth of this is brought home by the reactions to the North–South report. Here we have a text explicitly written for Northern politicians and appealing (apparently) to their instincts for enlightened self-interest. Yet what has been the response? The Brandt Commission's call for more aid, for trading reforms, and for greater global management, has met with some sort of acclaim in Scandinavia and the Netherlands, and also in Japan (which alone of the trilateral blocs–see Table 5.5–has a measurable trading dependence upon the South). In the USA, by contrast, and in the UK and West Germany, the report's recommendations have been all but ignored by the governments in power. Indeed since its publication the USA has become more and not less protectionist, and it has joined the UK and West Germany in actually cutting the percentage of its GNP which it makes over as official development assistance.[35] Nor has there been any tangible progress at the various international summit meetings demanded by Brandt. Writing of the Cancun summit meeting of Autumn 1981, the Brandt Commissioners say that: '[it] fell far short of our expectations. It produced no new guidelines nor any clear impetus for future negotiations. It did not even come close to launching the idea of a world economic recovery programme' (Brandt, 1983, p. 2).[36]

Brandt II, monetarism and the geopolitics of debt

Why should this be the case? Either the USA and its allies are being persistently wilful, or downright irrational, in ignoring their mutual interests, or these mutual interests have little meaning for them. Without wishing to suggest that governments are always entirely rational it seems to me that we must assume the latter. I have already noted that a Northern government can have only a small interest in boosting its aid flows to the South if it believes that the South will have the temerity to use the money to buy goods from its rivals (and the practice of tying is designed to stop this). The same point can be made more generally by considering the weaknesses of the Brandt Commission's more recent call for a global response to the debt crisis.

In this last sub-section I will argue that the Brandt Commissioners have presented a more than able critique of the monetarist perspective on the so-called debt-bomb. I will assume, too, that they are broadly correct in their recommendation for a route out of this crisis. The world economy badly needs a Northern-led reflation, and the South badly needs access to a greater pool of neutral money (more SDRs). What the Commissioners have not been able to see, however, and this bears upon their failure to look beyond *the* North and *the* South, is the very real opposition to these proposals that will come from the USA. It falls to Parboni to show that the USA has a vested interest in maintaining the hegemonic position of the dollar, and will continue to resist a greater allocation of SDRs so long as it can use this financial seignorage to ward off the economic onslaught of its more competitive allies. It falls to Parboni, too, to provide us with a consistent geopolitical economy. One implication of his work is that the Brandtian goal of an easing of North-South tensions may yet depend on a prior resolution of the geopolitical disputes now racking *The Disintegrating West*.[37]

Monetarism: Lal and Beenstock revisited   It is useful to begin with the monetarist perspective, not just because this is the Commission's own starting-point, but because it reminds us that much of the present talk about a global 'debt-bomb' (Palmer, 1983) is wildly apocalyptic. It rests on a curiously conservative misunderstanding of the role of credit which quotes rising absolute debt totals and debt/export ratios as signs of the impending and inevitable demise of the capitalist world banking system. Monetarists are right to reject this mode of thinking, for such a vision fails to understand three simple points.

First, the absolute tenfold increase in debt over the past decade is a nominal figure only. In real terms the South's debt has probably only doubled over this period. Second, this apparently low debt exposure is not gainsaid by the high, and supposedly more threatening, debt/export ratios which debt-bomb proponents are fond of quoting. As Deepak Lal puts it 'most of these ratios are meaningless. For as long as a borrower can utilise a foreign loan productively to yield a rate of return at least equal to the real interest cost of borrowing and can convert the equivalent domestic resources into foreign exchange, the foreign borrowing can pose no problem' (Lal, 1983b, p. 18). Precisely. Debt in itself is not a bad thing. So long as it is used productively it is indeed a precondition of development and it is no coincidence that the countries most often cited as the fuses of the debt-bomb are the very ones that enjoyed the highest rates of output and export growth in the 1970s (Table 5.7). In any case, says Lal, their debt/export ratios are not high by historical standards: 'the ratio of long-term debts to exports of non-oil developing countries of 1.1 in 1982 is well below the lowest ratios of 2.2 for China and Japan in 1913 and a fraction of those for Canada and South Africa. There was little talk of a debt crisis then' (Lal, 1983b, p. 18).

TABLE 5.7 *Third World debt and development, 1970–80*

| Country | Average annual growth rates, % | | Debt service* as a percentage of: | | | |
| | Output 1970–80 | Exports 1970–80 | GNP | | Exports of goods and services | |
			1970	1980	1970	1980
Mexico	5.2	13.4	2.1	4.9	24.1	31.9
Brazil	8.4	7.5	0.9	3.4	18.9	22.9
Argentina	2.2	9.3	1.9	1.4	21.5	16.6
Venezuela	5.0	−6.7	0.7	4.9	2.9	13.2
South Korea	9.5	23.0	3.1	4.9	19.4	12.2
Chad	−0.2	−4.0	1.0	3.1	3.9	n.a.
Niger	2.7	12.8	0.6	2.2	3.8	2.3
El Salvador	4.1	1.5	0.9	1.2	3.6	3.5
Ghana	−0.1	−8.4	1.1	0.6	5.2	6.0
Ethiopia	2.0	−1.7	1.2	1.1	11.4	7.6

*Debt service is the sum of interest payments and repayments of principal on external public and publicly guaranteed medium and long-term debt.

SOURCE World Bank, *World Development Report* (1982), Tables 2, 8 & 13

Finally, it is not the case that a return to private commercial lending as the main form of North – South capital flow is 'bound' to precipitate a banking crisis. For a monetarist such a scenario is blind to the grid of inter-bank lines and central banks now in place to ward off the sort of collapse in domestic monetary supplies which we saw fifty years ago, and quite at odds with the real history of the 1930s. In Lal's judgement the defaults then 'were the result and not the cause of the Great Depression', which is to say that commercial markets were closed to Third World countries prematurely. What has happened since is that a fiction has emerged wherein:

the trauma of these defaults [has] coloured post-war views about the desirability of private flows of capital between countries. The Bretton Woods system was regarded by the then US Secretary of the Treasury . . . as the achievement of his lifelong ambition to drive the usurious moneylenders from the temple of international finance (ibid).

Perhaps so. Certainly most geographers who are prepared to forego a rather crude view of the evils of debt will recognise the merit of some of these propositions. They might even endorse Lal's conclusion that:

Much of the talk of a Third World banking crisis threatening the Western banking system is exaggerated. It stems from a misunderstanding in both North and South of the consequences of a return to private commercial lending as the main form of capital flow from rich to poor countries (Lal, 1983b, p. 18).

But does it follow from this that there is no secular, long-run malaise in the international monetary system? I think this is a more controversial claim, though it is worth stating that it is in keeping with the neo-classical view of interdependency. For Michael Beenstock:

What is going on at present is a liquidity crisis rather than a solvency crisis which is therefore likely to be a *temporary* problem. As global inflation is squeezed out of the system real interest rates will tend to abate and financial distress in the Third World will ease. At the same time global policies of *sound money* and the associated permanent reduction in world inflation will trigger a *spontaneous* economic recovery as real wages, real interest rates and real stocks of wealth and money balances revert to *normal* levels (Beenstock, 1983a, p. 23. Emphasis added).

From this it follows that it is quite wrong to combat a temporary crisis by a new round of institution building – 'nurturing a world central bank conceived in the spirit of unsound money' he says – or by strengthening IMF quotas, increasing SDR allocations to the tune of $10–12billion per year, or increasing IMF resources by

$10–11 billion dollars under the General Agreement to Borrow. That would simply fuel global inflation and signal the fact that some Northern countries are willing to be 'monetarist at home but Keynesian abroad . . . actually accepting the central thesis of Brandt' (Beenstock, 1983a, p. 23).

In fact such a fear was quite unfounded, as Professor Beenstock must have known. Most Northern governments have been at pains to disassociate themselves from the idea of a global banking crisis. Instead, they have maintained a tight-lipped silence which tells its own story: crisis, what crisis? Nor is this gainsaid by the fact of the IMF having its quotas raised by 50 per cent in 1983. This may be 50 per cent too much for Professor Beenstock but it is a long way short of an endorsement of the proposals of Brandt II. Far less does it come to terms with that Commission's underlying philosophy or analysis.

Brandt II: Common crisis Brandt's analysis opposes the monetarist interpretation at two points. First of all it joins with the debt-bomb proponents in denouncing the infelicities and imperfections of the international private capital market that is the altar of the New Right. Second, it points up the necessarily contradictory and depressive effects of pursuing monetarist policies of competitive deflation at an international level.

Private capital markets At first glance the Brandt Commission's strictures on the role of private capital are straightforward enough. It is in favour of them so long as they have the support of the international institutions and the central banks. Probe a little deeper, though, and it is clear that there is more to it than this. Because the Commissioners' view of bank-lending to sovereign countries has grown out of its reading of the past ten or so years of world economic history, it emphasises three points.

First, volatility: it is not the Commission's belief that private capital flows can or should be relied upon to provide the lion's share of development finance; still less that it should be made the *raison d'être* of a diminished role for the Bretton Woods institutions (the IMF, the IDA and the IBRD). This would quite overlook the fact that present trends to private finance are less a result of some pilgrimage back to the 'norms' of market economics than the product of the peculiar, and probably unrepeatable, circumstances that followed OPEC's distortion of economic and financial markets in 1973–4. Then, for the first time since the 1930s, the private markets were liberated to play a role in the Third World not just because certain legal restrictions were lifted (which is Lal's point), but because vast numbers of petro-dollars were flooding on to the Euromarkets from OPEC members with a limited import capacity (see Hoogvelt, 1982, pp. 46–50; and Johnson, 1983, pp. 148–9). Similarly, it would overlook the fact that the World Bank and the International Development Association are meant to serve a rather different set of clients than the private banks. Their customers are not so much the credit-worthy NICs as the low income countries at the bottom of the international league table.

Following on from this there is the question of geographical coverage, or what the Commissioners refer to as the 'herd behaviour' of those banks who followed the lead of their big brothers in lending to just a few countries; notably Brazil, Mexico, Argentina and South Korea. This might well make sense in terms of a simple supply and demand calculus (Mexico demanded $X billion so it got $X billion) but the Commissioners doubt whether the principles of 'sound finance' have been best served by a system which allocated cash as if there were no tomorrow, and which has been divorced from any manner of external control. Yet this is arguably what happened. Not only have the major banks maintained a strict security on their credit portfolios and debt exposures (from each other and from their shareholders: Rodgers, 1983) but tales abound of banks ignoring the usual checks on the securities offered by their clients. The lure of a quick profit simply proved too much. With interest rates well above the London Interbank Offered Rate (LIBOR) spread, and commissions of 0.125 per cent to be made on most deals, bankers fell over themselves to set up billion dollar loans which appeared to be not only profitable but copper-bottomed. After all they were lending to national governments. Quite. But whether the stability of the financial system has been strengthened by banks such as Citicorp and Chase Manhattan lending more than their equity value and losing their Triple-A credit ratings as a result (Palmer, 1983, p. 6) is another moot point.

Third, there is the question of short-term versus long-term debts. Here the Commissioners would point out that whilst it may be true, *pace* Lal, that the ratio of long-term debt to exports in selected Latin American countries is not high by historical standards, this is hardly the point. What matters is that the trend away from multilateral official capital flows has been paralleled by an inevitable contraction in the amortisation periods of the loans offered to the Third World. Private banks are not in the business of lending long. (Five to seven years is typical, hence the post-OPEC crisis of 1981–3.) The implications of this are twofold. First, that a serious mismatch might arise between the long-run needs of developing countries for infrastructural finance and the recycling timetables of the private markets which prefer an investment profile better suited to short-run debt-servicing capacities. (One thinks of the apparently wasteful gigantism that lies behind so much of Latin America's public debt: nuclear power plants, hotels, luxury apartment blocks and the like – Rettie, 1983.) Second, it suggests that the dependence of South upon North may be forged anew by tying the development chronologies of the former to the monetary (that is, interest-rate) rhythms of the latter.

International Monetarism   This brings us to the second, and perhaps more important, debate between Brandt and Beenstock: on the impact of international monetarism. It is the Brandt Commission's bold charge that the counter-inflationary policies now being pursued by Northern governments, far from providing the conditions of world recovery and Southern development, are actively pulling the rug from under it. They are not alone in this judgement. It is a common claim amongst Keynesian economists that even if monetarist policies make sense within individual OECD countries (which they dispute) they can be disastrous when pursued in a beggar-thy-neighbour fashion on the international stage (see Bird, 1981; Kaldor, N., 1983). This is so for two main reasons. First there is the question of recession. It seems self-evident to a non-monetarist economist that high-interest-rate policies to control the money supply restrictively in any one country – and especially the USA – must induce a copy-cat policy in the polities of its competitors, if only to safeguard their currencies against exchange rate fluctuations set in motion by capital flows to the high-interest-rate areas. Yet this must in turn set in train the sort of world slump in which we now find ourselves; with the imports of the industrial nations stagnant, with the exports of the developing countries rising at a mere 1 per cent per year (as against 8 or 9 per cent growth rates in the later 1970s), and with real commodity prices at their lowest levels for thirty years. Second, there is the question of the direct effect that high interest rates have on the repayment of Third World debt. Here the Commissioners are convinced that the present crisis has emerged because the Third World countries have been made the unwitting victims of a peculiar scissors crisis, or catch-22 (see Figure 5.1). On the one hand they have seen their export markets fall away in the wake of the OECD recession. But at the same time they have been forced to pay off a greatly increased debt-burden just as real interest rates rose from 6 per cent in 1976 to 15 per cent in early 1982, and just as the dollar (in which most of the loans are to be repaid) strengthened in the teeth of these same interest rate policies. As Jay Palmer reminds us, each 1 per cent rise in these interest rates 'added an estimated $2 billion to the developing countries' annual debt bill' (Palmer, 1983, p. 8).

The debt crisis   This is a lot of money by any standards, and it is the scale of this problem, plus the Commissioners' critique of international monetarism which has led Brandt to a rather different outlook on the present crisis from that of most neo-classical economists. The perspective of the Commission strikes a reasonable balance between millenarianism and complacency. On the one hand it points out the valuable role of the major banks in recycling the OPEC surpluses to selected (perhaps too selected) countries, but at the same time it stresses the essentially unplanned, and thus volatile, nature of this lending, and the dangers of relying on what both Beenstock and Howe take to be axiomatic: a spontaneous fall in real interest rates leading to a spontaneous world recovery. This is simply not on, say the Commissioners. Any spontaneity in the system is surely of a disequilibrating nature, with counter-inflationary policies in one part of the globe encouraging slump and protectionism elsewhere, and thus a further round of devaluation and/or higher interest rates to combat this. Indeed, for all the pieties emerging from Williamsburg about a commitment to lower interest rates, the American administration's failure to cut its record budget-deficits should (on strictly monetarist criteria) induce a fresh surge in American interest

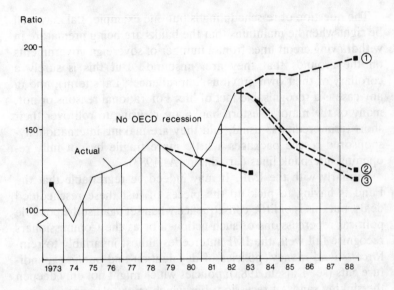

Scenarios

1. Major adjustment by borrowing countries, minimal OECD recovery
2. Partial adjustment by borrowing countries, moderate OECD recovery
3. Major adjustment by borrowing countries, moderate OECD recovery

SOURCE Morgan Guaranty (after Frances Williams)

FIGURE 5.1 *The debt/export ratios of 21 major developing country borrowers (average of beginning and end-year total debt as a percentage of exports of goods and services)*

rates, and lest this be taken as a sign that things have to get worse before they get better, let us recall that time is the essential factor in the present debt-crisis. However meaningless debt/export ratios might be in the long run, and in a boom, the fact that they are heading quickly to the 200 mark in many LDCs cannot but generate a set of economic and political problems now, as the Commissioners fully appreciate.

The question of re-scheduling is but one example. Lal may well be right when he maintains that the banks are being premature in withdrawing credit lines from a number of sovereign governments on the grounds that they are 'unsound'. But this is surely a corollary of their own previous 'imprudence' (Lal's term), and in any case is a recognisable fact of life. For rational reasons or not, many of the major Western banks are refusing to roll over their short-term credits as usual, and they are making internationally-sponsored rescue packages a little more fragile by not fully re-opening interbank lines (Friedman, A. 1983).

Similarly with the IMF. It may indeed be regrettable that the Fund is having to pick up the pieces of just these rescheduled deals, but this is of little consequence when set against the possible political repercussions of such action. For as the Commissioners recognise full well, the IMF intercedes almost invariably to reinforce 'sound money' policies of devaluation and public expenditure cuts (see Katseli, 1983); policies which might not only deepen the sinking sands of recession, but which might also provoke just that measure of political resistance ('instability': Brandt, 1983, p. 35) which monetarists rightly perceive as a threat to international recovery.

Finally, what if the worst does come to the worst? Suppose some bank from, say, the American mid-West threatens to pull down the whole interbank house of cards to teach the 'reds' or the bad-debtors a lesson. (According to one Frankfurt banker this nearly happened in 1981 when the German banks lived in fear that 'some small US bank was going to play patriot and show those Communists a thing or two by calling in their debt' – quoted in Palmer, 1983, p. 8). Or suppose that the Latin American countries collectively follow John Rettie's advice and take as their creed a bowdlerisation of Marx's famous apophthegm: debtors unite, you have nothing to lose but your interest.[38] What then? Well very likely the system would survive. As Figure 5.2 makes clear, it is stronger than some seem to think, but its stability could only be guaranteed at a price, for the precondition of saving the system in such circumstances would be nothing less than a 'tax' on Northern citizens. Again, this is hardly the ideal way to kick-start the magic circle of spontaneous growth which is so vital to the monetarist case.

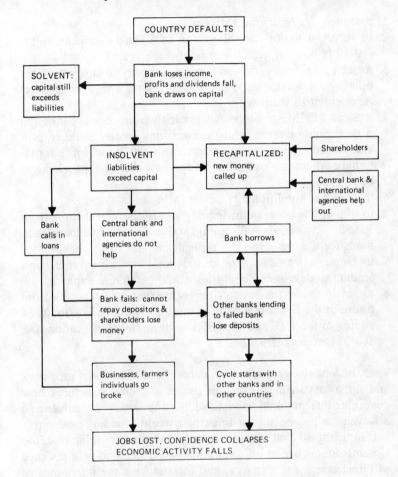

SOURCE   Michael Prest, *The Times* 3 February 1983.

FIGURE 5.2   *What happens after a default?*

Proposals For all these reasons, the Brandt Commissioners have
come to reject the fatalistic charms of monetarism, and to put
forward a set of proposals which go far beyond the anaemic
re-equipping of the IMF which took place in 1983. As far as we are
concerned, the most important of these proposals are as follows:

1. to double (at least) the IMF quotas;
2. to secure a major new allocation of Special Drawing Rights (10–12 billion per year for at least three years);
3. to set up an emergency borrowing authority to support developing countries through enlargement and reform of the General Agreement to Borrow;
4. to allow the IMF to borrow increasingly from central banks and from capital markets, whilst encouraging central banks to provide additional short-term deposits to the Bank for International Settlements so that its bridge-financing operations might be expanded;
5. to relax the conditionality of the IMF;
6. to step up the programme lending arm of the World Bank from 10 to 30 per cent of total lending, and to secure a real increase in funds for the Seventh IDA replenishment;
7. to create a framework of confidence in which private bank lending to developing countries would be able to expand;
8. to set in motion an authoritative international review of the future of the Bretton Woods institutions, with the possibility of adding to the IMF and the IBRD a third global institution, the World Development Fund.

Parboni and the geopolitics of debt   Together, these proposals add up to a stinging attack on the institutional structures now governing international finance, whilst at the same time advancing a Keynesian prospectus for reflating a world economy in slump.[39] It is in this spirit that I would commend them. If nothing else, the Commissioners are to be congratulated for demanding a package of direct action for recovery, and for attacking the impotence of the free-market Friedmanites (Beenstock's cries of 'gloomy economics' and 'global *dirigisme*' notwithstanding).

However global *dirigisme* depends on global goodwill and it is on this more practical issue that I think the Commissioners' programme falls down. Their prospectus amounts to (another) call for the governments of the North to see sense and to join together in collective action against the 'common crisis'. At no point do they suspend their belief, common to 'most observers of the international economy . . . that the real role of governments, codified in the Keynesian stereotypes, has been tirelessly to defend the mechanisms that safeguard the harmony of international relations' (Parboni, 1981, p. 88). Nor do they consider that:

the crisis may not be the result of so-called objective factors [at all] but is fundamentally the fruit of a grand inter-imperialist conflict the stakes of which is the global redivision of economic and political power between the USA on the one hand and the major powers of the second world – Germany and Japan – on the other (Parboni, 1981, p. 118).

Perhaps this is to be expected, but it is in marked contrast to the more challenging thesis of Parboni's *The Dollar and Its Rivals* (see also Aglietta, 1982). For here is a text which not only faces up to current realities (the Cancun failure, the rise of protectionism, US–European conflicts on East–West trade, US opposition to any decline in the dollar standard and so on) but does so in a way which eschews both the charges of irrationality that course through the Brandt reports (see Corbridge, 1982b) and the stereotypes of American malevolence so often found on the Left. Instead it makes use of a carefully crafted argument to ground a polemic on inter-imperialism in the changing contours of one key geopolitical fact: the unrivalled ability of post-war US governments to ward off the long-run decline of their economy by resort to devaluation and the extraction of financial seignorage.

Let me elaborate on this, because it is still not a common claim in geography. For Parboni, it is a truism that the USA has long opposed the philosophy of 'concerted action' which once presidential advisor, Feldstein (1983), believes to be at the core of international Keynesianism. Keynes himself may have been the first to feel this chill wind when his plans for an international bank with the power to issue notes crumbled in the face of a US-sponsored IMF which would do no more than intervene in foreign exchange and balance-of-payments problems, but he was by no means the last. Throughout the 1950s and 1960s the USA opposed the introduction of the SDR, and even today, when a miserly allocation of SDRs points fleetingly to the future, the USA clings to the hope that its protégé might remain in the mould of its now defunct antecedents: the British Exchange Equalisation Fund and the American Stabilisation Fund (see Harrod, 1972, p. 639).

Why should the USA take this 'negative' stance (Brandt, 1983, p. 34)? This is a question that is less often asked and it is here that Parboni's geopolitics come into their own. In essence his argument runs like this. Consider the position of the US economy at the end of the Second World War, he says. Undoubtedly this was then at a peak, with its 62 per cent share of world manufacturing output presaging nothing except a period of relative decline.[40] The question then is what could the USA do to stave off this decline. One option open to it would be to ensure that investment and accumulation rates within the USA stayed ahead of its emergent competitors, but given the post-war propensity of US capital to flow out of the country this presupposed an unlikely degree of economic planning. Then again, it could act to make domestic investment more profitable by attacking the power of organised labour, but this too raised the prospect of unwelcome political opposition. However there was a third option, an international option. By making use of the relatively closed nature of the US economy (its import/GNP ratio of 0.15 is less than half that of its European rivals) the USA could hope to undercut its competitors by a policy of persistent dollar devaluation. This would induce only a limited degree of inflation at home and could be secured by running up huge balance-of-payments deficits worldwide, and simply printing dollars to cover them. The only conditions for such action were as follows. First, it presupposed that the USA would act to defend the hegemonic position of the dollar as the world's generally accepted reserve currency; which it did. (The reason for this is that countries would only allow the USA to build up balance-of-payments deficits against them so long as the dollar 'alone' could be used by central banks to settle accounts and intervene in foreign exchange markets, and by private firms to conduct international trade: see Frieden, 1983.) Second, it presupposed that the USA would if necessary break its Bretton Woods commitments to maintain the value of the dollar at a nominal fixed exchange rate, and to maintain its convertibility into gold. This latter agreement was critical because the threat of a rush into gold cautioned US governments against excessive dollar devaluations (see also Argy, 1981, Part 1).

Of course what I have outlined here are only the parameters of US financial action. Parboni is not claiming that, in practice, the USA has maintained a bullish monetary policy since 1945. Not at all. Throughout the 1950s US economic supremacy was so assured that its government was content to present itself as a benevolent despot, providing 'the world with the "collective blessing" of economic stability while extracting no direct advantages for its own economy' (Parboni, 1981, p. 50). To this end it not only used its own trade surpluses and ability to issue international reserve money to 'finance the accumulation of reserves by the rest of the world through . . . aid and military assistance' (Parboni, 1981, p. 49). It also allowed its economic partners to 'devalue their own money relative to the dollar and to maintain discriminatory practices against American goods for long periods' (ibid). Throughout this period the interest of the USA was not in extracting direct advantage, but in attaining 'indirect gains such as those produced by the general political reinforcement of the Western world made possible by the post-war economic boom and the development of trade on a grand scale' (ibid, p. 50).

The 1960s are another matter, for then the USA's economy began to come under pressure from its erstwhile satellites, Germany and Japan. With these two countries biting into its export markets and surpassing its rate of fixed capital formation and productivity growth (see Table 5.8), the USA was forced to run up balance-of-payments deficits just to pay its way (and to sustain the Vietnam offensive). This induced precisely those pressures that it wished to avoid: a movement into gold, and demands for new international forms of credit.

Clearly something had to give way, and on 15 August 1971 President Nixon unilaterally withdrew the USA from its Bretton Woods commitment to maintain the convertibility of the dollar into gold. According to Parboni the significance of this one event cannot be overstated. Henceforth the USA would not use its reserve currency position for the general good, but would instead 'unhesitatingly pursue its own national interest and [so] become the principal source of perturbation of the international economy' (Parboni, 1981, p. 50).

This worked in two ways. First, by escaping the trap of gold convertibility, the USA was free to 'finance its own deficits with payments in its own currency, without having to resort to financial assets abroad previously accumulated through foreign surpluses' (ibid, p. 41). This it did. Between 1970 and 1978 the USA ran up a current account deficit of more than $30 billion, an act no other country could even imagine and one bound to accelerate the international transmission of inflation already under way when OPEC put up its prices in 1973–4 (see Table 5.9). Indeed it is Parboni's belief that the mid-1970s rise in raw material prices was largely made possible by the USA's ability to import oil and other

TABLE 5.8   *The relative decline of the United States economy,*
            1950–77

(a) *Annual growth rates of industrial productivity, 1950–76 (in %)*

USA	2.8
Japan	8.3
France	5.0
Germany	5.4
Italy	4.3
Great Britain	2.6

(b) *Annual growth rates of total fixed capital stock excluding*
    housing, 1950–77 (average of stocks, net and gross, in %)

	1950–70	1971–7
USA	3.8	3.0
Japan	8.8	7.9
France	5.4	6.3
Germany	6.2	4.8
Italy	5.1*	5.0*
Great Britain	3.9	3.7

*net stock only

(c) *Evolution of shares of world exports in manufactures (in %)*

	1956	1970	1976
USA	25.5	18.5	17.3
Japan	5.7	11.7	14.6
France	7.9	8.7	9.8
Germany	16.5	19.8	20.6
Italy	3.6	7.2	7.1
Great Britain	18.7	10.8	8.7

SOURCE Parboni (1981) *The Dollar and Its Rivals*, p93.

commodities at will, by printing more dollars. In his own words 'The ease with which the United States is able to appropriate foreign resources makes a serious policy of energy saving and increases in domestic oil production much less compelling' (Parboni, 1981, p. 52).

TABLE 5.9 *Evolution of some items of the United States balance of payments (in thousands of millions of dollars)*

	(1)	(2)	(3)	(4)
1960–9	+23.3	+41.2	−23.7	+15.5
1970	+0.4	+2.2	−4.2	−7.4
1971	−2.8	−2.7	−4.9	−9.0
1972	−7.9	−6.8	−3.1	+2.2
1973	+0.4	+0.5	−2.3	−0.7
1974	−3.3	−5.3	−5.3	−1.9
1975	+11.9	+9.0	−4.8	−8.4
1976	−1.4	−9.3	−2.4	−6.9
1977	−15.2*	−31.2	−3.5	−4.2
1978	−15.9*	−34.1	−4.0	−16.6
Total	−33.8	−70.2	−34.5	−52.9

(1) Current account balance
(2) Balance of trade (f.o.b.)
(3) Balance of direct investment, of the USA abroad and of foreign investment in the USA, net of disinvestment and reinvestment of earnings
(4) Variation of the net position abroad of credit agencies
*As of 1977 the current account includes earnings of direct foreign investment that are re-invested; the unfavourable current account balance is correspondingly diminished.
SOURCE Parboni (1981) *The Dollar and Its Rivals*, Table 2.

At the same time this resort to international deficit financing allowed the Americans to push through a persistent devaluation of the dollar. (This is the second aspect to dollar 'seignorage'). The main purpose of this was to restore US competitiveness, but its unintended(?) effect was to induce the European economic stagnation of the late 1970s (and indirectly the world slump and international debt crisis of the 1980s). This is so because Germany's response to the increased US competition that ensued was to step up its export drive by extending cheap credits to potential customers and by improving the technological quality of German manufactured goods. Both prongs of Germany's export strategy – cheap credits and industrial restructuring – required domestic deflation. Thus 'In order to maintain international competitiveness, Germany is then forced into domestic recession and, because the rest of Europe is dependent on German orders, Europe is forced into recession along with Germany' (Frieden, 1983, p. 92).[41]

In one way or another, then, the recent financial strategy of the USA has not been a happy one.[42] Outside its shores it has created frightening bouts of both inflation and recession, and when set alongside the German dominance of the European Monetary System it has allowed just two major powers to dictate economic circumstances to the rest of the world, often against their best interests. As ever, Parboni sums this up best. In a polemical passage that is worth quoting at some length, and in preference to further consideration of his more technical points, he argues that:

> Here again the preponderance of imperialist interests at the expense of weak countries is evident. The United States and Germany agree in rejecting any enlargement of official financial mechanisms [cf. Brandt] which would enable the weak countries to deal more effectively with potential problems related to their concession of credit to newly industrialising countries in order to sell their complex products, or would enable the new countries to go into debt more independently and to select their own suppliers of financing. The various plans to increase official international liquidity have been systematically sabotaged – or in the best of cases sharply reduced in scope – by joint action by the United States and Germany . . . The United States and Germany, in conflict over the maintenance of industrial and technological leadership, join together in the commercial exploitation of the rest of the world (Parboni, 1981, p. 138).

Implications   Of course it may be objected that this is past history and that since President Reagan came to power there has been such a sea-change in US financial affairs that Parboni's thesis is now out of touch. After all, the *direct* roots of the present debt crisis are surely to be found in the strong dollar policies of the current US administration and not in the weak dollar era that preceded them.[43]

Maybe so, but in a sense this misses the point, or so I would urge by way of conclusion. For one thing it is not apparent that recent events are inconsistent with Parboni's thesis. On the contrary, he would maintain that the 'monetarist' about-turn of the later Carter and early Reagan Presidencies (it is not a matter of personalities) is very much a product of the long-term contradictions of the weak-dollar decade of the 1970s. In effect it was forced upon the Americans by the severe crisis of confidence which shook the dollar in 1978. By this time quite reasonable fears were springing up in the financial community that the strategy of dollar devaluation was promoting a degree of international inflation that made another wave of raw materials price rises inevitable, and it was this that demanded a movement into the mark, yen, Swiss franc or pound simply to preserve the value of long-term assets. As Parboni puts it:

> Under the pressure of both the internal financial establishment and the monetary authorities of other countries (especially Germany), and terrified of an influx of funds to the US market and of the threatened rise in raw materials prices, the Carter administration finally decided, in November 1978, to stabilise the dollar, primarily through credit measures (Parboni, 1981, p. 15).

Just as crucially, though, this objection fails to understand the true purpose of *The Dollar and Its Rivals*. As I read it, this is not to provide predictions on this or that short-run scenario; though Parboni is not averse to the odd moment of speculation. (See, for example, his claim that the strong-dollar era will be shortlived because it 'has more drawbacks than advantages for the US economy. It does help to reduce inflation . . . but it also debilitates America's industrial structure and undermines its competitive position' (Parboni, 1983, p. 95). Rather it is Parboni's intention to provide us with an empirically consistent interpretation of the present crisis which has as its core what I would call a 'geopolitical economy'. This consists of a number of interlocking propositions, as we have seen, but the demands it makes of future geographies fall under two main headings. First, it asks us to begin our accounts of development or of crisis by deconstructing the received categories of North and South or core and periphery. By all means let us acknowledge that national economic actions are constrained – especially in the South, and especially in the UK, the centre of transnational finance capital – but let us recognise also that there are still inter-regional rivalries shaping the (Northern) world economy and conditioning many responses to the North–South issue. These rivalries may yet make a space for more effective Southern political action. Second, it enjoins us to put particular emphasis upon the geopolitical strategy of the USA as a long-run determinant of global development and perturbation. The USA is not just another core power. It is a threatened giant with unrivalled capacities for autonomous (and often aggressive) economic and political actions.

5.4   Conclusions

As ever there is a long way to go. This chapter may have given the impression that US economic and foreign policies are in some sense expressive of a political consensus in that country. In reality things are a good deal more complicated, as my own admonition of Brandt would lead one to expect. A more sensitive analysis of US foreign policy than that of Parboni would pay attention to those changing self-perceptions of the USA's role in the world system so admirably mapped out by Henrikson (1980). It would also acknowledge the shifting and rather curious textures of US policy-making which have taken that country from what Fred Halliday (1983) calls Cold War I to Cold War II. Of critical importance here is the ongoing debate between the isolationism still maintained by many US conservatives (and evident in a continuing distrust of 'soft' Europe and Europeans) and the more outward-looking strategies of global containment and managerialism pioneered by the likes of MacArthur and Rockefeller respectively.[44]

For all that there are still some positive signs. In political geography pre-eminently, there is an increasing mistrust of the more simplistic centre–periphery models still widely favoured in economic geography. Saul Cohen's work comes to mind as a case in point. He has substantially revised his earlier work on *Geography and Politics in a World Divided* (1973) to map out a new account of 'Global Geopolitical Equilibrium'. The basis of the new equilibrium, Cohen suggests, will be found in the resolution of the current conflict between globalism and regionalism. Cohen adopts the framework of general systems theory to argue that all organisms, and this includes the world system, must proceed from an undifferentiated state through differentiation and then specialisation and on to hierarchical integration. In his view we are now entering this final phase as industrialisation begins to secure the rise of such second level regional powers (his model has five levels) as Egypt, Brazil, Nigeria and Saudi Arabia. As a result of 'their new found strength [he says] second order powers have narrowed the political gap between themselves and the major powers' (Cohen, 1982, p. 228). More crucially, they have helped to fill the gaps which previously allowed the five premier powers (the USA, USSR, EEC, Japan and China) an unlimited and aggressive global reach. Much like the more radical sub-imperialism models proposed by Galtung (1976) and Gibson and Horvarth (1983), Cohen foresees a future of growing complexity in which 'the South or the Developing World is not a unified entity' (Cohen, 1982, p. 239), and in which 'policy-makers must deal with states in accordance with their appropriate levels of power, if restoration of international equilibrium is to be achieved' (ibid, p. 230).

In my view this latter sentiment comes perilously close to an endorsement of a spheres of influence and balance of terror model of world geopolitics, and I would want to resist both its moral underpinnings and its rather too harmonious vision of the future. Such a vision is clearly at odds with the less optimistic, Parbonistyle, geopolitical economy for which I have already expressed a preference. Nevertheless, Cohen's work has the signal value of resisting the simplisticism of North and South. Like his colleague Agnew (1983), Cohen recognises the dangers of an 'exceptionalist' American foreign policy, and he is sensitive to the new constraints and opportunities that have emerged in a world system still coming to terms with a declining US hegemony, with an expanding socialist bloc, and with the disintegration of a uniformly weak South.

To this extent, too, these are pieces of work which sit comfortably with the general tenor of this chapter. The thrust of Cohen's work (or Agnew's or Gottman's, 1980) is clearly not to deny the relevance of a centre–periphery perspective *per se*. Nor is it my intention to gloss over the very real hostilities that the South will continue to face in any grandiose North–South forums (or, indeed, on any occasion when their policies, individually or collectively, conflict with the geopolitical imperatives of one or more of the trilateral powers). Our aim, I think, is an end to needless didacticism. For us, as for Paul Claval, speaking of the 'economic field' and of North and South:

> The opposition of the centre and periphery seems to belong more to the category of expressive images than to that of coherent theories. Many spatial mechanisms of power show a tension between the margins and the heart of the system, but to lead everything back to that dialectic is unrealistic; it risks hiding the deeper causes of the lack of balance in the modern world (Claval, 1980, p. 70).

As capitalism continues to change its spots, to push and probe into new industries and new countries, this will be ever more the case. On the one hand developments will ensure that no one country is able to exist in a vacuum unpressured by the actions of its rivals and allies. The increasing transnationalisation of industry and finance will see to that. At the same time, this very transition, together with an associated growth in telecommunications, will ensure that the world system does not remain frozen forever into a fixed set of spatial haves and have-nots. As new lines of political action are opened up, including those forced on nation-states by transnationalisation, so the central truth of capitalist development will be confirmed; the world system does not just persist, it changes.[45]

6
Conclusion

'The world system does not just persist, it changes': the truth of this statement should be so obvious as to require no special pleading. Sadly, though, this is not always the case. This review of radical development geography has identified a sub-discipline poised uncertainly between two different intellectual traditions. On the one hand lies the path of dogma and determinism (wherein capitalism and its laws of motion are assumed to remain essentially unchanged in time and space). On the other hand lies the path of critical engagement (wherein the emphasis is upon capitalism's temporal and spatial variation and its conditions of existence). Quite which tradition will prevail is not yet clear, as there are pointers in both directions.[1] At stake, though, are two issues of real importance; two issues which have run throughout this book and to which I must return in this conclusion.

The first issue concerns the way in which geographers theorise time and space in their accounts of differential development. For too long radical development geography has preoccupied itself with models of the capitalist world system which assign no more than a formal role to time and space. This is especially true of the work of the neo-Marxists. For the followers of Frank and Wallerstein capitalism has been 'essentially' the same since the sixteenth and seventeenth centuries, and it remains 'essentially' the same in the highlands of New Guinea, in the latifundia of South America, in the newly industrialising countries of South-east Asia and in the urban societies of Europe and North America. A somewhat modified formalism is evident, too, in the accounts of structural Marxism. Rey, in particular, advances a three-stage model of capitalist and pre-capitalist articulation in which the periphery gradually gives up its character to the core (see section 2.4). More recently, this tradition has been continued by David Harvey. Harvey's remarkable work on *The Limits to Capital* (1982) depends upon a model of capitalist crisis management which sees in time and space two 'fixes' to capitalism's unyielding crisis of over-accumulation.[2] To recapitulate: Harvey sees in the credit system a 'prospect of spreading fixed capital costs over more than one cycle of production and thus of attenuating the imbalance between Department 1 and Department 2 which results from capitalist competition' (as summarised by Kearns, 1984, p. 413). When this temporal fix comes undone – because of the loss of confidence it occasions in the value of money – capitalism turns to the spatial fix of imperialism. Following Lenin, Harvey argues that imperialism presents new opportunities for the restoration of profits, but only for a short while. Harvey concludes that imperialism must finally bring the capitalist system to world war, and probable nuclear Armageddon, as the imperialist countries fight one another for a diminishing supply of virgin lands.

This sort of determinism is not at all what I have in mind when I talk of time, space and conditions of existence. Harvey's account not only fails to explain why the spatial fix is more important than other fixes (devaluation, for example, or cartelisation) but it also fails to specify how the systemic requirements of capitalism are to be identified by agents capable of pandering to them. This returns us to the old problem of structural causality (see Chapter 1). As Kearns points out 'This is not just a question of inserting a theory of the state, an omission Harvey concedes, [it] involves an explicit consideration of a range of agents from the joint-stock companies to the World Bank' (Kearns, 1984, p. 413). Amongst these agents I would include the environment, the transnational corporations and the nation-state; the point being that an account of the changing dynamics of the modern world system must have recourse to a range of 'explanatory variables' which occupies a middle-level between capitalism-in-general and the individual and his or her class. If we are really to grasp the fundamentally different impact that the capitalist world system has had on (say) Brazil and Taiwan, then we must have done with models of capitalist development which oppose a fixed core and a fixed periphery (neo-Marxism) or which theorise the Third World in terms of the needs ('fixes') of the imperialist powers alone (structural Marxism). More positively, our accounts of differential development must recognise that the dynamics of a changing capitalist world economy are always mediated by conditions of existence (population growth rates, gender relations, state policies and so on) which vary in space and time and which are not directly at the beck and call of a grand 'world system'. This, I trust, is the message of Chapters 3, 4, and 5.

The second issue is scarcely less important for it concerns the conduct of academic debate. Throughout this book I have had cause to comment on an attitude of 'us and them' which pervades some parts of radical development studies. In Chapter 3 this penchant for confrontation was evident in the arena of demography, in Chapter 4 it surrounded the 'facts' of industrialisation, and in Chapter 5 it was apparent in the North–South controversy. The point I wish to make here is the simple one that radical development geography has nothing to gain from such an attitude. To suppose that one can defend a shaky argument on epistemological grounds is self-deluding. Worse than this it is self-defeating. If radical development geography is to claim the future which is surely its own, it must begin to take seriously the arguments of those who are not immediately drawn to its conclusions.

Notes

1 Introduction

1. Clearly there are other propositions that one can think of: notably on the erosion of national sovereignty and on the commercialisation of Third World agriculture. The concept of a paradigm is used throughout as a convenient shorthand; it does not imply any endorsement of Kuhn's vision of scientific changes.
2. Content analysis, of course, is a crude way of measuring academic fashions: it takes no account of column inches or of changes in editorial policy and it says nothing about citation structures (as a proxy for 'impact' or 'importance'). Nevertheless, an increased interest in economic development issues is surely evident and it is all the more remarkable for occurring at a time when human geography journals are multiplying apace. (On this 'explosion of specialisms' see Johnston, 1979, and Munton and Goudie, 1984).
3. I say 'renaissance' because a concern for 'things foreign' has always existed in geography. One suspects that if Keeble had considered the immediate post-war, or even inter-war, period he would have uncovered a vast literature on economic or 'colonial' development. See, for example, Fairgreave (1932), Gilbert and Steel (1945) and Church (1948). See also Farmer's (1983a) recent review paper. The saddening thing is that geography is today becoming more parochial and more insular. Although development geography has 'come of age' the number of research students now working on these issues is declining. (On this, and on policies towards research funding, see Thrift, 1985).
4. Rostow (1960), Hirschman (1958), Hoselitz (ed.) (1960), North (1961).
5. The importance of radical development geography may be understated here by the absence of articles published in Antipode.
6. Because this book is about the assumptions and procedures underlying radical development geography *specifically*, I do not discuss geography's long and honourable tradition of 'environmental–area'' studies. As far as personal prejudices are concerned, it will become clear that my own hopes for future development geography lie very much with a theoretically informed, empirical 'field' geography. My own preferences are for the sort of geography pioneered by Forde (1948) and Farmer (1957, 1977) – amongst others – and now being

refashioned by scholars including Bayliss-Smith (1982), Bayliss-Smith and Wanmali (eds) (1984), Carlstein (1982), Harriss, B. (1984) and Harriss, J. (1981).

7. Major textbooks disavowing the diffusionist paradigm include Brookfield (1975), Buchanan (1972), De Souza and Foust (1979) and Mabogunje (1980). More recent additions include Harvey (1982), Smith, N. (1984) and Forbes (1984). Unfortunately, Forbes's book only became available to the author after the completion of the manuscript. I must record here my broad agreement with the book's thesis and with its well-placed critique of articulation theory. If I have a criticism of Forbes's book it is that it still considers 'class' and 'relations of production' to the exclusion of their conditions of existence. This lack of balance (as I see it) is then written into the short empirical chapters that comprise Part III of Forbes's text.

8. Obviously there are exceptions: see Abumere (1979), Chisholm (1982).

9. A not-dissimilar logic is evident in the work of the most recent *dependencia* theorists: see Palma (1978). Palma uses the term *dependencia* to embrace three related traditions: the theory of underdevelopment school associated with Frank; the 'obstacles to development' group led by Sunkel; and the dependency-as-method school linked with Cardoso.

10. Perhaps a glossary would be useful here! Although I have labelled this second failing 'determinism' it should be obvious that this sin could be described in a number of different ways, for its consequences are indeed wide. In particular, the determinism associated with a rationalist version of structural Marxism is marked by a necessary *teleology* (the idea of self-reproduction) and by a stark *essentialism* (the concept of totality is employed in such a way that capitalism-in-general is made into an all-embracing entity to which a whole series of secondary effects – maybe cultural or environmental–demographic – must be referred back). In the latter context the phrase 'determinant in the last instance' is especially compelling and I would join a number of colleagues in arguing for a less structural type of 'Marxism' than this. See Duncan and Ley (1982) and Gregory (1978, 1981).

11. Auty (1979), Worsley (1979). The 'Third World', the 'South', the 'periphery' and the 'underdeveloped world' are used interchangeably in this text.

12. See Chisholm (1982, especially Chapter 3), Swindell (1979) and Cole (1981) for three very different, but all at times acerbic, appreciations. On Hindess and Hirst's (arguably) narrow conception of epistemology see Thompson (1984).

13. See note 10.

14. Corbridge (1982).

15. For a critical review of the major urban issues see Gilbert and Gugler (1981). On capitalism and peasant farming see Goodman and Redclift (1981). This text reveals the huge extent of this one field.

16. As a review paper, not as a comprehensive review of the literature.

2   Capitalism, development and underdevelopment

1. Dos Santos (1973), for example, and Furtado (1963). This book is concerned mainly with Anglo-Saxon radical development studies. In the work of French geographers the theories of Samir Amin looms large. My own view of Amin (1976, 1977) is in line with that of Henry Bernstein who has argued that Amin's theoretical efforts are 'a compendium of virtually every proposition ever advanced by under-development theory, assembled in a chaotic manner' (Bernstein, 1979, p. 84). Hence Amin's absence here: see also Smith, S. (1981).
2. That is, the extraction of surplus value by continuous technological change and improvement.
3. See Palma (1978).
4. Baran defines the actual economic surplus as the difference 'between society's actual current output and its actual current consumption' (Baran, 1973, p. 132). The potential economic surplus is defined as the 'difference between the output that could be produced in a given natural and technical environment with the help of employable pro-ductive resources and what might be regarded as essential consump-tion' (ibid, p. 133).
5. Like Baran I am overlooking the exploitation and immiserisation that was one complement of this competitive 'golden age'. In Baran's work this oversight is symptomatic of the author's concern with the 'rational use of a surplus' rather than with the class-basis of its production.
6. Baran's work may best be seen as 'radical Keynesian'. Although *The Political Economy of Growth* developed out of a series of lectures delivered at Oxford University in 1955, it is clear that Baran's debt is to what he calls his Cambridge friends, notably Joan Robinson and Michael Kalecki.
7. Note, however, that Baran talks of the already 'highly developed capitalist West'.
8. Emmanuel (1972). This thesis is ably criticised by Bettelheim (1972), Kay (1975) and Pilling (1973). On its problematic determination of international prices see also Brewer (1980), chapter 9.
9. I say 'remembered heroes' because Paul Baran's work is absent from the bibliographies of most development geography textbooks: from Chisholm (1982), from Mabogunje (1980), from Dickenson *et al.* (1983), even from Brookfield (1975).
10. This is Frank's dedication of *Capitalism and Underdevelopment in Latin America* (1967).
11. ECLA refers to the United Nations Economic Commission for Latin America. Its leading light was Prebisch, a sort of 1950s international Keynesian who offered a powerful critique of conventional interna-tional trade theory. In essence, he argued that comparative advantage theory legitimised the perpetual under-industrialisation of the per-iphery because it ignored the fact that factor markets, being more oligopolistic in the core, were sponsoring a long-run terms of trade

decline in the Third World. The solution proposed by ECLA was protected import-substitution. (This has since been revised).

12. The feudal–imperialist alliance defines the major Latin American landowners and the metropolitan bourgeoisie.

13. Based on Taylor, J. (1979) p. 85.

14. A fourth system would/will be a 'socialist world economy'.

15. Spain, for example, was a core country but it is now in the semi-periphery. Russia (or the Soviet Union) has moved the other way: from the semi-periphery to the core. In a recent text Wallerstein has expanded upon these movements in an illuminating way. Instead of welcoming such mobility as a sign that development is possible within a capitalist world system, Wallerstein suggests that this 'game of geographical musical chairs' [*sic*] only occludes the continuing stratification which characterises 'the world system' (Wallerstein, 1984, p. 9). This is like telling a fan of Aston Villa that it matters not at all whether his team finishes first or twenty-second in the English First Division; what matters is that there are always eleven teams in the top half of the table and eleven teams in the bottom half!

16. This argument demands to be taken seriously. Marx's definitions are not sacred and if the Wallerstein approach helps us to determine more accurately Third World pasts and futures so much the better. The problem is that it does not. I shall argue later that Wallerstein's account actually prevents a sensitive empirical and political analysis of particular Third World countries and classes. It may also be instructive that Wallerstein puts the term 'the relations of production' in quotation marks.

17. The phrase is Agnew's (1982). I should point out that Agnew himself is critical of this attempt to 'sociologise the geographical imagination by turning spatial categories into causes' (Agnew, 1982, p. 159).

18. See also Palma (1978 p. 903), who talks of Frank's mechanico-formal method.

19. That is, derived from the logic of Adam Smith's *The Wealth of Nations*.

20. To be fair, Wallerstein tried to head off this criticism, which had previously been put to Frank, by suggesting that the difference 'between the gleb serf of the Middle-Ages [pre-capitalist] and the slave or worker on an *encomienda* in sixteenth century Hispanic America [capitalist] . . .was threefold: the difference between assigning 'part' of the surplus to a market and assigning 'most of the surplus'; the difference between production for a local market and a world market; the difference between the exploiting classes spending the profits, and being motivated to maximise them and partially reinvest them' (Wallerstein, 1974, p. 126). It will be clear that I do not accept this suggestion. This is not because Wallerstein is being 'un-Marxist' – whatever that might mean – but because he is being imprecise. Though ingenious, Wallerstein's part of/most of distinctions do not allow for a careful theorisation of capitalist development. See also Culley, 1977.

21. Nor has he changed his mind: see Frank (1983) for a deeply pessimistic view of 'autonomous socialism'.
22. Smith, T. C. (1957). See also Nakamura (1966) and Halliday, J. (1975).
23. Bill Warren's (1980) optimistic views on peripheral industrialisation are discussed in Chapter 4.
24. I nearly said 'teleology' until I re-read Mouzelis' careful discussion: Mouzelis (1980).
25. That is, concentrated and centralised.
26. Which they are not: see Marx (1976, chapters 17 and 25).
27. See Chapter 4.
28. Classical and neo-Marxism come closest to a meeting of minds with Luxemburg and Baran.
29. See Harriss, J. (1980), Bernstein (1977) and Palma (1978) respectively.
30. This is a contentious point: see Terray (1972) and Hindess and Hirst (1975).
31. Note that a slave under the lineage system had a number of rights and expectations that he would not have under merchant capitalism : Rey (1971).
32. The vagueness of the terminology here is instructive.
33. See Foster-Carter (1978).
34. Note that Frank and Wallerstein also emphasise a concern for totalities. Wallerstein says: 'I am not calling for a multidisciplinary approach to the study of social systems, but for a unidisciplinary approach' (Wallerstein, 1974, p. 11).
35. That is, a notion of relative autonomy which means just that (in formal, grammatical terms); not a concept loaded with ideas of structural causality.
36. I am not sure where one draws the line when defining Marxism, nor if it matters.
37. Thus, whilst it is sobering to reflect on the Chilean tragedy, and on US intervention in El Salvador and Nicaragua, it is also worth reminding ourselves of the Cuban experience, and of the historical victory of Haiti's 'Black Jacobins' (James, 1980).

3   Capitalism, determinism and development

1. See Malthus (1970), chapter 5. Malthus later modified his views in his essay of 1803. I am not concerned with this change of heart here: for informative discussions see Woods (1982), Glacken (1967).
2. See Horvarth (1974).
3. Rightly, too, given the propensity of some theorists to engage in so-called 'lifeboat ethics' [sic], or the idea that some one-third of the world must be left to die in order that the other two-thirds may live. See Hardin (1968) for such a view, and Poleman (1977) for a scathing critique.

4. Malthus (1970), chapters 8–12.
5. See Gregory (1980) for an incisive critique of the politics implicit in such a technocratically conceived systems theory. Miles and Irvine (1979) make a similar point in a more detailed discussion of the Limits to Growth (1972).
6. This is not (or should not be) an invitation to relativism. One can still accept or reject an argument in terms of its internal consistency. This can include the way in which a discourse handles and transforms data sets.
7. On reflection 'Malthusian' may be the wrong label for Lord Anti-Aid, as he has recently been dubbed by the Observer (April 1984). Re-reading Bauer (1976) I am inclined to see him as a polemicist both for *laissez-faire* economics (in countries like Taiwan and South Korea) and for a rather crude version of environmental determinism whereby many African and South Asian countries are written off as tempera-mentally ill-suited to development because of an adverse climate. A social Darwinian, free-market Malthusian perhaps? (On Bauer's 'dis-paraging of development economics', see Toye, 1983).
8. When pressed by Sir Bernard Braine, who challenged him over the fact of population control in Asiatic Japan, Bell responded by saying that this was an exception. Moreover, whilst population control may possibly occur elsewhere in the distant future, 'meanwhile the sugges-tion is that the people of the temperate zone have a moral responsi-bility to feed and to keep alive an increase in 2500 million in the next twenty years in the tropical and equatorial regions. These are the considerations that underlie the Brandt report. My complaint about it is not its lack of good intentions, but that it has not faced the implications of what it proposes, but has taken refuge behind fashion-able phrases that are too glibly exchanged among pseudo-liberals in all parts of politics and in all parts of the western world' (Hansard, 16 June 1980, vol. 986 [192/3], col. 1268).
9. Later in his life Mao embraced official birth control programmes with some vigour. By 'early Maoist' I am referring to the Mao of the Cultural Revolution. At this time high population growth rates were positively encouraged: Yuan-Tien (1980).
10. See Hindess and Hirst (1977), ch. 1. It follows that one cannot ignore someone's findings simply because they claim to have produced them under such-and-such a rubric.
11. A minor irony here is that Harvey's latest book, *The Limits to Capital* (1982), attacks Cutler *et al.* for this very sin. Writing about the term 'mode of production' Harvey contends that the 'debate has gone from the unnecessarily obscure and difficult . . .to the ridiculous . . .and [has] reached its nadir of self-destructiveness in the work of Hindess and Hirst (1977) and Cutler *et al.* (1978)' (Harvey, 1982, p. 25). It is a common mistake on the Left to assume that these two later texts are without empirical and political significance and that they adopt the sterile logic of Hindess and Hirst (1975).
12. Elvin's use of the phrase is not to be confused with that of Clifford

Geertz whose book on *Agricultural Involution* (1963) is still a landmark in social scientific discussions of the relationship between colonialism, demography and the environment. Unlike Elvin, Geertz
focuses on the particular relations of production characteristic of a
given social information (Indonesia).

13. Elvin also suggests that the Chinese Communist Party was wrong to
blame the 'feudal–imperialist' alliance for the state of the country
they took over in 1949. By implication too he is critical of Maoist
policies of land redistribution since 1949. For a rather different view
of life in 1930s China, see Tawney (1966) and Ch'en (1936).

14. Defined in true Paul Baran style as 'the potential surplus above mass
consumption', but given the support of a fairly extensive empirical
presentation.

15. Marx (1976), ch. 32.

16. Unless one follows Fanon's line on the lumpenproletariat leading the
revolution in the Third World: Fanon (1967).

17. See Ratcliffe (1978) for a restatement of the Mamdani thesis.

18. See Hansard 986 (192/3).

19. Crude sociobiology only: Hirst and Woolley (1982) are right to attack
the knee-jerk Leftism which rejects all sociobiology as racist. 'While
holding no brief for the main substance of Wilson's theory [E.O.
Wilson's *Sociobiology*, 1975, a flawed but not unsophisticated text],
and being equally appalled by his numerous gaffes when it comes to
discussing human social relations in what are virtually no more than
casual asides, it is not clear in some of these [radical] ripostes how *any*
attempt to account for significant human attributes or behaviours in
terms of genetic transmissions or in terms of natural selection, could
ever be other than a neo-fascist ideological onslaught' (Hirst and
Woolley, 1982, p. 71. Emphasis in the original. See also the final
section of this chapter).

20. Kropotkin (1902). See also Galois (1976) and Breitbart (1981).

21. The phrase is Schmidt's (1971). The critique I shall develop of radical
development theory's anti-environmentalism is not, of course, to be
confused with the very penetrating work now being done by some
'Marxists' on capital and ecology: see, for example, Gorz (1982) and
Bahro (1983). A more direct influence on the critique developed here
is Timpanaro (1978). Less impressive is Redclift (1984).

22. Farmer reminds us that Indian agriculture has often been described as
'a gamble in the rains' (Farmer, 1983, p. 11).

23. See Wendler and Eaton (1983) for a qualified endorsement of the
Charney model, though one which halves the Charney team's assumed desert/non-desert albedo differential.

24. I am dealing here with the rice Green Revolution. For a wider
discussion see Chandler (1979), chs 1 and 2.

25. Readers may feel that this is a classic example of 'oppositional'
reasoning on Frank's part. Still, his influence remains substantial, and
Chisholm may be right to detect a tinge of such reasoning in Bradbury's account of resource-based dependency in Canada: see
Chisholm (1982), p. 133 on Bradbury (1979).

26. For an overview see Ishikawa (1983), Nolan (1983) and Watson (1983).
27. See MacEwen (1982) and Pollitt (1982).
28. See Pollitt (1982), Table 9.
29. Marx deals with the practicalities of socialist construction most persuasively in 'The Critique of the Gotha Programme' (1974). Nove leaves us in no doubt, however, that Marx, as well as many of his later followers, did at times define socialism in Utopian terms. Nove himself believes that the case for modern socialism 'should be stressing the importance of externalities' in contemporary capitalism (Nove, 1983, p. 5).
30. And of Stalin perhaps: see Maltley's (1966) classic paper on the Soviet environmental debates.
31. See Burgess (1982) and Slater (1982), amongst others.
32. See Steven Rose's critique in *Not in Our Genes* (1984).
33. Morris (1971).
34. Neither Nove nor I are arguing that divisions of labour are quite without flexibility, or that income and wealth differentials have to be as obscenely wide as they are in the UK today.

4   Capitalism, industrialisation and development

1. Not everyone on the Left of course. In radical geography circles John Friedmann (and friends) continues to argue for an 'agropolitan' approach to development (see Friedmann, 1981; Friedmann and Douglass, 1978; Friedmann and Weaver, 1979) whilst others warn against urban bias. The role of industrialisation in a unified development strategy is clearly an important issue, but it is not central to this essay.
2. See Bukharin (1972).
3. A false proposition since endorsed by the World Bank's Helen Hughes. She maintains that 'at the end of World War II the developing countries had almost no industrial capacity' (Hughes, 1980, p. 11). In fact India, alone, was then the world's tenth most significant industrial power.
4. Blaut (1973), Peet (1978), Slater (1973) amongst others.
5. See McGee (1974) and Browett (1981).
6. For an interesting discussion of M. N. Roy and the relationship between Moscow and the Indian Communists – from the latter's perspective – see Azad (1980).
7. I will comment later on Warren's selective choice of Third World countries – for example Malta and Spain. Of interest here is the way in which manufacturing employment figures are presented in the absence of corollary figures on service and agricultural sector employment.
8. 'Prostitutes are often classified with beggars and thieves, but their occupation must be regarded as socially beneficial in cities with large male immigrant populations' (Warren, 1980, p. 216).

9. Though it should be said that Warren does not accept that inequality is on the rise: Warren (1980) p. 250.
10. Cf. Warren on stagnationism.
11. Notably Arrighi (1978), Frank (1981), Fröbel (1982) and Andreff (1984). Frank and Frobel have occupied neo-Smithian and neo-Ricardian positions at different times.
12. After Fröbel (1982).
13. He attributes the original phrase to Helen Hughes.
14. See also Gibson and Horvarth (1983) p. 180.
15. 'On balance, the 1970s and the NICs provide solid grounds for a further development and refinement of analysis from the dependency perspective' (Bienefeld, 1981, p. 94).
16. See Taylor and Thrift (1982) and the more extensive bibliographies of the following industrial geographers: Labasse (1975), Stewart (1976), Walker and Storper (1981) and Hayter and Watts (1983).
17. Subject to a whole host of counterveiling tendencies of course!
18. Peet praises the 'world structural theories' of radical development geography for seeing 'the particular as a version of the whole' (Peet, 1983, p. 105). See also Landsberg (1979), Szymanski (1977) and Wheelwright (1980).
19. But not just the Left. Sanjaya Lall and Frances Stewart figure prominently in the ensuing discussion.
20. The main tax incentives are pure tax holidays, modified tax holidays (dependent on levels of investment) and cost lowering incentives.
21. Vaitsos (1973).
22. Neither Newfarmer nor Topik are professional geographers but their paper appears in Taylor and Thrift's *The Geography of Multinationals* (1982).
23. See Seidman (1974).
24. More exactly, how are we to judge this issue given IBM's recently successful defences against anti-trust legislation in the USA and in the EEC?
25. Lall's point is clearly correct but one wonders if his newfound confidence in the TNCs justifies transfer pricing to the extent of 300 per cent and more.
26. In India the industrial bourgeoisie has 'settled' for a significant public sector involvement in most of the aforementioned industries.
27. See Streeten (1975) and Kemp (1983). See also the continuing debate between Lipton (1968, 1977) and Byres (1972, 1974, 1979). I have summarised this latter controversy in Corbridge (1982).
28. See Thomas (1980) and Taylor and Thrift (1982).
29. Definitions of the NICs vary widely. Frank's six countries comprise a minimal grouping. At the other end of the spectrum the World Bank defines sixteen countries as 'semi-industrialised': Frank's six plus Egypt, Columbia, the Philippines, Turkey, Greece, Portugal, Spain, Yugoslavia, Argentina and Israel (World Bank: World Development Report, 1983, pp. 87–8).
30. The term is Hamilton's (1983).

31. Again, this is too generalised: even Brazil and Mexico have their marked dissimilarities – see Gereffi and Evans (1981), Eckstein and Hagopian (1983).

32. In particular I would object to the air of 'necessary correlation' that Lamb implies: for example, between the new industrialisation and repression. For a more considered view see Sheahan (1980).

33. Barrett and Whyte suggest that Taiwan's recent development is 'deviant' in so far as it is still dependent and yet it enjoys rapid growth and development. In a reply which is indicative of the extraordinary special pleading into which some critics will enter on behalf of the indefensible (that is, crude dependency theory), Heather-Jo Hammer maintains that Taiwan did not become dependent until the late 1960s and is thus only just about to underdevelop. Apparently the negative consequences of dependency operate at a fifteen-year lag and the years of Japanese colonialism and US aid imperialism are not to count as real dependency. In a marvellously understated reply to this reply, Barrett and Whyte suggest that 'We find this distinction between external reliance and dependency . . . rather vague and highly idiosyncratic' (Barrett and Whyte, 1984, p. 937). Quite.

34. Over the same period per capita growth of GNP averaged six per cent annually. The figures for Korea are equally impressive. From 1960 to 1977 its GNP per capita grew at a rate of 7.4 per cent annually, whilst it annual export growth rate averaged a phenomenal 33.1 per cent (World Bank – World Development Report, 1979, Tables 1 and 8). On Korea's growth with the equity' see Rao (1978), Westphal (1977), Watanabe (1972) and Hasan (1976).

35. According to Barrett and Whyte (1982), Taiwan received $1.7 billion from the USA (1952–68), which accounted for 40.7 per cent of gross domestic capital formation between 1952 and 1960 and 12 per cent between 1960 and 1968. Since the later 1960s domestic capital formation has been boosted mainly by direct foreign private investment and international bank lending: see Galenson (1979).

36. And South Korea: 94 per cent of its operational farm units lie within the size range 0.1–3.0 hectares. Moreover it is not enough to ridicule these successes by pointing out that the south-east Asian countries are all city-states or small countries. In terms of geographical area this may be true, but in terms of population size South Korea is 'larger' than Argentina or Colombia, while Taiwan is 'larger' than Australia, Venezuela and Peru (since mid-1980). On Korean agriculture see Douglass (1983).

37. In other words the typical goods demanded by the vast mass of Taiwanese farmers in the 1950s and 1960s were such things as two-wheel tractors, power-tillers and tubewells (Johnston and Kilby, 1975, chapter 7; Y-M. Ho, 1980). In a country with a bimodal distribution of operational land holdings (such as Pakistan and most of South America) the rural demand profile is heavily biased to the 'needs' of a wealthy elite. This has implications not only for the Mercedes and combine syndrome, but for all those who claim that

countries should obey their relative demand and price signals, even where these signals are emerging from a violently distorted economic structure. I will come back to this.

38. Real wages grew at a rate close to 5.2 per cent a year over the period of 1960–78. Probably the main reason for this is that Taiwan's afore-mentioned land reforms and rural industrialisation discouraged the sort of massive rural to urban migration that is often the source of a cheap and 'unskilled' urban labour force. In terms of real wages and productivity rates it is clear that Taiwan is not a cheap labour area (in terms of NIDL theorising) but that its main attraction is a skilled and educated workforce well able to cope with (and attract) technologi-cally more demanding activities. Finally, it is not the case that Tai-wan's agricultural sector has suffered markedly in this drive to industrialisation. From 1950 to 1970 agricultural output grew at an average annual rate of 4.38 per cent (while population grew at 3.37 per cent annually). This growth was achieved almost entirely by new cultivation techniques, by the introduction of new seeds, by multi-cropping and by the application of chemical fertilisers (see Lee, 1974).

39. See Baldry *et al.* (1983) for a general overview. On Taiwan see Galenson (1979).

40. In Bangladesh 'about 30 per cent of rural households are landless, and another 30 per cent own less than 0.4 hectares of land . . . while the top 5 per cent of rural households . . . owned about 40 per cent of the total agricultural land in the country' (Hossain and Jones, 1983, pp. 163 and 169).

41. The post-war government in Taiwan was dominated by the exiled supporters of Chiang Kai-Shek.

42. In an 'Essay on the Process of Industrial Development and Alterna-tive Development Strategies', Balassa writes: 'The reference to 'alternative development strategies' in the title of the essay reflects my view as to the importance of the choice of policies for industrial and economic development' (Balassa, 1981, p.2).

5   Capitalism, interdependency and development

1. See also his claim that 'There are today no socialist systems in the world economy any more than there are feudal systems because there is only one world system' (Wallerstein, 1979, p.35).

2. This is clearly true if one takes Radice at his word: an autonomous economic strategy is no longer possible, but it is evident that he means rather more than this. Radice argues that a more or less autonomous strategy was feasible until recently and that it gained academic and political credence in the work of Keynes. By implication he traces the death of Keynesianism not to Milton Friedmann, but to the interna-tionalisation of capital. Again, this is a fair point but I think he takes it too far. In practice all national governments (and all political activists

working to secure national governments) have to act as if national economic planning can make a difference – which it surely does. The only alternative is to wait on events.

3. An ultra-imperialism of the North or core: Murray (1971).

4. That is, the EEC and Japan.

5. Often known as the World Bank Group.

6. United Nations Yearbooks (various).

7. On aid as the new 'white man's burden', see Byres (1972a).

8. I will explain the reasons for this later on. For an interesting account of these early negotiations see chapter 13 of Roy Harrod's (1972) account of *The Life of John Maynard Keynes*.

9. United Nations Conference on Trade and Development.

10. It is worth recalling that the Club of Rome was the original sponsor of RIO.

11. The 'New' neo-classical tag is Beenstock's (1983). Clearly there is a difference between neo-classical economics and monetarism, but Beenstock straddles this gap without too much discomfort.

12. Both groups advocate selective protectionism.

13. See Coakley and Harris (1983).

14. And more recently Norway. Between 1977 and 1983 Norway's average ODA/GNP ratio was 0.94: see World Bank, *World Development Report* (1983), Table 18.

15. World Bank, *World Development Report* (1981).

16. See Hawkins 1970, chapter 2.

17. See Payer (1982).

18. See Independent Group on British Aid (1982).

19. Lappé, Collins and Kinley (1980) clearly concur.

20. A geographer, and essentially an 'aid reformer'.

21. World Bank, *World Development Report* (1980)–India, Indonesia and Bangladesh.

22. The Carter Administration did seek to build a human rights dimension into its aid programme, though with important caveats.

23. Again, on 1983 World Bank definitions.

24. Tarrant's correlation coefficient maps cereal aid from the EEC against calories available per capita in selected Third World countries. On certain other definitions of need or poverty – for example GNP per capita – the coefficient is somewhat higher. The UK statistic is based on a life expectancy index of need.

25. Argentina and Uruguay were two other (then) dictatorships which gained in a similar way: Lappé *et al.* (1980).

26. Remember Blaut's claim that 'there is no real foreign aid (save Green Berets and guns)' (Blaut, 1978, p. 310). See also Wellings (1982).

27. The Group of 77, formed in 1964, is a common bargaining front for the South. It now has more than 120 members.

28. Unlike the IMF: see Payer (1974).

29. At least that was the intention: Hoogvelt (1982), p. 93.

30. See Tarrant (1981) and Woolcock (1982).

31. See also Seers (1981) and Singer (1980). No doubt the USSR is equally culpable but there are few statistics available on this. For a

discussion of OPEC's increasingly important, but very Arab-oriented, aid programme see Shihata and Mabro (1979) and Iqbal (1983).

32. An exception is Elson (1982).
33. I accept that it is not always wise to draw a hard-and-fast distinction between realisation and accumulation crises.
34. This is not a view I share: it is steeped in ultra-Leftist teleology and determinism.
35. World Bank: *World Development Report* (1983).
36. Compare this with the naive optimism of Wiarda (1982).
37. The title of a book by Mary Kaldor (1978).
38. Rettie (1983), see also Bird (1983). On the threat of a second debt shock, see Delamaide (1984). On the role of the transnational banks and the Euromarkets, see Stallings (1982) and Griffith-Jones (1982). On the need to revise the criteria of financial allocation, see Killick (1981) and Robinson (1981).
39. Brandt (1983).
40. See also Dendrinos (1984) and Davis (1984) for two very different confirmations.
41. See also Block (1977), Brett (1983) and the recent reviews of Roddick (1984) and Edwards (1984). For a useful geographical contribution, see Leahy and Hill (1981).
42. Blanchard and Dornbusch argue that 'At the centre of world macro-economics stand the US budget, the US cut long-term real rate of interest and the international value of the dollar' (1984), p. 89). See also Willett (1983). There is a danger here of course that the US is put in a no-win position: that a high dollar and a low dollar are each blamed for crisis and recession. Whilst I am aware of this, and of the need to revise Parboni's interpretation to take account of the strong-dollar era, it seems to me that his central point is being reinforced. The USA still retains an immense and unrivalled economic power by virtue of the dollar's pre-eminent role in the world monetary system.
43. That is, as a result of high real dollar interest rates.
44. An excellent discussion of these competing ideologies (which do not always reduce to specific party political interests) can be found in Sanders (1983). He is especially informative on Rockefeller's role (and motives) in resurrecting international Keynesianism (see pp. 126–8). In geography, Hoffman (1982) has tried to trace back the roots of American foreign policy still further. See also Cline (1980) and Hart (1983).
45. For a general, if often very pessimistic, assessment of the prospects for national development strategies, see Bienefeld and Godfrey (eds) (1982) and Seers (1981a).

6 Conclusion

1. Amongst the more recent contributions Browett (1981) and Harvey (1982) in very different ways continue the deterministic tradition.

Less economistic accounts of class and gender can be found in Forbes (1984) and Zelinsky *et al.* (1982).

2. I say remarkable because *The Limits to Capital* is a typically serious and intense study of Marxism in which some chapters – notably the chapter on theories of rent – are simply outstanding. What I am contesting here is the overall architecture of Harvey's book: its willingness to treat capitalism as a set of necessary laws and tendencies and its unwillingness to engage with the non-Marxist literature on (possible) crisis formation and displacement under capitalism.

Bibliography

Abumere, S. (1979) 'The Diffusion of Economic Development in Bendel State, Nigeria', *Geographiska Annaler*, 61, 103–111.

Adam, G. (1975) 'Multinational Corporations and Worldwide Sourcing', in H. Radice (ed.) *International Firms and Modern Imperialism* (Harmondsworth: Penguin).

Aglietta, M. (1982) 'World Capitalism in the Eighties', *New Left Review*, 137, 5–41.

Agnew, J. (1982) 'Sociologizing the Geographical Imagination: Spatial Concepts in the World System Perspective', *Political Geography Quarterly*, 1, 159–66.

Agnew, J. (1983) 'An Excess of "National Exceptionalism": Towards a New Political Geography of American Foreign Policy', *Political Geography Quarterly* 2, 151–66.

Amin, S. (1976) *Unequal Development* (London: Monthly Review).

Amin, S. (1977) *Imperialism and Unequal Development* (Hassocks: Harvester)

Anderson, M. (1980) *Approaches to the History of the Western Family, 1500–1914* (London: Macmillan).

Andreff, W. (1984) 'The International Centralization of Capital and the Re-ordering of World Capitalism', *Capital and Class*, 22, 58–80.

Anker, R. (1978) 'An Analysis of Fertility Differentials in Developing Countries', *Review of Economics and Statistics*, 60, 58–69.

Argy, V. (1981) *The Post-War International Monetary Crisis* (London: George Allen & Unwin).

Arrighi, G. (1970) 'International Corporations, Labour Aristocracies and Economic Development in Tropical Africa', in R. Rhodes (ed.) *Imperialism and Underdevelopment* (London: Monthly Review).

Arrighi, G. (1978) *A Geometry of Imperialism* (London: New Left Books).

Auty, R. (1979) 'Worlds Within the Third World', *Area*, 11, 232–5.

Auty, R. (1983) 'MNCs and Regional Revenue Retention in a Vertically Integrated Industry: Bauxite/Aluminium in the Caribbean', *Regional Studies*, 17, 3–17.

Auty, R. (1983a) 'Multinational Resource Corporations, The Product Life-Cycle and Product Strategy: The Oil Majors' Response to Heightened Risk', *Geoforum*, 14, 1–14.

Azad, P. S. (1980) *Prithvi Singh Azad in Lenin's Land* (New Delhi: Sterling).

Bach, W. (1979) 'Short-Term Climatic Alterations Caused by Human Activities: Status and Outlook', *Progress in Physical Geography*, 3, 55–83.

Bacha, E. and Taylor, L. (1978) 'Brazilian Income Distribution in the 1960s: "Facts", Model Results and the Controversy', *Journal of Development Studies*, 14, 271–97.

Baer, W. (1976) 'Technology, Employment and Development: Empirical Findings', *World Development*, 4, 121–30.

Bahro, R. (1983) *From Red to Green* (London: New Left Books).

Balassa, B. (1981) *The Newly Industrialising Countries in the World Economy* (Oxford: Pergamon).

Baldry, L., Haworth, N., Henderson, G. and Ramsey, H. (1983) 'Fighting Multinational Power: Possibilities, Limitations and Contradictions', *Capital and Class*, 20.

Baran, P. (1973) *The Political Economy of Growth* (Harmondsworth: Penguin).

Barney, G. (ed.) (1982) *The Global 2000 Report to the President* (Harmondsworth: Penguin).

Barrett, R. and Whyte, M. (1982) Dependency Theory and Taiwan: Analysis of a Deviant Case', *American Journal of Sociology*, 87, 1064–89.

Barrett, R. and Whyte, M. (1984) 'Reply to Hammer', *American Journal of Sociology*, 89, 937–40.

Bath, C. and James, D. (1976) 'Dependency Analysis of Latin America: Some Criticisms, Some Suggestions', *Latin American Research Review*, XI, 3–54.

Bauer, P. T. (1974) 'Foreign Aid, Forever?', *Encounter*, 42, 15–28.

Bauer, P. T. (1976) *Dissent on Development* (Cambridge, Massachusetts: Harvard University Press).

Bayliss-Smith, T. (1982) *The Ecology of Agricultural Systems* (Cambridge: Cambridge University Press).

Bayliss-Smith, T. and Wanmali, S. (eds) (1984) *Understanding Green Revolutions: Agrarian Change and Development Planning in South Asia* (Cambridge: Cambridge University Press).

Becker, D. (1984) 'Development, Democracy and Dependency in Latin America: A Post-Imperialist View', *Third World Quarterly*, 6, 411–31.

Beenstock, M. (1983) *The World Economy in Transition* (London: George Allen & Unwin).

Beenstock, M. (1983a) 'The Gloomy Economics of Willy Brandt', *Financial Times*, (March).

Bernstein, H. (1977) 'Notes on Capital and Peasantry', *Review of African Political Economy*, 10, 60–73.

Bernstein, H. (1979) 'Sociology of Underdevelopment versus Sociology of Development', in D. Lehmann (ed.) *Development Theory* (London: Frank Cass).

Bernstein, H. (1982) 'Industrialisation, Development and Dependence', in H. Alavi and T. Shanin (eds) *Introduction to the Sociology of Developing Countries* (London:Macmillan).

Bettelheim, C. (1972) 'Theoretical Comments', in A. Emmanuel, *Unequal Exchange* (London:Monthly Review).

Bienefeld, M. (1981) 'Dependency Theory and the Newly Industrialising Countries: Towards a Reappraisal', in D. Seers (ed.) *Dependency Theory: A Critical Re-Assessment* (London: Frances Pinter).

Bienefeld, M. and Godfrey, M. (eds) (1982) *The Struggle for Development: National Strategies in an International Context* (Chichester: John Wiley).

Bird, G. (1981) 'Developing Country Finances: Present and Future', *Futures*, 13, 191–205.

Bird, G. (1983) 'Interest Rate Subsidies on International Finance as a Means of Assisting Low Income Countries', *World Development*, 11, 515–25.

Birke, L. (1984) 'Outgrowing Selfish Genes', *New Socialist*, 16, 40–2.

Blaikie, P. (1978) 'The Theory of Spatial Diffusion of Innovations: A Spacious Cul-de-Sac', *Progress in Human Geography*, 2, 268–95.

Blanchard, O. and Dornbusch, R. (1984) 'US Deficits, the Dollar and Europe', *Banca Nazionale del Lavoro Quarterly Review*, 148, 89–113.

Blaut, J. (1970) 'Geographic Models of Imperialism', *Antipode*, 2, 65–85.

Blaut, J. (1973) 'The Theory of Development', *Antipode*, 5, 22–6, reprinted in R. Peet (ed.) *Radical Geography* (London: Methuen, 1978).

Blaut, J. (1976) 'Where was Capitalism Born?', *Antipode*, 8 1–11, reprinted in R. Peet (ed.) *Radical Geography* (London: Methuen, 1978).

Block, F. (1977) *The Origins of International Economic Disorder*, (Berkeley: University of California Press).

Bornscheir, V. Chase-Dunn, C. and Rubinson, R. (1978) 'Cross-National Evidence of the Effects of Foreign Investment and Aid on Economic Growth and Equality: A Survey of Findings and a Re-Analysis', *American Journal of Sociology*, 84, 651–83.

Boserup, E. (1967) *The Conditions of Agricultural Growth* (London: George Allen & Unwin).

Boserup, E. (1970) 'Present and Potential Food Production in Developing Countries', in W. Zelinsky *et al.* (eds), *The Geographer and His Crowding World* (Oxford: Oxford University Press).

Boserup, E. (1981) *Population and Technology* (Oxford: Basil Blackwell).

Bradbury, J. (1979) 'Towards an Alternative Theory of Resource-Based Town Development in Canada', *Economic Geography*, 55, 147–66.

Bradby, B. (1980) 'The Destruction of Natural Economy', in H. Wolpe (ed.) *The Articulation of Modes of Production* (London: Routledge & Kegan Paul).

Brandt, W. (Chairman of the Brandt Commission) (1980) *North-South: A Programme for Survival* (London: Pan).

Brandt, W. (Chairman of the Brandt Commission) (1983) *Common Crisis, North-South: Co-operation for World Recovery* (London: Pan).

Breitbart, M. (1981) 'Peter Kropotkin: The Anarchist Geographer', in D. Stoddart (ed.) *Geography, Ideology and Social Concern* (Oxford: Basil Blackwell).

Brenner, R. (1976) 'Agrarian Class Structure and Economic Development in Pre-Industrial Europe', *Past and Present*, 70, 30–75.

Brenner, R. (1977) 'The Origins of Capitalist Development: A Critique of Neo-Smithian Marxism', *New Left Review*, 104, 25–92.

Brett, E. A. (1983) *International Money and Capitalist Crisis*, (London: Heinemann).

Brewer, A. (1980) *Marxist Theories of Imperialism*, (London: Routledge & Kegan Paul).

Brookfield, H. (1975) *Interdependent Development*, (London: Methuen).

Browett, J. (1981) 'Development, The Diffusionist Paradigm and Geography', *Progress in Human Geography*, 4, 57–79.

Browett, J. (1982) 'On the Role of Geography in Development Geography', *Tijdschrift voor Economische en Sociale Geographie*, 72, 155–.61.

Buchanan, K. (1970) *The Transformation of the Chinese Earth* (Edinburgh: Bell & Sons).

Buchanan, K. (1972) *The Geography of Empire* (Nottingham: Spokesman).

Buchanan, K. (1973) 'The White North and the Population Explosion', *Antipode*, 3, 7–15.

Bukharin, N. (1972) *Imperialism and World Economy* (London: Merlin).

Bundy, C. (1979) *The Rise and Fall of the South African Peasantry* (London: Heinemann).

Burgess, R. (1982) 'The Politics of Urban Residence in Latin America', *International Journal of Urban and Regional Research*, 6, 465–79.

Burton, I. Kates, R. and White, G. (1978) *The Environment as Hazard* (New York: Oxford University Press).

Byres, T. J. (1972) 'Industrialisation, the Peasantry and the Economic Debate in the Post-Independence Period', in A. Bhuleskar (ed.) *Towards a Socialist Transformation of the Indian Economy* (Bombay: Popular Prakashan).

Byres, T. J. (1972a) 'The White Man's Burden in a Neo-Colonial Setting', in T. J. Byres (ed.) *Foreign Resources and Economic Development* (London: Frank Cass).

Byres, T. J. (1974) 'Land Reform, Industrialisation and the Marketed Surplus in India: An Essay on the Power of Urban Bias', in D. Lehmann (ed.) *Agrarian Reform and Agrarian Reformism* (London: Faber).

Byres, T. J. (1979) 'Of Neo-Populist Pipe Dreams', *Journal of Peasant Studies*, 6, 210–44.

Cain, M. (1977) 'The Economic Activities of Children in a Village in Bangladesh', *Population and Development Review*, 3, 201–27.

Cain, M. (1982) 'Perspectives on Family and Fertility in Developing Countries', *Population Studies*, 36, 159–75.

Caldwell, J. (1977) 'The Economic Implications of High Fertility: An Investigation with Nigerian Survey Data', *Population Studies*, 31, 15–27.

Caldwell, J. (1978) 'A Theory of Fertility: From High Plateau to Destabilisation', *Population and Development Review*, 4, 553–77.

Caldwell, J. Reddy, P. and Caldwell, P. (1984) 'The Determinants of Fertility Decline in India', in T. Dyson and N. Crook (eds), *India's Demography* (New Delhi: South Asian Publishers).

Cannon, T. (1975) 'Geography and Underdevelopment', *Area*, 7, 212–16.

Cannon, T. (1977) 'Natural Disasters and the Third World', in N. Smith, M. Forbes and M. Kershaw (eds) *Geography, Social Welfare and Underdevelopment* (St Andrews' Geographers Special Publication 2).

Cardoso, F. H. (1977) 'The Consumption of Dependency Theory in the US' *Latin American Research Review*, XII, 7–24.

Cardoso, F. H. and Faletto, E. (1979) *Dependency and Development in Latin America* (Berkeley: University of California Press).

Carlstein, T. (1982) *Time, Resources, Society and Ecology – Volume 1*, (London: George Allen & Unwin).

Cassen, R. (1976) 'Population and Development: A Survey', *World Development*, 4, 785–830.

Cassen, R. (1978) *India: Population, Economy, Society* (London: Macmillan).

Chambers, R., Longhurst, R. and Pacey, A. (eds) (1981) *Seasonal Dimensions to Rural Poverty* (London: Frances Pinter).

Chandler, R. (1979) *Rice in the Tropics*, (Boulder: Westview).

Charlesworth, J. (1957) *The Quaternary Era, With Special Reference to Glaciation* (London: Arnold).

Charney, J., Stone, P. and Quirk, W. (1975) 'Drought in the Sahara: A Biogeophysical Feedback Mechanism', *Science*, 187, 434–5.

Charney, J., Stone, P. and Quirk, W. (1976) 'Reply to Ripley', *Science*, 191, 100–2.

Ch'en, H. S. (1936) *Landlord and Peasant in China: A Study of the Agrarian Crisis in South China*.

Chenery, H., Ahluwalia, M., Bell, C., Duloy, J. and Jolly R. (1974) *Redistribution With Growth* (Oxford: Oxford University Press).

Chesneaux, J. (1979) *China: The People's Republic, 1949–1976* (Hassocks: Harvester).

Chetley, A. (1979) *The Baby-Milk Scandal* (London: War on Want).

Chinn, D. (1979) 'Rural Poverty and the Structure of Farm Household Income in Developing Countries: Evidence from Taiwan', *Economic Development and Cultural Change*, 27, 283–302.

Chinn, D. (1982) 'Growth, Equity and Gini Coefficients: The Case of Taiwan', *Economic Development and Cultural Change*, 30, 871–86.

Chisholm, M. (1982) *Modern World Development: A Geographical Perspective* London: Hutchinson).

Chudnovsky, D. (1979) 'The Challenge by Domestic Enterprises to the TNC's Domination: A Case Study of the Argentine Pharmaceutical Industry', *World Development*, 7, 45–58.

Church, R. (1948) 'The Case for Colonial Geography', *Transactions of the Institute of British Geographers*, 14, 15–25.

Claval, P. (1980) 'Centre/Periphery and Space: Models of Political Geography', in J. Gottman (ed.) *Centre and Periphery: Spatial Variation in Politics* (London: Sage).

Clay, E. (1981) 'Environment, Technology and the Seasonal Pattern of Agricultural Employment in Bangladesh' (mimeo).

Cline, S. (1980) *World Power Trends and US Foreign Policy for the 1980s* (Boulder: Westview).

Coakley, J. and Harris, L. (1983) *The City of Capital* (Oxford: Basil Blackwell).

Cochrane, S. H. (1979) *Fertility and Education: What Do We Really Know?* (Baltimore: World Bank Staff Paper 26).

Cody, J., Hughes, H. and Wall, D. (eds) (1980) *Policies for Industrial Progress in Developing Countries* (Oxford: Oxford University Press).

Cohen, R. (1981) 'The New International Division of Labour, Multi-National Corporations and Urban Hierarchy', in M. Dear and A. Scott (eds) *Urbanization and Urban Planning in Capitalist Society* (London: Methuen).

Cohen, S. (1973) *Geography and Politics in a World Divided* (New York: Oxford University Press) 2nd edn.

Cohen, S. (1982) 'A New Map of Global Geopolitical Equilibrium: A Developmental Approach', *Political Geography Quarterly*, 1, 223–41.

Cole, J. P. (1981) *The Development Gap* (London: John Wiley).

Corbridge, S. (1982) 'Urban Bias, Rural Bias and Industrialisation: An Appraisal of the Work of Michael Lipton and Terry Byres', in J. Harriss (ed.) *Rural Development: Theories of Peasant Economy and Agrarian Change* (London: Hutchinson).

Corbridge, S. (1982a) 'Industrial Development in Tribal India: The Case of the Iron Ore Mining Industry, Bihar 1900–1980', in N. Sengupta (ed.) *Fourth World Dynamics: Jharkhand* (Delhi: Authors Guild).

Corbridge, S. (1982b) 'Interdependent Development? Problems of Aggregation and Implementation in the Brandt Report', *Applied Geography*, 2, 253–65.

Corbridge, S. (1984) 'Crisis, What Crisis? Monetarism, Brandt II and the Geopolitics of Debt', *Political Geography Quarterly*, 3, 331–45.

Corbridge, S. (forthcoming) 'Capitalism, Industrialisation and Development', *Progress in Human Geography*.

Corbridge, S. and Watson, P. (forthcoming) 'The Economic Value of Children: A Case Study from Rural India', *Applied Geography*.

Croll, E. (1983) 'Production versus Reproduction: A Threat to China's Development Strategy', *World Development*, 11, 467–81.

Culley, L. (1977) 'Economic Development in Neo-Marxist Theory' in B. Hindess (ed.) *Sociological Theories of the Economy* (London: Macmillan).

Cutler, A., Hindess, B., Hirst, P. and Hussain, A. (1977) *Marx's Capital and Capitalism Today – Volume 1* (London: Routledge & Kegan Paul).

Cutler, A., Hindess, B., Hirst, P. and Hussain, A. (1977) *Marx's Capital and Capitalism Today – Volume 21* (London: Routledge & Kegan Paul).

Darden, J. (1974) 'Population Control or a Redistribution of Wealth?', *Antipode*, 7, 50–2.

Davis, M. (1984) 'The Political Economy of Late Imperial America', *New Left Review*, 143, 6–38.

Delamaide, D. (1984) *Debt Shock* (London: Weidenfeld & Nicolson).

Dendrinos, D. (1984) 'The Decline of the US Economy: A Perspective from Mathematical Ecology', *Environment and Planning*, A16, 651–62.

De Souza, A. and Foust, J. (1979) *World Space Economy* (Columbus: Merrill).

Dickenson, J. P. *et al.* (eds.) (1983) *A Geography of the Third World* (London: Methuen).

Dos Santos, T. (1973) 'The Crisis of Development Theory and the Problem of Dependency in Latin America', in H. Bernstein (ed.) *Underdevelopment and Development* (Harmondsworth: Penguin).

Douglass, M. (1983) 'The Korean *Saemaul Undong*: Accelerated Rural Development in an Open Economy', in D. Lea and D. Chaudhri (eds) *Rural Development and the State* (London: Methuen).

Duncan, J. and Ley, D. (1982) 'Structural Marxism and Human Geography: A Critical Assessment', *Annals of the Association of American Geographers*, 72, 30–59.

Dunford, M. and Perrons, D. (1983) *The Arena of Capital*, (London: Macmillan).

Dupré, G. and Rey, P. P. (1973) 'Reflections on the Pertinence of a Theory of the History of Exchange', *Economy and Society*, 2.

Easterlin, R. (1975) 'An Economic Framework for Fertility Analysis', *Studies in Family Planning*, 6, 54–63.

Eberstadt, N. (1980) 'Recent Declines in Fertility in Less Developed Countries and what "Population Planners" May Learn From Them', *World Development*, 8, 37–60.

Eckstein, S. and Hagopian, F. (1983) 'The Limits of Industrialisation in the Less Developed World: Bolivia', *Economic Development and Cultural Change*, 32, 63–95.

Edwards, C. (1984) *The Fragmented World: Competing Perspectives on Trade, Money and Crisis* (London:Methuen).

Edwards, C., Biggs, S. and Griffith, J. (1978) 'Irrigation in Bangladesh: On Contradictions and Under-utilised Potential', *University of East Anglia: School of Development Studies*, Discussion Paper 22.

Ehrlich, P. (1972) *The Population Bomb* (London:Pan).

Elson, D. (1982) 'The Brandt Report: A Programme for Survival?', *Capital and Class*, 16.

Elvin, M. (1973) *The Pattern of the Chinese Past* (Stanford: Stanford University Press).

Emmanuel, A. (1972) *Unequal Exchange* (London: Monthly Review).

Emmanuel, A. (1974) 'Myths of Development versus Myths of Under-Development', *New Left Review*, 85, 61–82.

Enke, S. (1971) 'Economic Consequences of Rapid Population Growth', *Economic Journal*, 81, 800–11.

Ettama, W. (1979) 'Geographers and Development', *Tijdschrift voor Economische en Sociale Geographie*, 70, 66–74.

Ettama, W. (1983) 'The Centre – Periphery Perspective in Development Geography', *Tijdschrift voor Economische en Sociale Geographie*, 74, 107–19.

Evans, P. (1981) 'Recent Research on MNCs', *Annual Review of Sociology*, 199–223.

Eyre, S. (1978) *The Real Wealth of Nations* (London: Edward Arnold).

Fairgreave, J. (1932) *Geography of World Power* (London: University of London Press).

Fanon, F. (1967) *The Wretched of the Earth* (Harmondsworth: Penguin).

Farmer, B. H. (1957) *Pioneer Peasant Colonization in Ceylon* (Oxford: Oxford University Press).

Farmer, B. H. (ed.) (1977) *Green Revolution? Technology and Change in Rice Growing Areas of Tamil Nadu and Sri Lanka* (London: Macmillan).

Farmer, B. H. (1983) *An Introduction to South Asia* (London: Macmillan).

Farmer, B. H. (1983a) 'British Geographers Overseas, 1933–1983', *Transactions of the Institute of British Geographers*, 8, 70–9.

Fei, J., Ranis, G., and Kuo, S. (1979) *Growth With Equity: The Taiwan Case* (Oxford: Oxford University Press).

Feldstein, M. (1983) 'The World Economy Today: Signs of Recovery', *Economist*, 287, 87–92.

Fitzpatrick, P. (1980) *Law and State in Papua New Guinea* (London: Academic Press).

Forbes, D. (1984) *The Geography of Underdevelopment* (London: Croom Helm).

Forde, C. D. (1948) *Habitat, Economy and Society* (New York: Dutton).

Forrester, J. (1971) *World Dynamics* (New York: Wright & Allen).

Foster-Carter, A. (1978) 'The Modes of Production Controversy,' *New Left Review*, 107, 47–77.

Frank, A. G. (1967) *Capitalism and Underdevelopment in Latin America* (London: Monthly Review).

Frank, A. G. (1969) *Latin America: Underdevelopment or Revolution*, (London: Monthly Review).

Frank, A. G. (1972) *Lumpenbourgeoisie, Lumpendevelopment* (London: Monthly Review).

Frank, A. G. (1978) *Dependent Accumulation and Underdevelopment* (London: Macmillan).

Frank, A. G. (1979) 'Unequal Accumulation: Intermediate, Semi-Peripheral and Sub-Imperialist Economies', *Review*, II, 281–350.

Frank, A. G. (1980) 'North–South and East–West: Keynesian Paradoxes in the Brandt Report', *Third World Quarterly*, 2, 669–80.

Frank, A. G. (1981) *Crisis in the Third World* (London: Heinemann).

Frank, A. G. (1982) 'Asia's Exclusive Models', *Far Eastern Economic Review*, (25 June) 22–3.

Frank, A. G. (1983) 'Global Crisis and Transformation', *Development and Change*, 14, 323–46.

Frieden, J. (1983) 'Review: The Dollar and Its Rivals', *New Left Review*, 135, 91–6.

Friedman, A. (1983) 'The Search for a Banking Lifeboat', *Financial Times*, (15 March), 33.

Friedmann, J. (1981) 'The Active Community: Toward a Political–Territorial Framework for Rural Development in Asia', *Economic Development and Cultural Change*, 29, 235–61.

Friedmann, J. and Douglass, M. (1978) 'Agropolitan Development: Towards a New Strategy for Regional Planning in Asia', in L. Fu-Chen and K. Salih (eds) *Growth-Pole Strategy and Regional Development Policy: Asian Experiences and Alternative Approaches* (New York: Pergamon).

Friedmann, J. and Weaver, C. (1979) *Territory and Function: The Evolution of Regional Planning* (London: Edward Arnold).

Friedmann, J. and Wulff, R. (1976) *The Urban Transition* (London: Edward Arnold).

Fröbel, F. (1982) 'The Current Development of the World Economy: Reproduction of Labour and Accumulation of Capital on a World Scale', *Review*, V.

Fröbel, F., Heinrichs, J. and Kreye, O. (1980) *The New International Division of Labour* (Cambridge, Cambridge University Press).

Furtado, C. (1963) *The Economic Growth of Brazil* (Berkeley: University of California Press).

Galenson, W. (ed.) (1979) *Economic Growth and Structural Change in Taiwan* (Ithaca: Cornell University Press).

Galois, B. (1976) 'Ideology and the Idea of Nature: The Case of Peter Kropotkin', *Antipode*, 8, 1–16.

Galtung, J. (1976) 'Conflicts on a Global Scale: Social Imperialism and Sub-Imperialism – Continuities in the Structural Theory of Imperialism', *World Development*, 4, 154–65.

Geertz, C. (1963) *Agricultural Involution: The Process of Ecological Change in Indonesia* (Berkeley: University of California Press).

Geras, N. (1977) *The Legacy of Rosa Luxemburg* (London: New Left Books).

Gereffi, G. and Evans, P. (1981) 'Transnational Corporations, Dependent Development and State Policy in the Semi-Periphery: A Comparison of Brazil and Mexico', *Latin American Research Review*, 16, 31–64.

Gibson, K. and Horvarth, R. (1983) 'Global Capital and the Restructuring Crisis in Australian Manufacturing', *Economic Geography*, 59, 178–94.

Gilbert, A. and Gugler, J. (1981) *Cities, Poverty and Development: Urbanization in the Third World* (Oxford: Oxford University Press).

Gilbert, E. and Steel, R. (1945) 'Social Geography and its Place in Colonial Studies', *Geographical Journal*, 106, 118–31.

Girvan, N. (1976) *Corporate Imperialism: Conflict and Expropriation* (London: Monthly Review).

Glacken, C. (1967) *Traces on the Rhodian Shore* (Berkeley: University of California Press).

Glyn, A. and Harrison, J. (1980) *The British Economic Disaster* (London: Pluto).

Godfrey, M. and Langdon, S. (1976) 'Partners in Underdevelopment? The Transnationalisation Thesis in a Kenyan Context', *Journal of Commonwealth and Comparative Politics*, 14, 42–63.

Gold, J. and Shepherd, I. (1983) 'An Interview with Ron Johnston', *Journal of Geography in Higher Education*, 7, 109–23.

Goodman, D. and Redclift, M. (1981) *From Peasant to Proletarian: Capitalist Development and Agrarian Transitions* (Oxford: Basil Blackwell).

Gore, C. (1983) 'Review of Modern World Development', *Environment and Planning*, A15, 1424–5.

Gore, C. (1984) *Regions in Question* (London: Methuen).

Gorz, A. (1982) *Farewell to the Working Class* (London: Pluto).

Gottman, J. (1980) 'Organising and Re-organising Space', in J. Gottman (ed.) *Centre and Periphery: Spatial Variation in Politics* (London: Sage).

Goudie, A. (1977) *Environmental Change* (Oxford: Clarendon Press).

Goudie, A. (1981) *The Human Impact: Man's Role in Environmental Change* (Oxford: Basil Blackwell).

Goudie, A. (1983) 'Desertification', in R. Johnston *et al.* (eds.) *A Dictionary of Human Geography* (Oxford: Basil Blackwell).

Gould, P. (1970) 'Tanzania, 1920–1963: The Spatial Impress of the Modernisation Process', *World Politics*, 22, 149–70.

Grahl, J. (1983) 'Restructuring in West European Industry', *Capital and Class*, 19.

Gray, R. (1974) 'The Decline of Mortality in Ceylon and the Demographic Effects of Malaria Control', *Population Studies*, 28, 205–29.

Greer, C. (1979) *Water Management in the Yellow River Basin of China* (London: University of Texas Press).

Gregory, D. (1978) *Ideology, Science and Human Geography* (London: Hutchinson).

Gregory, D. (1980) 'The Ideology of Control: Systems Theory and Geography', *Tijdschrift voor Economische en Sociale Geographie*, 71, 327–42.

Gregory, D. (1981) 'Human Agency and Human Geography', *Transactions of the Institute of British Geographers*, 6, 1–18.

Gregory, D. (1983) 'Capitalism', in R. Johnston *et al.* (eds) *The Dictionary of Human Geography* (Oxford: Basil Blackwell).

Griffith-Jones, S. (1982) 'Transnational Finance and Latin American National Development', *Institute of Development Studies Discussion Paper* 175.

Grigg, D. (1979) 'Ester Boserup's Theory of Agrarian Change: A Critical Review', *Progress in Human Geography*, 3, 69–84.

Halliday, F. (1983) *The Making of the Second Cold War* (London: Verso).

Halliday, J. (1975) *A Political History of Japanese Capitalism* (London: Monthly Review).

Hamilton, C. (1983) 'Capitalist Industrialisation in the Four Little Tigers of East Asia', in P. Limqueco and B. MacFarlane (eds) *Neo-Marxist Theories of Development* (London: Croom Helm).

Hammer, H. J. (1984) 'Comment on "Dependency Theory and Taiwan: Analysis of a Deviant Case"', *American Journal of Sociology*, 89, 932–7.

Hansen, A. (1944) *Readings in Business Cycle Theory* (Philadelphia: Merrill).

Hardin, G. (1968) 'The Tragedy of the Commons', *Science* (13 December).

Hare, F., Kates, R. and Warren, A. (1977) 'The Making of Deserts: Climate, Ecology and Society', *Economic Geography*, 53, 334–46.

Harriss, B. (1984) *State and Market* (Delhi: Concept).

Harriss, J. (1980) 'Contemporary Marxist Analysis of the Agrarian Question in India', *Madras Institute of Development Studies, Working Paper* 14.

Harriss, J. (1981) *Capitalism and Peasant Farming: Agrarian Structure and Ideology in Northern Tamil Nadu* (Bombay: Oxford University Press).

Harrod, R. (1972) *The Life of John Maynard Keynes* (Harmondsworth: Penguin).

Hart, J. (1983) *The New International Economic Order: Conflict and Co-operation in North–South Economic Relations, 1974–1977* (London: Macmillan).

Harvey, D. (1978) 'Population, Resources and the Ideology of Science', in R. Peet (ed.) *Radical Geography* (London: Methuen).

Harvey, D. (1982) *The Limits to Capital* (Oxford: Basil Blackwell).

Hasan, P. (1976) *Korea: Problems and Issues in a Rapidly Growing Economy* (Baltimore: John Hopkins Press).

Hawkins, E. (1970) *The Principles of Development Aid* (Harmondsworth: Penguin).

Hayter, R. and Watts, H. (1983) 'The Geography of Enterprise: A Reappraisal', *Progress in Human Geography*, 7, 157–81.

Hayter, T. (1971) *Aid as Imperialism* (Harmondsworth: Penguin).

Hayter, T. (1981) *The Creation of World Poverty* (London: Pluto).

Heer, D. and Smith, D. (1968), Mortality Level, Desired Family Size and Population Increase', *Demography*, 5.

Henrikson, A. (1980) 'America's Changing Place in the World: From "Periphery" to "Centre"?', in J. Gottman (ed.) *Centre and Periphery: Spatial Variation in Politics* (London: Sage).

Hill, J. and Scannell, H. (1983) *Due South: Socialists and World Development* (London: Pluto).

Hindess, B. and Hirst, P. (1975) *Pre-Capitalist Modes of Production* (London: Routledge & Kegan Paul).

Hindess, B. and Hirst, P. (1977) *Modes of Production and Social Formation* (London: Macmillan).

Hirschman, A. (1958) *The Strategy of Economic Development* (New Haven: Yale University Press).

Hirst, P. and Woolley, P. (1982) *Social Relations and Human Attributes* (London: Tavistock).

Ho, Ping-ti (1959) *Studies on the Population of China, 1368–1953* (Oxford: Oxford University Press).

Ho, S. P. S. (1978) *Economic Development of Taiwan, 1860–1970* (New Haven: Yale University Press).

Ho, S. P. S. (1979) 'Decentralised Industrialisation and Rural Development: Evidence from Taiwan', *Economic Development and Cultural Change*, 28, 77–96.

Ho, Y-M. (1980) 'The Production Structure of the Manufacturing Sector and its Distributional Implications: The Case of Taiwan', *Economic Development and Cultural Change*, 28, 321–43.

Hoffman, G. (1982) 'Nineteenth Century Roots of American World Power Relations', *Political Geography Quarterly*, 1, 279–92.

Holland, S. (1976) *Capital Versus the Regions* (London: Macmillan).

Holland, S. (1981) 'Militarism, Monetarism and Multinationals', *New Socialist*, 2, 8–12.

Hoogvelt, A. (1982) *The Third World in Global Development* (London: Macmillan).

Horvarth, R. (1974) 'Machine Space', *Geographical Review*, 64, 167–88.

Hoselitz, B. (1952) *The Progress of Underdeveloped Areas* (Chicago: Chicago University Press).

Hoselitz, B. (ed.) (1960) *Theories of Economic Growth* (New York: Free Press of Glencoe).

Hossain, M. and Jones, S. (1983) 'Production, Poverty and the Co-operative Ideal: Contradictions in Bangladesh Rural Development Policy', in D. Lea and D. Chaudhri (eds) *Rural Development and the State* (London: Methuen).

Hughes, H. (1980) 'Achievements and Objectives of Industrialisation', in J. Cody, H. Hughes and D. Wall (eds) *Policies for Industrial Progress in Developing Countries* (Oxford: Oxford University Press).

Hymer, S. (1975) 'The Multinational Corporation and the Law of Uneven Development', in H. Radice (ed.) *International Firms and Modern Imperialism* (Harmondsworth: Penguin).

Independent Group on British Aid (1982) *Real Aid: A Strategy for Britain* (London: IGBA).

Iqbal, Z. (1983) 'Arab Concessional Assistance, 1975–81', *Finance and Development*, 20, 31–3.

Ishikawa, S. (1983) 'China's Economic Growth since 1949: An Assessment', *China Quarterly* (1983) 94, 242–81.

Jackman, R. (1980) 'A Note on the Measurement of Growth Rates in Cross-National Research', *American Journal of Sociology*, 86, 604–17.

Jackman, R. (1982) 'Dependence on Foreign Investment and Economic Growth in the Third World', *World Politics*, 34, 175–96.

James C. L. R. (1980) *The Black Jacobins* (London: Allison & Busby).

Jenkins, R. (1984) 'Divisions over the International Division of Labour', *Capital and Class*, 22, 28–57.

Johnson, D. (1977) 'The Human Dimensions of Desertification', *Economic Geography*, 53, 317–21.

Johnson, R. (1983) 'The Great Debt Explosion', *New Society* (January) 148–9.

Johnston, B. F. and Kilby, P. (1975) *Agriculture and Structural Transformation* (Oxford: Oxford University Press).

Johnston, R. (1979) *Geography and Geographers: Anglo-American Human Geography since 1945* (London: Edward Arnold).

Johnston, R. (1984) 'The World Is Our Oyster', *Transactions of the Institute of British Geographers*, 9, 443–59.

Kaldor, M. (1978) *The Disintegrating West* (London: Allen Lane).

Kaldor, N. (1983) *The Economic Consequences of Mrs Thatcher* (London: Duckworth).

Kamarck, A. (1976) *The Tropics and Economic Development: A Provocative Inquiry into the Poverty of Nations* (Baltimore: John Hopkins Press).

Kaplinsky, R. (1979) 'Export-Oriented Growth: A Large International Firm in a Small Developing Country', *World Development*, 7, 825–34.

Katseli, L. (1983) 'Devaluation: A Critical Appraisal of the IMF's Policy Prescriptions', *American Economic Review*, 73, 359–63.

Kaufman, R., Chernotsky, H. and Geller, D. (1975) 'A Preliminary Test of the Theory of Dependency', *Comparative Politics*, 7, 303–30.

Kay, G. (1975) *Development and Underdevelopment* (London: Macmillan).

Kearns, G. (1984) 'Review Article: Making Space for Marx', *Journal of Historical Geography*, 10, 411–17.

Keeble, D. (1967) 'Models of Economic Development', in R. Chorley and P. Haggett (eds) *Models in Geography* (London: Methuen).

Kemp, T. (1983) *Industrialisation in the Non-Western World* (London: Macmillan).

Khalifa, A. (1976) 'The Influence of Wife's Education on Fertility in Rural Egypt', *Journal of Biosocial Science*, 8, 53–60.

Kidron, M. (1971) 'Memories of Development', *New Society*, 17, 360–66.

Killick, A. (1981) 'Euromarkets Recycling of OPEC Surpluses: Fact or Myth?', *The Banker*, 131, 15–23.

Kirk, M. (1984) 'The Return of Malthus? The Global Demographic Future, 2000–2050', *Future*, 16, 124–38.

Kitching, G. (1980) *Class and Economic Change in Kenya: The Making of an Africa Petite-Bourgeoisie* (London: Yale University Press).

Knodel, J. and Pichit, P. (1973) 'Thailand: Fertility and Family Planning among Rural and Urban Women', *Studies in Family Planning*, 4, 229–55.

Koestler, A. (1980) *Bricks to Babel* (London: Picador).

Komarov, B. (1980) *The Destruction of Nature in the Soviet Union* (London: Pluto).

Kropotkin, P. (1902) *Mutual Aid: A Factor of Evolution* (London: Heinemann).

Kuo, L. (1972) *The Technical Transformation of Agriculture in Communist China* (New York: Praeger).

Kuznets, S. (1974) *Population, Capital and Growth* (London: Heinemann).

Labasse, J. (1975) 'The Geographical Space of Big Companies', *Geoforum*, 6, 113–24.

Laclau, E. (1979) *Politics and Ideology in Marxist Theory* (London: Verso).

Lal, D. (1983) *The Poverty of 'Development Economics'* (London: IEA).

Lal, D. (1983a) 'Time to Put the Third World Debt Threat into Perspective', *The Times*, (6 May) 18.

Lal, R. (1968) 'Literacy and Population Growth', *Population Review*, 12, 55–9.

Lall, S. (1975) 'Is Dependence a Useful Concept in Analysing Underdevelopment?', *World Development*, 3, 799–810.

Lall, S. (1980) *The Multinational Corporation* (London: Macmillan).

Lall, S. (1983) 'The Rise of Multinationals from the Third World', *Third World Quarterly*, 5, 618–26.

Lall, S. (1984) 'Transnationals and the Third World: Changing Perceptions', *National Westminster Bank Quarterly Review* (May) 2–16.

Lamb, G. (1981) 'Rapid Capitalist Development Models: A New Politics of Dependence?' in D. Seers (ed.) *Dependency Theory: A Critical Re-Assessment* (London: Frances Pinter).

Lamb, H. (1966) *The Changing Climate* (London: Methuen).

Lamb, H. (1977) *Climate: Past, Present and Future* (London: Methuen).

Landsberg, M. (1979) 'Export-Led Industrialisation in the Third World: Manufacturing Imperialism', *Review of Radical Political Economics, 11*.

Lanning, G. and Mueller, M. (1979) *Africa Undermined* (Harmondsworth: Penguin).

Lappé, F. and Collins, J. (1982) *Food First* (London: Sphere).

Lappé, F. Collins, J. and Kinley, D. (1980) *Aid as Obstacle* (San Francisco: IFDP).

Leahy, E. and Hill, J. (1981) 'The Spatial Distribution of International Monetary Reserves', *Geographical Review*, 71, 64–82.

Lee, G. (1971) 'Rosa Luxemburg and the Impact of Imperialism', *Economic Journal*, 81, 847–62.

Lee, T. H. (1974) 'Food Supply and Population Growth in Developing Countries: A Case Study of Taiwan', in N. Islam (ed.) *Agricultural Policy in Developing Countries* (London: Macmillan).

Lenin, V. I. (1970) *Imperialism: The Highest Stage of Capitalism*, (Peking: Foreign Languages Press).

Lenin, V. I. (1974) *The Development of Capitalism in Russia* (Moscow: Progress).

Lewis, W. A. (1955) *The Theory of Economic Growth* (London: George Allen & Unwin).

Lewis, W. A. (1978) *The Evolution of the International Economic Order* (Princeton: Princeton University Press).

Lewthwaite, G. (1966) 'Environmentalism and Determinism: A Search for Clarification', *Annals of the Association of American Geographers*, 56, 1–23.

Leys, C. (1975) *Underdevelopment in Kenya* (London: Heinemann).

Lim, D. (1983) 'Fiscal Incentives and Direct Foreign Investment in LDCs', *Journal of Development Studies*, 19, 207–12.

Lim, L., Bide, H., Osnos, S. and Haggard, S. (1982) 'A Second Look at the NICs', *Far Eastern Economic Review*, (6 August) 54–6.

Lindert, P. (1980) 'Child Costs and Economic Development', in R. Easterlin (ed.) *Population and Economic Change in Developing Countries* (Chicago: Chicago University Press).

Lipietz, A. (1982) 'Towards Global Fordism? Marx or Rostow', *New Left Review*, 132, 33–58.

Lipton, M. (1968) 'Strategy for Agriculture: Urban Bias and Rural Planning', in P. Streeten and M. Lipton (eds) *The Crisis of Indian Planning* (Oxford: Oxford University Press).

Lipton, M. (1977) *Why Poor People Stay Poor: A Study of Urban Bias in World Development* (London: Temple Smith).

Long, N. (1975) 'Structural Dependency, Modes of Production and Economic Brokerage in Peru', in I. Oxaal, A. Barnett and D. Booth (eds) *Beyond the Sociology of Development* (London: Routledge & Kegan Paul).

Luxemburg, R. (1972) *The Accumulation of Capital* (London: Allen Lane).

MacEwan, A. (1982) 'Revolution, Agrarian Reform and Economic Transformation in Cuba', in S. Jones, M. Murmis and P. Joshi (eds) *Rural Poverty and Agrarian Reform* (Dakar: Enda).

MacFarlane, B. (1983) 'Political Economy of Class Struggle and Economic Growth in China, 1950–1982', *World Development*, 11, 659–72.

McGee, T. G. (1974) 'In Praise of Tradition: Towards a Geography of Anti-Development', *Antipode*, 6, 30–47.

McGee, T. G. (1978) 'Western Geography and the Third World', *American Behavioural Scientist*, 22, 93–114.

Mabogunje, A. (1973) 'Manufacturing and the Geography of Development in Tropical Africa', *Economic Geography*, 49, 1–20.

Mabogunje, A. (1980) *The Development Process: A Spatial Perspective*, (London: Hutchinson).

Malthus, T. (1970) *An Essay on the Principle of Population* (Harmondsworth: Penguin).

Maltley, I. (1966) 'The Marxist Approach to the Geographical Environment', *Annals of the Association of American Geographers*, 56, 97–111.

Mamdani, M. (1972) *The Myth of Population Control* (London: Monthly Review).

Mandel, E. (1968) *Marxist Economic Theory: 2 Volumes* (London: Merlin).

Manners, G. (1981) 'Our Planet's Resources', *Geographical Journal*, 147, 1–22.

Martinelli, A. (1982) 'The Political and Social Impact of Transnational Corporations', in H. Makler, A. Martinelli and N. Smelser (eds) *The New International Economy* (London: Sage).

Marx, K. (1967) *The Communist Manifesto* (Harmondsworth: Penguin).

Marx, K. (1974) 'The Critique of the Gotha Programme', in D. Fernbach (ed.) *Karl Marx: The First International and After* (Harmondsworth: Penguin).

Marx, K. (1976) *Capital, Volume 1* (Harmondsworth: Penguin).

Meadows, D. H., Meadows, D. L., Randers, J. and Behrens, W. (1972) *The Limits to Growth* (London: Pan).

Meillassoux, C. (1964) *Anthropologie Economique Des Gouro De Côte d'Voire*, (Paris: Mouton).

Meillassoux, C. (1971) *The Development of Indigenous Trades and Markets in Western Africa* (Oxford: Oxford University Press).

Meillassoux, C. (1972) 'From Reproduction to Production', *Economy and Society*, 1, 93–105.

Meillassoux, C. (1981) *Maidens, Meal and Money: Capitalism and the Domestic Community* (Cambridge: Cambridge University Press).

Meillassoux, C. (1983) 'The Economic Bases of Demographic Reproduction: From the Domestic Mode of Production to Wage-Earning', *Journal of Peasant Studies*, 11, 50–61.

Melrose, D. (1982) *Bitter Pills* (Oxford: Oxfam).

Miles, I. and Irvine, J. (1979) 'Social Forecasting: Predicting the Future or Making History?' in I. Miles and J. Irvine (eds) *Demystifying Social Statistics* (London: Pluto).

Moran, T. (1978) 'Multinational Corporations and Dependency: A Dialogue for Dependistas and Non-Dependendistas', *International Organisation*, 32, 79–100.

Morris, D. (1971) *The Naked Ape* (London: Corgi).

Moulder, F. (1977) *Japan, China and the Modern World Economy* (Cambridge: Cambridge University Press).

Mouzelis, N. (1978) *Modern Greece: Facets of Underdevelopment* (London: Macmillan).

Mouzelis, N. (1980) 'Modernisation, Underdevelopment, Uneven Development', *Journal of Peasant Studies*, 7, 353–74.

Mueller, E. (1982) 'The Allocation of Women's Time and Its Relation to Fertility', in R. Anker *et al.* (eds) *Women's Roles and Population Trends in the Third World* (London: Croom Helm).

Muller, M. (1974) *The Baby Killer* (London: War on Want).

Muller, M. (1982) *The Health of Nations* (London: Faber).

Mumy, G. (1979) 'Economic Systems and Environmental Quality', *Antipode*, 11, 26–33.

Munton, R. and Goudie, A. (1984) 'Geography in the UK, 1980–1984', *Geographical Journal*, 150, 27–47.

Murphey, R. (1967) 'Man and Nature in China', *Modern Asian Studies*, 1, 313–33.

Murray, R. (1971) 'The Intensification of Capital and the Nation–State', *New Left Review*, 67, 84–109.

Nakamura, J. (1966) *Agricultural Production and Economic Development in Japan, 1873–1922* (Princeton: Princeton University Press).

Neff, L. (1969) 'Dependency Rates and Savings Rates', *American Economic Review*, 59, 886–96.

Nelson, R. (1958) 'A Theory of the Low-Level Equilibrium Trap in Under-Developed Countries', *American Economic Review*, 48.

Newfarmer, R. (1979) 'TNC Takeovers in Brazil: The Uneven Distribution of Benefits in the Market for Firms', *World Development*, 7, 25–43.

Newfarmer, R. and Topik, S. (1982) 'Testing Dependency Theory: A Case Study of Brazil's Electrical Industry', in M. Taylor and N. Thrift (eds) *The Geography of Multinationals* (London: Croom Helm).

Nolan, P. (1983) 'Decollectivization of Agriculture in China, 1979–1982', *Economic and Political Weekly*, 32/33, 1395–1406, 1434–1441.

North, D. C. (1961) *The Economic Growth of the United States, 1790–1860* (New York: Englewood Cliffs).

Nove, A. (1983) *The Economics of Feasible Socialism* (London: George Allen & Unwin).

Page, H. and Lesthaeghe, R. (eds) (1981) *Child Spacing in Tropical Africa: Tradition and Change* (London: Academic Press).

Palloix, C. (1975) 'The Internationalisation of Capital and the Circuit of Social Capital', in H. Radice (ed.) *International Firms and Modern Imperialism* (Harmondsworth: Penguin).

Palloix, C. (1977) 'The Self-Expansion of Capitalism on a World Scale', *Review of Radical Political Economics*, 9, 1–28.

Palma, G. (1978) 'Dependency: A Formal Theory of Underdevelopment or a Methodology for the Analysis of Concrete Situations of Under-Development?', *World Development*, 6, 881–924.

Palmer, J. (1983) 'The Debt-Bomb Threat', *Time Magazine* (10 January) 4–11.

Papanek, G. (1973) 'Aid, Foreign Private Investment, Savings and Growth in Less Developed Countries', *Journal of Political Economy*, 81, 120–30.

Parboni, R. (1981) *The Dollar and Its Rivals: Recession, Inflation and International Finance* (London: Verso).

Parboni, R. (1983) 'Capital and the Nation–State: A Reply to Frieden', *New Left Review*, 137, 87–96.

Parry, M. (1978) *Climatic Change: Agriculture and Settlement* (London: Dawson).

Past & Present (1978) *Symposium on Brenner*, 78, 79, 80 (Oxford: Past & Present Society).

Patel, M. (1983) 'Drug Costs in Developing Countries and Policies to Reduce Them', *World Development*, 11, 195–204.

Payer, C. (1974) *The Debt Trap: The IMF and the Third World* (London: Monthly Review).

Payer, C. (1982) *The World Bank: A Critical Analysis* (London: Monthly Review).

Pearson, L. (1970) (Chairman of the Pearson Commission) *Partners in Development* (London: Pall Mall).

Peet, R. (1978) 'The Development of Radical Geography in the US', in R. Peet (ed.) *Radical Geography* (London: Methuen).

Peet, R. (1982) 'International Capital, International Culture', in M. Taylor and N. Thrift (eds) *The Geography of Multinationals* (London: Croom Helm).

Peet, R. (1983) 'The Global Geography of Contemporary Capitalism', *Economic Geography*, 59, 105–111.

Perkins, D. (1969) *Agricultural Development in China, 1368–1968* (Edinburgh: Edinburgh University Press).

Petras, J., McMichael, P. and Rhodes, R. (1978) 'Industrialisation in the Third World', in J. Petras, *Critical Perspectives on Imperialism and Social Class in the Third World* (London: Monthly Review).

Phillips, A. (1977) 'The Concept of Development', *Review of African Political Economy*, 8, 7–20.

Pilling, G. (1973) 'Imperialism, Trade and 'Unequal Exchange': The Work of Arghiri Emmanuel', *Economy and Society*, 2, 164–186.

Poleman, T. (1977) 'World Food: Myth and Reality', *World Development*, 5, 383–94.

Pollitt, B. (1982) 'The Transition to Socialist Agriculture in Cuba' (mimeo).

Post, K. (1978) *Arise Ye Starvelings: The Jamaican Labour Rebellion of 1938 and its Aftermath* (The Hague: Martin Nijhoff).

Radice, H. (1984) 'The National Economy: A Keynesian Myth?', *Capital and Class*, 22, 111–40.

Rao, D. C. (1978) 'Economic Growth and Equity in the Republic of Korea' *World Development*, 6.

Rapp, R. (1983) 'Peasants into Proletarians from the Household Out', in J. Mencher (ed.) *Social Anthropology of Peasantry* (Bombay: Somaiya).

Ratcliffe, J. (1978) 'Social Justice and Demographic Transition: Lessons from India's Kerala State', *International Journal of Health Services*, 8, 123–44.

Rawski, T. (1979) 'Economic Growth and Employment in China', *World Development*, 7, 767–82.

Redclift, M. (1984) *Development and the Environmental Crisis* (London: Methuen).

Repetto, R. (1979) *Economic Equality and Fertility in Developing Countries* (Baltimore: John Hopkins Press).

Rettie, J. (1983) 'Debtors Unite', *Guardian* (26 May) 18.

Rey, P. P. (1971) *Colonialisme, Neo-Colonialisme et Transition au Capitalisme* (Paris: Maspero).

Rey, P. P. (1973) *Les Alliances des Classes* (Paris: Maspero).

Riddell, B. (1981) 'The Geography of Modernisation in Africa: A Re-Examination', *Canadian Geographer*, 25, 290–9.

280   *Bibliography*

Ripley, E. A. (1976) 'Drought in the Sahara: Insufficient Geophysical Feedback?' *Science*, 191, 100.

Riskin, C. (1975) 'Surplus and Stagnation in Modern China', in D. Perkins (ed.) *China's Modern Economy in Historical Perspective* (Stanford: Stanford University Press).

Robinson, J. (1981) 'Is it Possible to Assess Country Risk?', *The Banker*, 131, 71–9.

Roddick, J. (1984) 'Crisis, 'Seignorage' and the Modern World System', *Capital and Class*, 23, 121–34.

Rodgers, P. (1983) 'A Tale of Two Cities and of Two Standards', *Guardian* (9 March) 19.

Rose, S. (1984) *Not in Our Genes* (Harmondsworth: Penguin).

Ross, R. J. (1983) 'Facing Leviathan: Public Policy and Global Capitalism', *Economic Geography*, 59, 144–60.

Rostow, W. W. (1960) *The Stages of Economic Growth: A Non-Communist Manifesto* (London: Cambridge University Press).

Rowthorn, B. (1980) 'Imperialism in the Seventies – Unity or Rivalry?', in B. Rowthorn, *Capitalism, Conflict and Inflation* (London: Lawrence & Wishart).

Rushdie, S. (1983) *Shame* (London: Cape).

Sampson, A. (1974) *The Sovereign State: The Secret History of ITT* (London: Coronet).

Sanders, J. (1983) *Peddlars of Crisis* (London: Pluto).

Santos, M. (1974) 'Geography, Marxism and Underdevelopment', *Antipode* 6, 1–9.

Sauer, C. (1956) 'The Agency of Man on the Earth', in W. C. Thomas (ed.) *Man's Role in Changing the Face of the Earth* (Chicago: University of Chicago Press).

Schiffer, J. (1981) 'The Changing Post-War Pattern of Development', *World Development*, 9.

Schmidt, A. (1971) *The Concept of Nature in Marx* (London: New Left Books).

Schumacher, E. (1973) *Small is Beautiful* (London: Blond & Briggs).

Schumm, S. and Lichty, R. (1965) 'Time, Space and Causality in Geomorphology', *American Journal of Science*, 263, 110–19.

Seccombe, W. (1983) 'Marxism and Demography', *New Left Review*, 137, 22–47.

Seers, D. (1980) 'North–South: Muddling Morality and Mutuality', *Third World Quarterly*, 2, 681–92.

Seers, D. (1981) 'Development Options: The Strengths and Weaknesses of Dependency Theories in Explaining a Government's Room to Manoeuvre', in D. Seers (ed.) *Dependency Theory: A Critical Re-Assessment* (London: Frances Pinter).

Seers, D. (1981a) 'Massive Transfers and Mutual Interests', *World Development*, 9.

Seidman, A. (1974) 'The Distorted Growth of Import-Substitution Industry: The Zambian Case', *Journal of Modern African Studies*, 12, 601–31.

Semple, E. (1911) *Influences of Geographic Environment* (New York: Holt).

Sengupta, N. (1982) 'Tank Irrigation in Gangetic Bihar', A. N. Sinha Institute, Patna, discussion paper.

Sheahan, J. (1980) 'Market-Oriented Economic Policies and Political Repression in Latin America', *Economic Development and Cultural Change*, 28, 267–91.

Shihata, I. and Mabro, R. (1979) 'The OPEC Aid Record', *World Development*, 7, 161–73.

Singer, H. (1980) 'The Brandt Report: A North-Western Point of View', *Third World Quarterly*, 2, 694–700.

Sklar, R. (1976) 'Post-imperialism: A Class Analysis of Multinational Corporate Expansion', *Comparative Politics*, 9, 75–92.

Slater, D. (1973) 'Geography and Underdevelopment – I', *Antipode*, 5, 21–53.

Slater, D. (1977) 'Geography and Underdevelopment – II', *Antipode*, 9, 1–31.

Slater, D. (1982) 'State and Territory in Post-Revolutionary Cuba', *International Journal of Urban and Regional Research*, 6, 1–33.

Slicher van Bath, B. H. (1963) *The Agrarian History of Western Europe, AD 500–1850* (London: Edward Arnold).

Smil, V. (1984) *The Bad Earth: Environmental Degradation in China* (London: Zed Press).

Smith, D. M. *et al.* (1976) 'Separation in South Africa', Queen Mary College, London, Occasional Paper 6.

Smith, N. (1984) *Uneven Development: Nature, Capital and the Production of Space* (Oxford: Basil Blackwell).

Smith, S. (1981) 'The Ideas of Samir Amin: Theory or Tautology', *Journal of Development Studies*, 17, 5–21.

Smith, T. C. (1957) *The Agrarian Origins of Modern Japan* (Stanford: Stanford University Press).

Snyder, D. (1974) 'The Economic Determinants of Family Size in West Africa', *Demography*, 11, 613–28.

Sobhan, R. (1979) 'The Politics of Food and Famine in Bangladesh', *Economic and Political Weekly*, 14, 1973–9.

Sobhan, R. (1983) *The Crisis of External Dependence: The Political Economy of Foreign Aid to Bangladesh* (London: Zed Press).

Soja, E. W. (1968) *The Geography of Modernization in Africa* (Syracuse: Syracuse University Press).

Stallings, B. (1982) 'Euromarkets, Third World Countries and International Political Economy', in H. Makler, A. Märtinelli and N. Selser (eds) *The New International Economy* (London: Sage).

Stewart, F. (1972) 'Choice of Techniques in Developing Countries', *Journal of Development Studies*, 9, 99–121.

Stewart, F. (1973) 'Trade and Technology', in P. Streeten (ed.) *Trade Strategies for Development* (London: Macmillan).

Stewart, F. (1978) *Technology and Underdevelopment* (London: Macmillan).

Stewart, J. S. (1976) 'Linkages and Foreign Direct Investment', *Regional Studies*, 10, 245–58.

Streeten, P. (1975) 'Industrialisation in a Unified Development Strategy', *World Development*, 3, 1–9.

Stycos, J. and Weller, R. (1967) 'Female Working Roles and Fertility', *Demography*, 4, 210–17.

Sunkel, O. (1973) 'Transnational Capitalism and National Disintegration in Latin America', *Social and Economic Studies*, 22, 132–76.

Susman, P. and Schutz, E. (1983) 'Monopoly and Competitive Firm Relations and Regional Development in Global Capitalism', *Economic Geography*, 59, 161–77.

Sutcliffe, B. (1972) 'Imperialism and Industrialisation in the Third World', in R. Owen and B. Sutcliffe (eds) *Studies in the Theory of Imperialism* (London: Longman).

Swindell, K. (1979) 'Labour Migration in Underdeveloped Countries', *Progress in Human Geography*, 3, 239–59.

Szymanski, A. (1977) 'Capital Accumulation on a World Scale and the Necessity of Imperialism', *The Insurgent Sociologist*, 7, 35–53.

Tarrant, J. (1981) 'Food as a Weapon? The Embargo on Grain Trade Between USA and USSR', *Applied Geography*, 1, 273–86.

Tarrant, J. (1982) 'EEC Food Aid', *Applied Geography*, 2, 127–41.

Tawney, R. H. (1966) *Land and Labour in China* (London: Macmillan).

Taylor, J. (1979) *From Modernisation to Modes of Production* (London: Macmillan).

Taylor, M. and Thrift, N. (eds) (1982) *The Geography of Multinationals*, (London: Croom Helm).

Taylor, P. (1981) 'Political Geography and the World Economy', in A. Burnett and P. Taylor (eds) *Political Studies from Spatial Perspectives* (Chichester: Wiley).

Terray, E. (1972) *Marxism and 'Primitive' Societies* (London: Monthly Review).

Thirlwall, A. (1978) *Growth and Development* (London: Macmillan) 2nd edn. (3rd edition pub. 1983).

Thomas, M. (1980) 'Explanatory Frameworks for Growth and Change in Multi-Regional Firms', *Economic Geography*, 56, 1–17.

Thompson, J. B. (1984) *Studies in the Theory of Ideology* (London: Edward Arnold).

Thrift, N. (1985) 'Taking the Rest of the World Seriously?', *Environment and Planning*, A, 17, 7–24.

Timpanaro, S. (1978) *On Materialism* (London: New Left Books).

Tinbergen, J. and Dolman, J. (1977) *Reshaping the International Order* (London: Hutchinson).

Todaro, M. (1981) *Economic Development in the Third World* (London: Longman).

Toye, J. (1983) 'The Disparaging of Development Economics', *Journal of Development Studies*, 20, 87–107.

UNESCO (1978) *Transnational Corporations in World Development* (New York: United Nations).

Vaitsos, C. (1973) 'Bargaining and the Distribution of Returns in the Purchase of Technology by Developing Countries', in H. Bernstein (ed.) *Underdevelopment and Development* (Harmondsworth: Penguin).

Vernon, R. (1978) *Storm Over the Multinationals* (New York: Harvard University Press).

Vernon, R. (1979) 'The Product Life Cycle Hypothesis in a New International Environment', *Oxford Bulletin of Economics and Statistics*, 41, 255–68.

Vlassoff, M. (1979) 'Labour Demand and Economic Utility of Children: A Case Study in Rural India', *Population Studies*, 33, 415–28.

Vlassoff, M. (1982) 'Economic Utility of Children and Fertility in Rural India', *Population Studies*, 36, 45–59.

Wade, R. (1981) 'The Social Response to Irrigation', *Journal of Development Studies*, 16, 3–26.

Walker, R. and Storper, M. (1981) 'Capital and Industrial Location', *Progress in Human Geography*, 5, 473–509.

Wallerstein, I. (1974) *The Modern World System* (New York: Academic Press).

Wallerstein, I. (1979) *The Capitalist World Economy* (Cambridge: Cambridge University Press).

Wallerstein, I. (1984) *The Politics of the World Economy* (Cambridge: Cambridge University Press).

Ward, B. (1966) *Spaceship Earth* (London: Pan).

Warren, B. (1971) 'How International is Capital?' *New Left Review*, 68, 83–8.

Warren, B. (1973) 'Imperialism and Capitalist Industrialisation', *New Left Review*, 81, 3–44.

Warren, B. (1980) *Imperialism: Pioneer of Capitalism* (London: New Left Books).

Watanabe, S. (1972) 'Exports and Employment: The Case of the Republic of Korea', *International Labour Review*, 495–526.

Watson, A. (1983) 'Agriculture Looks for "Shoes that Fit": The Production Responsibility System and Its Implications', *World Development*, 11, 705–30.

Watts, M. (1983) 'Hazards and Crises: A Political Economy of Drought and Famine in Northern Nigeria', *Antipode*, 15, 24–34.

Wellings, P. (1982) 'Aid to the Southern African Periphery: The Case of Lesotho', *Applied Geography*, 2, 267–90.

Wendler, G. and Eaton, F. (1983) 'On the Desertification of the Sahel Zone', *Climatic Change*, 5, 365–80.

Westoby, J. (1979) '"Making Green the Motherland": Forestry in China', in N. Maxwell (ed.) *China's Road to Development* (Oxford: Praeger).

Westphal, L. (1977) 'Industrial Policy and Development in Korea', *World Bank Staff Working Paper 263*.

Wheelwright, E. (1980) 'The New International Division of Labour in the Age of the Transnational Corporation', in J. Friedmann *et al.* (eds) *Development Strategies in the 1980s* (University of Sydney: Development Studies Colloquium 1).

284 Bibliography

White, B. (1976) 'Population, Involution and Employment in Rural Java', *Development and Change*, 7, 267–90.

Wiarda, H. J. (1982) 'Cancun and After: The USA and the Developing World', *Political Science*, 15, 40–6.

Willett, T. (1983) 'US Monetary Policy and World Liquidity', *American Economic Review*, 73, 43–7.

Wilson, E. O. (1975) *Sociobiology* (Cambridge, Massachussets: Harvard University Press).

Wolf, E. (1982) *Europe and the People Without History* (London: Faber).

Wolpe, H. (1972) 'Capitalism and Cheap Labour Power in South Africa', *Economy and Society*, 1, 425–56.

Wolpe, H. (ed.) (1980) *The Articulation of Modes of Production* (London: Routledge & Kegan Paul).

Woods, R. (1982) *Theoretical Population Geography* (London: Longman).

Woolcock, S. (1982) 'East/West Trade: US Policy and European Interests', *The World Today*, 38, 51–9.

World Bank (1984) *World Development Report, 1984* (Oxford: Oxford University Press).

Worsley, P. (1979) 'How Many Worlds?', *Third World Quarterly*, 1, 100–8.

Yuan-Tien, H. (1980) *Population Theory in China* (New York: Sharpe).

Zelinsky, W. (1970) 'The Geographer and his Crowding World: Cautionary Notes Towards the Study of Population Pressures in the Developing Lands', in W. Zelinsky, L. Kolinski and M. Prothero (eds) *Geography and a Crowding World* (Oxford: Oxford University Press).

Zelinsky, W., Monk, J. and Hanson, S. (1982) 'Women and Geography: A Review and Prospectus', *Progress in Human Geography*, 6, 317–66.

Author Index

285

Subject Index